Beyond the Nouveau Roman

Berg French Studies

General Editor: John E. Flower

John E. Flower and Bernard C. Swift (eds), *François Mauriac: Visions and Reappraisals*

- Forthcoming -

Richard Griffiths, *The Use of Abuse: The Polemics of the Dreyfus Affair and its Aftermath*

Alec G. Hargreaves, *Immigration and Identity in Beur Fiction: Voices from the North African Community in France*

Malcolm Cook, *Fictional France: Social Reality in the French Novel, 1775–1800*

Nicholas Hewitt, *Intellectuals and the New Right in Postwar France*

Colin Nettelbeck, *Forever French: The United States Exile 1939–1945*

David Looseley, *Culture and Politics in Contemporary France*

Alan Morris, *Harmed Resistance: Writers and 'la Mode rétro' in Post-Gaullist France*

Alan Clark, *Paris Peasant: François Mitterrand and the Modernisation of France*

Beyond the Nouveau Roman

Essays on the Contemporary French Novel

Edited by
Michael Tilby

BERG

New York / Oxford / Munich
Distributed exclusively in the US and Canada by
St Martin's Press, New York

First published in 1990 by
Berg Publishers Limited
Editorial offices:
165 Taber Avenue, Providence, RI 02906, USA
150 Cowley Road, Oxford OX4 1JJ, UK
Westermühlstraße 26, 8000 München 5, FRG

British Library Cataloguing in Publication Data

Beyond the nouveau roman : essays on the contemporary
    French novel. – (Berg French studies).
    1. Fiction in French, 1945– — Critical studies
    I. Tilby, M. J. (Michael J.)
    843′.914′09

ISBN 0–85496–611–0

Library of Congress Cataloging-in-Publication Data

Beyond the nouveau roman : essays on the contemporary French novel /
    edited by Michael Tilby.
        p.   cm.
    ISBN 0–85496–611–0
    1. French fiction—20th century—History and criticism.
    I. Tilby, Michael.
    PQ672.B49 1989
    843′.91409—dc20   89–35886

Printed in Great Britain by
Billing & Sons Ltd, Worcester

This volume of essays is dedicated
to the memory of Ann Duncan

Contents

Bibliographical Note

The reader will find at the end of each chapter a list of the principal works of the author in question, followed by a selection of secondary material to aid further study. In the case of those authors who have attracted a good deal of critical attention, the bibliographies list only those studies that have been judged to be of particular interest. A somewhat fuller listing of criticism has been attempted in the case of the other novelists. Except where stated otherwise, references within chapters are to the editions listed in the bibliographies. Where no place of publication is given, it should be assumed that a French-language title was published in Paris and an English-language title in London.

Introduction

For all the hostility it raised, the *nouveau roman* in its classic phase, as represented by the challenging fictions of Robbe-Grillet, Butor, Sarraute and Claude Simon, has tended to dominate our perception of the evolution of the French novel in the twentieth century. Bolstered by developments in literary theory that arose in part precisely in order to make sense of this new novelistic practice, the work of the *nouveaux romanciers* represented a convincing case for the identification of authenticity in the novel with the purely self-referential. Many of the features that had previously given the novel its specificity and *raison d'être* were swept away. Only a restricted readership was able to see this in terms of a revitalisation; a more widespread view was to see it as having destroyed a form that had represented authoritatively both the external world and its essential significance. The idea of a crisis in the novel was not new to France (the notion can be traced back at least as far as the 1890s[1]), but the question of where the genre was to go after the *nouveau roman* was more easily raised than answered.

Gradually the challenge posed by the *nouveau roman* was taken up. In the case of those novelists such as Philippe Sollers and Maurice Roche who identified themselves with the avant-garde journal *Tel Quel*, it was a matter of claiming that Robbe-Grillet and those associated with him had not gone far enough. Encouraged by the continually evolving explorations in the realm of theory that were spearheaded by Roland Barthes, they saw it as their task to proceed to a systematic extension of strategies that had hitherto constituted no more than a clearing of the ground. As Leslie Hill in his essay on the *Tel Quel* group shows, a novel such as Sollers's *Drame* exemplifies a much more radical practice of writing, to the extent that 'what is being described cannot be captured within the realm of story at all'. Where Robbe-Grillet had parodied traditional narrative structures, the *Tel Quel* novelists abandoned them altogether. The retention of the label '*roman*' takes on an ironic ring; this new practice of writing

1. See Michel Raimond, *La Crise du roman* (Corti, 1967).

is pursued beyond the boundaries that separate genres. That these works, rather than those of the *nouveaux romanciers*, marked the end of the road for the novel in a recognisable form is neatly exemplified by the change of direction that Sollers's own work was to undergo in the 1980s.

Much more widespread, however, has been the tendency to express fundamental dissatisfaction with the allegedly self-imposed limitations of the *nouveaux romanciers*. Of the novelists represented in this volume, some have expressed scant interest in the *nouveau roman*, while others have gone a good deal further in voicing their dislike for its tenets. Marie-Claire Blais, for example, has declared herself to be 'presque indifférente' to the work of the new novelists. For his part, Patrick Modiano, as Alan Morris makes clear, has been careful to distance himself from both the viewpoint and the practices of Robbe-Grillet. He is on record as having declared to one of his interviewers: 'Enfin la littérature pour la littérature, les recherches sur l'écriture, tout ce byzantinisme pour chaires et colloques, ça ne m'intéresse pas'.[2] Similarly, Michel Tournier affects to have turned his back on 'une certaine école moderne [. . .] qui s'efforce de faire éclater les limites de la littérature'.[3] He makes great play of the traditional form of his writing: 'Je me suis mis à l'école la plus romanesque qui soit, le naturalisme. Une école qui vous fait sentir l'odeur des choses et des gens, qui commence avec Zola, continue avec Jules Renard, Colette, Henri Pourrat, Genevoix'.[4] Presenting himself as the professional philosopher turned amateur novelist, he relishes the opportunity this gives him to fulminate against those who can permit themselves the luxury of demolishing their own houses: 'Non aux romanciers nés dans le sérail qui en profitent pour tenter de casser la baraque'.[5] Patrick Grainville, the youngest of the novelists whose work is studied in this volume, is, as David Gascoigne shows, still more dismissive of 'des textes disloqués, incompréhensibles, absolument refermés sur eux-mêmes'.

Most of the novelists included in the present volume are united in their rejection of the unprecedentedly high degree of textual self-referentiality that the *nouveaux romanciers* maintained as their goal. This is not least because they see concerns beyond those of a narrowly literary nature as continuing to demand new forms of expression. Monique Wittig, whose writing at first sight suggests

2. See Jean-Louis Ezine, *Les Ecrivains sur la sellette* (Editions du Seuil, 1981), p. 22.
3. Michel Tournier, *Le Vent Paraclet* (Gallimard, Collection Folio, 1979), p. 180.
4. See Ezine, *Les Ecrivains sur la sellette*, p. 225.
5. Tournier, *Le Vent Paraclet*, p. 195.

that it has been strongly influenced by those *nouveaux romanciers* who had preceded her in the lists of that enterprising publishing house *Editions de Minuit*, has, as Jean Duffy stresses, none the less been concerned from the outset to use her writing as a vehicle for a commitment to a distinct extra-literary credo, that of a militant feminism. Throughout the work of such different writers as Agustin Gomez-Arcos, Modiano and Tournier, there is a similar determination to recognise the need for the novel to engage with some of the more traumatic experiences that have called into question the right of our inherited cultural traditions to be regarded as civilised.

At the same time, although the *Tel Quel* writers and Monique Wittig stand apart by reason of the closeness with which some of their procedures follow on from the iconoclasm of the *nouveaux romanciers*, the practice of a number of the other authors featured here suggests that they have not been unmarked by the new novelists' radical undermining of traditional narrative, however much they may profess to dislike such a stance. Tournier's position is in fact much less unequivocal than the polemical author of *Le Vent Paraclet* would have us believe. He may well characterise the practice of the *nouveaux romanciers* as 'ce côté Meccano', but he is nevertheless prepared to support Jean-Louis Ezine's proposition that his novels are 'constructed' rather than 'written'.[6] If the *nouveau roman* is for him to be equated with 'excessive formalism', he recognises that his own compositions require him to engage in some kind of justification of formalism. He is led to take refuge in the wholly positive achievement represented by Bach's *Art of the Fugue* (a choice of model that, it may be assumed in view of Tournier's admiration for Gide, consciously recalls the practice of the author of *Les Faux-Monnayeurs*). As for his compositions, it is clear that 'some of the formal aspects of Tournier's novels are less reassuringly traditional than he implies',[7] with the consequence that they exhibit instabilities that are indeed familiar from the work of the new novelists. More generally, the novelists with whom we are concerned often show continuity with the *nouveaux romanciers* in respect of what David Coward calls, with reference to Marguerite Duras, the author's 'technical boldness and consequent demands upon the reader'. It may indeed be possible on occasion to detect an assumption that the reader will bring to these new compositions the skills that he has learnt as a reader of Robbe-Grillet. But if the reader of Duras's *L'Amante anglaise* needs to

---

6. See Ezine, *Les Ecrivains sur la sellette*, p. 227.
7. Colin Davis, *Michel Tournier: Philosophy and Fiction* (Oxford, Clarendon Press, 1988), p. 4.

accommodate the alternative accounts of events contained within that text, it is apparent that the author's motivation is not that of aligning herself with the new novelists themselves. The experimentation is justified only as a means of service to ends of a greater human significance. The same is true, as Ann Duncan shows us, of the narrative sophistication employed by Gomez-Arcos; his work reveals him to be a humanist at heart. Rosemary Lloyd in turn emphasises Marie-Claire Blais's compulsive concern with experimentation. Although Blais has little truck with the cerebrality of the *nouveau roman*, her novel-writing too is founded on the realisation that no narrative discourse may be taken for granted.

For the majority of the novelists discussed in this volume, the *nouveau roman* was an unavoidable reference point. Yet the extent to which their work engages squarely with the challenge represented by the *nouveau roman* varies considerably, as consequently does the usefulness of a consistent comparison between it and the practice of the novelists concerned. The authors of the essays that follow will not therefore necessarily begin by situating the novelists' works in the context of the *nouveau roman*. Instead the *rapprochement* is allowed to emerge at moments that are felt to be most appropriate, so as not to confer upon these works a spurious polemical or confrontational intent.

The novelists in question cannot be regarded as forming a distinct group or school. Yet in many cases, their work reveals features that together allow us to identify certain similarities in these attempts to give the novel a new direction after the *nouveau roman*. Initially, the most striking trend is towards a studied avoidance of recognisable contemporary French settings. There is a new readiness to exploit and explore cultural traditions that transcend national boundaries and to re-open the question of the relationship between the present and the historical past. In formal terms, this is associated with a still more widespread avoidance of mimetic representation of characters and their world. There is implicit agreement that there can be no return to the ambition to capture the world's reflection. Instead, extravagance and distortion are used in various ways to challenge accepted pictures. Prominent in these writings is an eschewal of anything that the reader might be tempted to regard as 'realism', followed by a delight in the imaginative potential of fiction that is realised most notably through the cultivation of the realms of fantasy and myth, though the latter are rarely seen as ends in themselves. These are forms of writing that often bring into being characters that seize the reader's attention by virtue of their excessive attributes. The sophistication of the self-conscious artistry prevents such novels from merely re-establishing practices that held sway before the work of Robbe-Grillet. Yet they inevitably re-design the map of French literary traditions. It is perhaps not insignificant, for example, that both the oldest and the youngest of the novelists discussed share an interest in a writer widely regarded hitherto as being of relatively minor importance, Henry de Montherlant, and that the writings of Céline (especially his more aggressive and shapeless post-war compositions) take on a new centrality for Sollers, as well as for Modiano and for Grainville.

The temptation to give this volume a title that highlighted a common feature or trend has nevertheless been resisted, since that would risk creating a misleading impression of uniformity. It has not been our intention, either, to suggest that the novelists who have been included constitute the practitioners to be thought most worthy of critical attention. Although many of them would necessarily figure in any discussion of the contemporary French novel, they have been selected essentially as examples of the rich diversity of writing that continues to characterise French fiction. As will be evident from the individual select bibliographies that accompany these essays, it has been our endeavour to include both novelists who are relatively well known and some who are much less familiar. There is without doubt room for a further collection of essays that would include discussion of the work of, for example, J.-M.G. Le Clézio and Georges Perec.

The decision to begin with an essay devoted to Marguerite Yourcenar was taken partly in order to include the work of a novelist who has consistently exhibited an exemplary independence of literary and intellectual fashions. At the same time, it is significant that Yourcenar's importance as a writer became much more widely accepted in the period after 1970, culminating in her election in 1981 as the first woman member of the French Academy. There can be little doubt that the direction taken by French fiction after the *nouveau roman* helped to create conditions that were much more conducive to the appreciation of her writing, which in so many respects appears self-consciously uncontemporary.

The reader will doubtless wonder in which direction the French novel will now proceed. Patrick Modiano has made no secret of his view that the novel has irretrievably lost the function and status it formerly enjoyed:

> En 1933, je suppose que tous les étudiants du Quartier Latin avaient fait de *la Condition humaine* leur livre de chevet. Il est exclu qu'un roman puisse être aujourd'hui le livre de chevet des jeunes lecteurs. [. . .] Faute d'audience, faute de pouvoir s'adapter au rythme du monde moderne, il y a simple-

ment le fait que le roman ne peut plus, à mon sens, déterminer ou orienter la sensibilité commune, comme il pouvait encore le faire au début de ce siècle. Bousculé par le cinéma et les moyens d'expression modernes, l'influence du roman est plus sournoise et réduite qu'au temps où il était interdit dans les pensionnats.[8]

What the subjects of the essays that follow will show, however, is that the almost total 'loss of innocence' experienced by the mid-twentieth-century French novel need not condemn the genre to break with the age-old capacity of storytelling to hold readers and academics spellbound. At the same time, if the new catholic exploitation of some of the most fundamental powers of fiction may be expected to attract still more recruits, it is perhaps equally likely that their creations will continue to entertain an oblique critical relationship with more familiar images of a world that we thought we knew.

M. T.

8. See Ezine, *Les Ecrivains sur la sellette*, pp. 25–6.

–1–

Marguerite Yourcenar

MICHAEL TILBY

'Tout être qui a vécu l'aventure humaine est moi' (M. Yourcenar, *Carnets de notes de 'Mémoires d'Hadrien'*)

'"Harry", said Basil Hallward, looking him straight in the face, "every portrait that is painted with feeling is a portrait of the artist, not of the sitter"' (O. Wilde, *The Picture of Dorian Gray*)

To consider Marguerite Yourcenar (who died in 1987) as a contemporary author is in an obvious sense paradoxical. Two years younger than Malraux, she was born two years before Sartre, in 1903. A considerable proportion of her writings appeared in the inter-war period; by the time she was little more than thirty she had published two books of poetry, a biography of Pindar and a volume of short stories, as well as her first three novels: *Alexis* (1929), *La Nouvelle Eurydice* (1931) – which was dismissed by its author as 'un mauvais roman' and never re-published – and *Denier du rêve* (1934). Her fourth novel, *Le Coup de grâce*, appeared in 1939. All four lack the self-conscious modernity of the truly influential French novels of the 1930s: they show few, if any, signs of a dissatisfaction with established fictional forms. Clearly, their author did not feel that the novelist was entering the 'ère du soupçon' later identified by Nathalie Sarraute. Yourcenar's pre-war novels indeed represent a recognisable attempt to continue admired traditions. One reader of *Le Coup de grâce* was able to conclude that the hero had fulfilled for his generation the role that Werther had performed for Goethe's contemporaries some 160 years before.[1] In her choice of both form and subject matter much of Yourcenar's early work bears the trace of her reading of Gide, whose influence in the French-speaking world was at its peak during her formative years.[2] The fact that she spent the

1. M. Yourcenar, *Les Yeux ouverts* (Le Centurion: Livre de poche, n.d.), p. 113.
2. Yourcenar's concern to play down any suggestion of a debt to Gide (see her 1963 preface to *Alexis*, and *Les Yeux ouverts*, pp. 63–5) is doubtless justifiable in view of her detachment from many Gidean stances and procedures, but the reader of her early *récits* may none the less sense that she is often writing within a Gidean context.

greater part of her life outside France caused her to remain uniquely estranged from what are usually regarded as the most significant intellectual trends of the pre- and post-war periods; her personal familiarity was more with such now faded figures as Henry de Montherlant or Jean Schlumberger.

Similarly, although Yourcenar's later essays and interviews show her undoubted concern with a range of contemporary problems and causes, the more substantial prose narratives of her maturity reveal a studious avoidance of contemporary settings. They can also be said to develop independently of the mid-century trend towards a radical questioning of the 'bourgeois novel'. Yourcenar's lack of concern to innovate or theorise with regard to the novel, or indeed to confine herself to the genre, is striking. (Her already noted pursuit of a variety of literary forms is extended in this period to take in the theatre.) Her work exhibits a brand of humanism that is manifestly at odds with some of the most cherished premises shared in recent years by members of the Parisian literary avant-garde, while being almost wholly immune to charges of naïveté or anachronism. On reading her highly revealing responses in interviews, especially with Matthieu Galey in the extensive conversations collected under the attractive title *Les Yeux ouverts* (1980), one is struck not only by the delight Yourcenar takes in talking about her fictional characters, but also by her unfashionable disinclination to discourse prescriptively about the novel as a genre. Throughout *Les Yeux ouverts* she reveals a fundamental desire that her fictions – and above all her characters – be correctly understood, since in her eyes they are very largely the product of conscious and sharply-focused intentions. The reader's sense-making activities are required first and foremost to pinpoint what the author herself had determined to illustrate clear-sightedly in respect of her characters' actions and beliefs. To this extent Yourcenar may be felt more often than not to be her own best commentator.

Although her early novels – finely wrought if relatively unambitious compositions – attracted on occasion the admiration of such discerning critics as Edmond Jaloux, it is, nevertheless, only since the war that Yourcenar's work has established her as a writer possessed of a truly powerful imagination and of a matchless gift for the reconstruction of time and place. This is a reputation that has been achieved on the basis of just two novels: *Mémoires d'Hadrien*, published in 1951, and her study of a rebellious spirit of the sixteenth century, *L'Œuvre au noir*, which appeared, not entirely inappropriately, in 1968. Distinctions of genre, so far as these post-war compositions are concerned, are, however, much less significant than one might expect. The publication in 1974 and 1977 of the first two volumes of a projected trilogy entitled *Le Labyrinthe du monde* ostensibly represented an entry into the realm of autobiography, though this is a label that sits rather uneasily on *Souvenirs pieux* and *Archives du nord*. Yourcenar shows scant interest in the events of her own individual past, preferring to present us with portraits of her ancestors on both sides of the Franco-Belgian border. The concluding volume of the trilogy, *Quoi? L'Eternité* (1988), though it contains intermittent pictures of Marguerite as a child, casts its net much wider than is usual in more conventional works of autobiography. Furthermore, Yourcenar herself has stressed the continuity between the post-war novels and *Le Labyrinthe du monde* on the ground that her form of autobiographical writing demands the same reconstruction of character from a range of fragmented sources. In fact, the continuity between all five of the compositions of her maturity – and it is with them that this essay is concerned – exists in other respects as well.

Yourcenar expects her readers to realise that her notions of past and present are more complex than the yardstick of an explicit concern with contemporary affairs will allow. She believes our culture to be threatened and our age to have acquired a problematical relationship to the past. To explore moments of that past, therefore, can very consistently be the reflection of a concern with the present. More generally, history for Yourcenar is not a series of sealed units. As a result, her novels are subtly different from many examples of historical fiction. Notwithstanding the painstaking researches she undertakes as part of her desire for historical authenticity, she clearly feels that the past only possesses vitality when seized in relation to a constantly evolving present. Even historical authenticity appears less important to her for its own sake than as a means of allowing her to experience her chosen setting in its physical immediacy, rather than as a set of abstractions to be illustrated. It is significant that when she recalls the circumstances under which *Mémoires d'Hadrien* was composed, she insists that it would have been rather different had it been written ten years later, not just because her life would have continued to enter new phases, but because the course of twentieth-century history would have changed. Without the end-product ever assuming the neat equivalence of allegory, the *Mémoires* (and above all the section entitled 'Tellus stabilita') were felt by their author to have been coloured by hopes placed in the United Nations after 1945. Ten years on, the reaction to Hadrien's achievement could not so easily have been the same. When, on another occasion, she describes the past as more 'alive' than the present, this recognises not only the way its components come together to suggest a meaningful picture, but also the constantly changing perspective from which it is viewed. Altogether, such a focus on the past opens up a richness that is felt to be absent from the apparently amorphous and directionless present. But there remains an acute awareness that such a view of the past is dependent on a fully developed sense of the present. What all this begins to show us is that Yourcenar's writing challenges in highly suggestive ways any simplified notion of chronology.

Such straightforward notions of chronology are further thrown into question by the genesis of Yourcenar's compositions. Both *Mémoires d'Hadrien* and *L'Œuvre au noir* were among her earliest projects, begun, then set aside as being beyond her powers as she then saw them. (The sheer range of the Emperor's experiences and beliefs is enough to explain why she considered the *Mémoires* to be one of those works 'qu'on ne doit pas oser avant d'avoir dépassé quarante ans' – *H*, p. 323.)[3] The most visible hallmark of Yourcenar's practice as a writer is almost certainly the frequency with which she was led to engage in the rewriting of works that she had published several decades previously. As a result, her compositions may frequently be regarded as belonging neither purely to her youth nor wholly to her maturity. When the original version of the project that was to become *L'Œuvre au noir* – an episode in what was then conceived as a vast historical fresco that would also have satisfied part of the compulsion that was later to give birth to *Le Labyrinthe du monde* – was discovered to be too ambitious, Yourcenar was content to construct out of her material, firstly, a story that remained unpublished and then, in 1934, the three short stories of *La Mort conduit l'attelage*. Some forty years later, with the completion of *L'Œuvre au noir* behind her, the story she had in 1934 entitled 'D'après Rembrandt' was reworked into two new compositions, both of which drew on the achievements represented by the full-scale novel. This is doubtless only the fullest example of the way in which the process of rewriting leads to the constant enrichment of an *œuvre* that devoted itself single-mindedly to a small number of projects present in one form or another from the outset. In some instances even the first version of a Yourcenar composition may be regarded as a form of rewriting, in that the author, not having the novelist's assumed predilection for imagining fictional situations,

3. Parenthetical page-references within the text are to the Gallimard Folio editions of Yourcenar's novels and autobiographical volumes and to the Livre de Poche edition of *Les Yeux ouverts*. The following abbreviations are used: *H=Mémoires d'Hadrien*, including the *Carnets de notes de 'Mémoires d'Hadrien'*; *ŒN=L'Œuvre au noir*; *SP=Souvenirs pieux*; *AN=Archives du nord*; *YO=Les Yeux ouverts*.

feels the need to begin with history, genealogy and other biographical records. Her starting point, in other words, is very largely a *written* world. For Yourcenar, it is clearly not so much the subject that is important as its treatment. And although there is only one completed version of *Mémoires d'Hadrien*, it is evident from remarks already quoted that here too Yourcenar was aware that the process of rewriting is potentially never-ending.

Much of the distinctiveness of Yourcenar's compositions stems from her determination that they should be allowed to gestate within her over a long period and become invested with the increasing maturity of her vision. The interrelationship between *œuvre* and life is therefore acutely felt by her. And it is on this, and on the various ways in which our chronological perspectives are overturned, that the claim these works have to universality depends. In all her compositions Yourcenar's essential ambition is to make sense of existence. The motives that dictate her adoption of characters who superficially bear little resemblance to their creator are doubtless many, but one reason, it may be assumed, is her sense of the insignificance of those characteristics that set her apart from her fellow men as an individual being. Through the largely admirable male figures whose perspectives dominate her mature writing, she is engaged in finding a guide for living, perhaps even an art of living. Life is seen as a complex experiment, and it is necessary for Yourcenar's purpose that her characters' lives be seen in their entirety and, in the case of her heroes, that the lives be both long and eventful. All five works of her maturity insist on death as an omnipresent phenomenon. Both Hadrien and Zénon are shown in the face of a death that serves to heighten their self-awareness. Hadrien's concluding exhortation to himself – 'Tâchons d'entrer dans la mort les yeux ouverts' (from which is derived the title of the interviews with Matthieu Galey) – could easily have been pronounced by Zénon, whose physiological learning gives to his self-monitoring a dimension that is denied the Roman emperor. What Yourcenar asks of her heroes is a wisdom based on a vision of things as they are and a commitment to their own individual concept of freedom. It is a measure of her personal adherence to such values that she remains alive to the weaknesses and vulnerability of the characters who so surely command her admiration. It is through these values likewise that she advocates the avoidance of both conventional responses and of a wholesale rejection of tradition.

Mémoires d'Hadrien, which takes the form of a letter from the Emperor to his chosen successor Marc Aurèle, is a far more ambitious work than any of the novels that Yourcenar had published before the war. Initially, Hadrien claims that it is his intention merely to report on the progress of the illness from which he is dying, but the letter soon turns into an account of his life from its earliest days to the present. He attempts to justify this full-blown autobiography on the grounds that he is drawing on his own experience to make good the deficiencies in the young Marc's education. The reader is more likely to conclude that the Emperor is responding to a deep-seated need to make sense of a life that he knows to bear little resemblance to his public image.

For Yourcenar herself the period in which her novel is set was not without significance. As early as 1927 she had underlined a striking statement she had come across in Flaubert's correspondence: 'Les dieux n'étant plus, et le Christ n'étant pas encore, il y a eu, de Cicéron à Marc Aurèle, un moment unique où l'homme seul a été' (*H*, p. 321). Yet however meticulous the research on which the *Mémoires* are based, and for all the sincere tributes paid to her achievement by historians of Ancient Rome, *Mémoires d'Hadrien* is not merely an attempt at an historical re-creation. 'Mon cher Marc' is only a nominal *destinataire* recalled occasionally for the sake of form; it is to a much wider readership that Hadrien's reflections are immediately addressed.

Death is a pervasive presence in the *Mémoires* and not just as a result of the temporal perspective from which Hadrien writes. Though he himself is not to be held entirely responsible, his reign begins and ends with executions. The principal challenge to his mastery of himself and therefore of those around him comes from the unexpected suicide of his beloved Antinoüs. At an early stage in his 'letter', Hadrien pronounces with some satisfaction: 'Je commence à connaître la mort' (p. 28). (We are told in the *Carnets de notes* that the only sentence to survive from the 1934 version was: 'Je commence à apercevoir le profil de ma mort'.) Throughout, there is a constant awareness of death as the reality which must be faced in any attempt to establish a philosophy of life.

That Hadrien is viewed by Yourcenar as a figure who is essentially to be admired is plain. She may justifiably protest at an over-hasty tendency to identify the character with his creator, but it is difficult for the reader not to feel that Hadrien's presence is, in part at least, the result of her distaste for the authorial first-person and that the project is motivated essentially by her desire to establish her own network of values. The most suggestive model of the relationship between the author and her character is perhaps provided *en abyme* in the text by the relationship between Hadrien and Plotine. As Hadrien observes, 'nous étions d'accord presque sur tout' (p. 95). While granting Hadrien a separate existence (and one that is not at odds with the historian's demand for accuracy), Yourcenar appears to have brought her character and herself to a meeting-point of like minds separated more by externals than by essentials.

The author's admiration for Hadrien as expressed outside the text is directed towards his lucidity. But there is much else to attract us in this autobiographer: his positive attitude towards what he feels is natural, his realism, his conscious avoidance of prejudices or extremes, as well as of fixed habits, and thus his open-mindedness and opposition to philosophical system, his refreshing questioning of positions, his determination to argue from direct experience, his dislike of disorder or chaos and the accompanying value he places on an aesthetic response to the world. His observation that 'le mot même d'idéal me déplairait comme trop éloigné du réel' (p. 111) follows naturally from the responses we have seen him make to specific experiences. He is candid in both his view of human nature and the way he sees the human condition, recognising his subjects as 'vains, ignorants, avides', and, less expectedly, 'inquiets' (p. 51), while confessing 'j'attends peu de chose de la condition humaine' (p. 313). Yet he avoids the related temptations of cynicism, pessimism and stoicism, all of which would represent his turning his back on the positive challenge presented by the world. Life is seen as a constant process of initiation and as involving a requirement to face up to perpetual paradox. His reiterated ambition is to become *himself*, a process which, among other things, entails accommodating the oscillation he experiences between a sense of feeling exceptional and the conviction that he is of no significance whatsoever.

It may often be the maxims Hadrien coins that arouse our admiration for him, but Yourcenar endows him with a character that both explains and is explained by the viewpoints these maxims express. The reader is in fact given the impression that Hadrien forges a character for himself, one that will allow him to make the most of the contradictory world in which he finds himself. More precisely, the act of becoming himself is seen principally in terms of accommodating the conflicting claims of self and the world. What allows Hadrien to emerge as a strong character and as someone who is able to experience the world directly is his cultivation of completeness and the reconciliation of opposites. He is, for example, the man of letters and the man of arms. An indication of the kind of self-representation that brings him most satisfaction can be seen from his description of himself astride his horse: 'Si on m'avait laissé le choix de ma condition, j'eusse opté pour celle de Centaure. Entre Borysthènes et moi, les rapports étaient d'une netteté mathématique: il m'obéissait comme à son cerveau, et non comme à son maître.' (p. 14). In other words, the ideal he projects consists of mind and body operating in perfect harmony.

Beginning with the memory of his schoolboy exercises in rhetoric, Hadrien also makes explicit reference to himself as Proteus (pp. 44 and 159), and there can be little doubt that he sees the cultivation of a Protean self as a source of strength. We are told of the ease with which he took over the responsibility of speech-writing for others, Trajan included. One section of his life-story bears the appropriate title '*Varius multiplex multiformis*'. That such possibilities were latent in Hadrien from the beginning is conveyed by the emphasis on his cultural make-up. He is not the pure Roman. On the contrary, he senses himself to be an outsider by virtue of his Spanish origins. Through education he considers his affinity to be not with Rome but with Athens. (The importance of Greece – both ancient and modern – for Yourcenar herself is apparent from many of her writings.) Yet if he has, in common with many of Yourcenar's characters, frequent opportunities to satisfy a yearning for travel, he remains unavoidably a Roman. This cultural amalgam leads him to appreciate the inadequacy of any one strand and gives him an ability to see beyond the perspective of his immediate surroundings. This Proteanism also goes some way towards explaining why his narrative exhibits so many of the hallmarks of creativity rather than merely reflecting the limited viewpoint of one individual.

Hadrien's sexuality is to an even greater degree *multiformis*. It is clear that no single companion can arouse in him the full range of physical and emotional responses for which he seeks an outlet, not even Antinoüs whose significance for Hadrien only takes on such extraordinary dimensions after his self-sacrifice. He thus engages in liaisons with young men essentially as a complement to his relationships with women. His only apparent requirement appears to be that such couplings should not lead to the formation of a bond or other restriction on his life. His favourite mistress is precisely the one who talks to him of the passion she feels for another man. Paradoxically, the urge for sexual gratification does not seem strong at all. For just as any individual sexual relationship appears to him incomplete, so sex is only one area in which this self seeks fulfilment. His relationship with Trajan's wife, in which the impossibility of consummation serves to highlight the intellectual affinity between them, is one of the most important in his life and is in no way demeaned by his awareness of her readiness to devote herself to his advancement. It is undeniable that the emotional climax of his life is occasioned by his love for Antinoüs and by the cult he instigates after the latter's suicide. Yet this neither makes homosexuality as such the true subject of the novel nor even authorises us to consider the work as foremost a love story. His relationship with Antinoüs is prized ultimately for the way it promotes further discovery of the self and its values.

In Hadrien, then, Yourcenar has succeeded in creating a character whose refinement in so many different domains exercises a powerful attraction. At the same time, the character's inability to consider himself to be in any fundamental way different from other men has the effect of making him less of a hero and more of a guide along the path to self-discovery. In an illuminating phrase his creator designates him 'un homme presque sage' (*H*, p. 328). It may none the less come as something of a surprise to find Yourcenar writing (again in the *Carnets de notes de 'Mémoires d'Hadrien'*): 'A de certains moments, d'ailleurs peu nombreux, il m'est même arrivé de sentir que l'empereur mentait. Il fallait alors le laisser mentir, comme nous tous' (p. 341). (Hadrien himself claims: 'J'y ai menti le moins possible' – p. 29.) We are not given many clues by the author herself as to the nature of this mendacity or lack of sincerity, but it is a tribute to her gift for characterisation that if we set aside our admiration for the Emperor and ask whether a presentation of his life by another might be less flattering, the text indeed assumes a new complexity.

Hadrien's very strengths may well be found to have their weaknesses. We do not necessarily find ourselves liking the character as much as we admire what he stands for. The lucidity may in fact act as something of a barrier, both in the relationships Hadrien has in life and in those the character entertains with us. He is an isolated figure not just by virtue of his position but also precisely because of his inability to see things as other than they are. He candidly confides at one point 'on m'aimait peu' (p. 50). The fact that he is prepared to catalogue the unattractive features of his behaviour (p. 66) does not automatically render him endearing. It is tempting to conclude that his ambition, which is revealed to us fitfully, was still more overriding than he is prepared to admit and would have been portrayed rather differently by an outside observer. As he himself recognises, his life might be more sharply defined by what he is *not* than by what he has been. There is always the risk, too, that the Protean ideal will lead to superficial diversity, a permanent sense of *disponibilité* rather than actual fulfilment. Hadrien displays justifiable pride in his achievements (the '*tellus stabilita*' of his coinage), yet his life follows a parabola: he undergoes a significant change after the death of Antinoüs. We may wonder whether he should not be held partially responsible for this young man's death. It is certainly doubtful whether his achievements bring him lasting satisfaction.

Ultimately, none of these shortcomings or unfortunate consequences destroys the essentially positive thrust of *Mémoires d'Hadrien*. In the absence of clear indications to the contrary, it is by no means certain that they represent part of what Yourcenar consciously set out to show. It is at least as likely that they follow naturally from the logic of Hadrien's character, as profoundly assimilated by his creator. What does invite recognition, however, is that Yourcenar is here eschewing idealism and realising in a highly convincing manner the ambition of her more laudable characters to face up to the limitations at the heart of the human condition.

Of all Yourcenar's post-war works, *L'Œuvre au noir*, arguably the most complex, is the only one to feature an entirely fictional central character. The lives of many different Renaissance thinkers and scientists go into Zénon's making. He is not predominantly any one of them. His close *parenté* with Hadrien, on the other hand, is evident. He is marked out by many of the same qualities. Yet as a result of his resolution to penetrate realms beyond the confines of accepted beliefs, his world view in *L'Œuvre au noir* is inevitably more enigmatic than that of the Roman statesman. At the same time the novel was considered by its author to be very much a product of the 1950s and 1960s, separated from *Mémoires d'Hadrien* by such events as Suez, Hungary and Algeria. Its central concern with rebellion and a quest for freedom was not without contemporary significance when it appeared in 1968, but it would be uncharacteristic of any of Yourcenar's works to reflect the mood of a mass movement. As Zénon observes (and we may be tempted to see here an indication of the author's personal experience), he had thought himself free at the age of twenty but now realises that it has taken him a lifetime to work towards such a state.

L'Œuvre au noir is again a work rooted in a profound familiarity with the author's chosen epoch and, more especially, with its modes of thought. Yourcenar indeed succeeds in evoking her sixteenth-century world with great immediacy, be it the everyday life of the Germano-Flemish commercial and banking world or the suppression of the Anabaptist rebellion at the siege of Münster. Zénon is published by no less a printer than Etienne Dolet in Lyons. And it is no mean achievement that the encounters with such figures as

Margaret of Austria and Catherine of Medici seem wholly acceptable. The novel recalls a turbulent Europe divided between king and emperor, Reformation and Counter-Reformation. (The title of Yourcenar's original youthful project had been *Remous*.) It was an age which, for the geographical centre of the novel, also meant foreign occupation. But Yourcenar's principal concern remains intellectual: the freedom of the mind in an age of political and religious repression. At one point, the young Zénon is described as 'ce David aux prises avec le Goliath scolastique' (*ŒN*, p. 40).

In Yourcenar's eyes merely to illustrate what historians have always known about the birth of the modern world would be otiose. And as was the case with *Mémoires d'Hadrien*, she explores in *L'Œuvre au noir* temptations and responses that did not die with the passing of her characters or with subsequent changes to religious and scientific orthodoxies. Her fictional world is the product of a belief in a substantial core of human experience that does not change. The fact that Wiwine's uncle, the curé of a church in Bruges, is, like Yourcenar's own paternal ancestors, a Cleenwerck is simply a playful indication of the way in which this novel is associated in the author's mind with a more personal historical continuity. There would indeed seem to be for her no clear separation between the activities and values of a Henri-Juste Ligre and those of his counterparts who peopled the world of her parents and grandparents. But all this is of minor interest alongside that which allows Yourcenar and her readers to feel that Zénon's life and the lessons he draws from it, far from being contained within an historical compartment, still possess power for a world that seemingly has been totally transformed.

So far as the title is concerned, the author herself offers essential enlightenment. Just over half-way through the novel, it is revealed that 'l'œuvre au noir' is an alchemical term designating the first of three stages in the Great Work: 'cet essai de dissolution et de calcination des formes qui est la part la plus difficile du Grand Œuvre' (p. 237). That this particular process could offer a suggestive model to a twentieth-century novelist had already been recognised by Yourcenar in her essay on Thomas Mann (1956). There, it is stated: 'le vieux terme des philosophes alchimistes convient à cette peinture par Mann des dissolutions et des résolutions de la substance humaine.'[4] Mann's views in *The Magic Mountain* are more generally compared to those of the 'grands occultistes humanistes de la Renaissance'. They have in common a perception of 'l'homme

---

4. M. Yourcenar, *Sous bénéfice d'inventaire*, nouvelle édition (Gallimard, Idées, 1978), pp. 298–9.

microcosme, formé de la même substance et régi par les mêmes lois que le cosmos, soumis comme la matière elle-même à une série de transmutations partielles ou totales, relié à tout par une sorte de riche capillarité'.[5] As Yourcenar goes on to note, this is quite alien to the Platonic or Christian opposition between body and soul. Yet for her the distinguishing feature of religion is precisely its capacity, as its etymology suggests, to link all things. (She admits to regarding herself as increasingly religious, though her beliefs clearly draw significantly on non-Christian sources.) This should not obscure the fact, however, that the formula 'œuvre au noir' also possesses a resonance beyond its function as an alchemical term and serves ultimately as an indicator of pessimism. Culturally, the novel traces the movement from the initial optimism of the Renaissance to the bleak practices of the Inquisition, whose exercise of torture places it in absolute opposition to Zénon's practice with regard to the body.

It is alchemy that encourages in Zénon a life of constant experimentation. His belief that it could bring him closer to the meaning of life motivates his journey from Bruges to León (home of a distinguished alchemist) in an ironic variation of the traditional pilgrimage to Compostella. One of the clearest indications of his method is to be found in the description of him, on his return from his extensive European travels, as 'plus avancé dans la voie qui consiste à tout nier, pour voir si l'on peut ensuite réaffirmer quelque chose, à tout défaire, pour regarder ensuite tout se refaire sur un autre plan ou à une autre guise' (p. 194). There are also abundant indications of his effort to see the individual mind and body as an amalgam of elements that reproduce in microcosm the behaviour of all matter.

This does not mean that Zénon exhibits all the characteristics of an alchemist of his time or that all his intellectual procedures or practices may legitimately be subsumed in the category of alchemy. The most celebrated quest of the alchemists – the manufacture of gold – is not at the centre of his concerns, though he does tell his cousin Henri-Maximilien that one day he expects this will prove possible. It is significant that most of the references to the production of gold are in the form of witticisms. Moreover, Zénon is, much more widely, 'un philosophe', as well as being a scientist and a doctor. He lists his diverse achievements, characterised by a curiosity for all kinds of knowledge, in the course of his conversation with Henri-Maximilien in Innsbruck (p. 159). Like Hadrien, his

5. Ibid., p. 271.

quest, announced at the age of twenty, is for *himself*. This is not to deny that alchemy colours each one of his activities, but it is a first indication that we should not see his life purely in terms of *arcana*. In her *note de l'auteur*, Yourcenar reminds us: 'on discute encore si cette expression [the formula 'œuvre au noir'] s'appliquait à d'audacieuses expériences sur la matière elle-même ou s'entendait symboliquement des épreuves de l'esprit se libérant des routines et des préjugés' (p. 459). And in a characteristic concluding reflection she adds: 'sans doute a-t-elle signifié tour à tour ou à la fois l'un et l'autre.' *Se libérer des routines et des préjugés* – there is much to indicate that this is the level on which Zénon's life is at its most suggestive, that it is as an account of an individual in search of his freedom that *L'Œuvre au noir* is essentially to be appreciated.

Yourcenar's observation about the uncertain status of alchemy in the sixteenth century is further valuable in that it sanctions us to see the portrayal of Zénon's procedures as intentionally mysterious or ambiguous. The glimpses we are given of his experiments are tantalisingly few. Just what he believes is, to a significant extent, shrouded in uncertainty. This of course contributes to the sense of mystery and danger associated with the questioning of orthodoxy. But, more importantly, it reflects this lucid individual's uncertainty about the nature of his own activities and about any attempt to understand the human world, a world he readily admits (p. 262) is 'fort confus'. 'Nous en savons moins sur les routes et le but d'une vie d'homme que sur ses migrations l'oiseau' (p. 417), he declares. The work would doubtless have seemed inauthentic if Zénon's strategies had been more clear-cut and of readily identifiable status.

The suggestiveness of this mystery and ambiguity (which is none the less accompanied by what we sense to be a sure grasp of general direction and of the essential way to proceed) is amply borne out by one of the most fundamental features of the composition – the almost self-conscious use of fire as a leitmotif. It occurs with such frequency as to be most evidently a challenge to interpretation. 'C'était', we are told, 'une de ces époques où la raison humaine se trouve prise dans un cercle de flammes.' Yet Zénon's adventure is associated principally with his recognition of himself as *fire*. His resolution to escape from the dangers that threaten him in Bruges eventually falters, for example, when he comes face to face with the sea, which is no place for this creature of Fire. All this is more than a reflection of the centrality of fire to the alchemist's experiments. Within the novel the element functions with all the ambiguity of a poetic symbol.

The reader, who is perhaps likely to entertain a degree of scepticism with regard to alchemy, has to be ready, like Zénon, to step outside his routines and prejudices. The curious structure of the novel is evidently designed to this end. *L'Œuvre au noir* opens with Henri-Maximilien, and the reader may suppose that the soldier–poet is to be the central character. With the introduction of the complementary Zénon at a doubtless symbolic cross-roads, there is the suggestion that both characters will be of equal importance to the novelist's purpose. The obviously contrived meetings between the two are in fact infrequent. Henri-Maximilien is, moreover, despatched to his death half-way through the novel. There is also curiously little about Zénon in the early sections. Later, many of the events of his life are conveyed to us only through the memories that he has retained after settling in Bruges. (The shortness of the chapter entitled 'Les derniers voyages de Zénon' is particularly striking.) Many events that the reader is tempted to assume are significant are mentioned only in passing. Zénon has, for instance, been involved with some colourful and influential figures on the European stage, but this part of his life remains unilluminated. This is essentially a means of making us accept that such events are not important in themselves. The physical journey is significant only as a stage in a development that is destined to continue far beyond; it is a means of discovering that the traveller is not led routinely to the discoveries he expects. Once again, as with *Mémoires d'Hadrien*, the vital perspective is that of looking back after a life-time of activity.

The final stage is that of maturity. Paradoxically (though not, of course, without parallel in French literature), Zénon experiences freedom in imprisonment and death. ('On n'est pas libre tant qu'on désire, qu'on veut, qu'on craint, peut-être tant qu'on vit' (p. 223), he muses at an earlier stage.) The alchemist is required to identify with the notion of life as imprisonment. Zénon exhorts himself not to try to understand (*comprendre*), but to experience (*subir*). We are thus offered a remarkable description of the philosopher's self-inflicted death, a physiological monitoring of the process until the moment of the narrator's unexceptionable final statement: 'c'est aussi loin qu'on peut aller dans la fin [not, we should note, 'l'histoire'] de Zénon.' The reader has already learnt of Zénon's approval for the (in fact spurious addition to the) quotation from Petronius recalled by Henri-Maximilien: 'le beau de la chose, approuva Zénon, est que votre auteur n'imagine même pas que le dernier jour d'un sage puisse être vécu autrement qu'en paix. Nous ferons en sorte de nous en souvenir à notre heure' (p. 166). The philosopher's approval is also forthcoming for the suicide of Pierre de Hamaere, a monk whom he otherwise detests.

This is a novel strewn with corpses (murders, suicides, deaths in war and from the plague) and differing attitudes towards death. *L'Œuvre au noir* is indeed a veritable *livre-cimetière*. Zénon's life can be seen as a long training in the acceptance of death as the only certainty. The section of the book that we experience in the present is marked by Zénon's relative indifference to his safety. His turning back from the sea has already been noted. Subsequently, his integrity will not allow him to play along with the charades necessary if he is to avoid the sentence of death. His is a death that is willed, a death that we admire, ultimately a necessary death that no one can prevent.

The whole of Zénon's life has been a preparation for this loss of self. The type of self that he first needs to cultivate is familiar from Hadrien. As Yourcenar puts it elsewhere, 'Tout voyageur est Ulysse – il se doit d'être aussi Protée' (*YO*, p. 306). In this respect Zénon too is favoured from birth. As the son of Hilzonde and Alberico de' Numi, he is the meeting point of complements: North (Bruges) and South (Florence–Rome), Catholic and Protestant (Hilzonde becoming an Anabaptist on her marriage to Simon Adriansen), lay and ecclesiastic (though it may be noted that the process of *complémentarité* is duplicated: Alberico may be a Catholic prelate but *numi* is Italian for the pagan gods; we are perhaps permitted also to detect a humorous allusion to Wagner's dwarf who has designs on the Rheingold). On the other hand, there is equal emphasis on this as a *chance* encounter, and it is significant that the coupling does not preside over Zénon's upbringing. He starts out a bastard and before long is an orphan, two privileged states seen as offering a degree of freedom, as in the works of Gide. (A parallel exists here with Zénon's half-sister Martha, a much more significant character than might be supposed. She is an example of potential that is wasted largely because she is a woman: 'Il [Zénon] avait été ce rebelle qu'elle [Martha] n'avait pas su être' – *ŒN*, p. 403.) Zénon indeed possesses a sense of difference that marks him out from the rest of the world. He is neither understood nor appreciated by most of his fellow-men. He could also be described as 'bisexual' (if that were not too ready-made a term). We note his uncertainty as to which of his own hypotheses explains his sexual behaviour. What is striking is his relative lack of concern as to which of them is the most convincing. Such indifference increases as he progresses towards the state of non-desire.

Presiding over his character is the concept of Renaissance man as formulated by Pico della Mirandola in his address to Adam, from which Yourcenar takes some appealing lines as her opening epigraph: 'Mais toi [...] par ton propre arbitre [...] tu te définis toi-même [...] Je ne t'ai fait ni céleste ni terrestre, mortel ou immortel, afin que de toi-même, librement [...] tu achèves ta propre forme' (my ellipses). The name Zénon is enigmatic. It is clearly intended to stand out from the heavy-sounding names of his milieu, be they Flemish, German, French or Latin. Beyond this, are we, for example, to think of the Zeno of the paradox beloved of the creator of 'Le Cimetière marin', of Zen, or simply of the concluding letter of the alphabet? The name of this character who does not appear to belong anywhere in particular is visibly part of his freedom to develop in different and complementary ways. His is an existence that lends itself to fictions: in the chapter entitled 'La Vie publique' the reader is treated to a list of sightings and rumours in place of the expected authoritative account of his doings. Once more, the writing is designed to detach the reader from his routines. Many of these reported sightings are plausible, and later evidence will sometimes reveal the extent to which they are founded on truth. But here too we are made to realise that the details of his journeying are not in themselves of much importance.

Much explicit reference is in fact made to Zénon's increasing sense of the irrelevance of his name. He feels that the name he assumes on his return to Flanders is no more arbitrary than the one he had originally been given. The process begins with his fellow countrymen forgetting his existence: 'Zénon cessait d'être pour eux une personne, un visage, une âme, un homme vivant quelque part sur un point de la circonférence du monde; il devenait un nom, moins qu'un nom, une étiquette fanée sur un bocal où pourrissaient lentement quelques mémoires incomplètes et mortes de leur propre passé' (p. 79). Much more significantly, by the time of the *mise au point* represented by the all-important chapter entitled 'L'Abîme', we read: '*Non habet nomen proprium*: il était de ces hommes qui ne cessent pas jusqu'au bout de s'étonner d'avoir un nom' (p. 209). An insistent notion in Zénon's thinking is the way the human body is matter which, as the alchemist observes to Henri-Maximilien (p. 146), renews itself entirely at least once every twenty years. This is a perspective that is re-emphasised in the opening sentence of 'L'Abîme': 'Peu à peu, comme un homme qui absorbe chaque jour une certaine nourriture finit par en être modifié dans sa substance, et même dans sa forme, engraisse ou maigrit, tire de ces mets une force, ou contracte en les ingérant des maux qu'il ne connaissait pas, des changements presque imperceptibles se faisaient en lui, fruit d'habitudes nouvelles qu'il s'était acquises' (p. 209).

Zénon's progression is in the direction of becoming a universal figure. In 'L'Abîme', we discover just how far his attitudes have taken him. Essentially, he has succeeded in breaking down categories:

> Le temps, le lieu, la substance perdaient ces attributs qui sont pour nous leurs frontières; la forme n'était plus que l'écorce déchiquetée de la substance; la substance s'égouttait dans un vide qui n'était pas son contraire, le temps et l'éternité n'étaient qu'une même chose, comme une eau noire qui coule dans une immuable nappe d'eau noire. Zénon s'abîmait dans ces visions comme un chrétien dans une méditation sur Dieu. (p. 213)

This last comparison, seemingly straightforward and innocuous, takes us to the heart of what makes Zénon an ambiguous and enigmatic character. We start by seeing him simply as an atheist: although, in this confused world where the boundaries between science, magic and religion are not boldly traced, it is possible to combine, as does Bartholommé Campanus, religion and alchemy, the latter has no doubt that 'son élève avait renoncé en secret aux consolations du Christ' (p. 38). What are we then to make of the fact that Zénon chooses as his pseudonym Sébastien Théus, apart, that is, from its appropriate connotation of martyrdom? At one level the name is purely fortuitous – the certificate he bought from a German widow was in the name of one Gott. But we are unlikely to halt our inquiry there. An obvious conclusion would be that the name underlines the extent to which Zénon has replaced God by Man (or himself) as his own deity. Yet there is much in the later stages of this work to make us unhappy with such an easy interpretation, starting with the closeness of the older Zénon to both the prior of the Cordeliers and the bishop, a position which, Yourcenar comments elsewhere (*YO*, p. 163), would have been inconceivable when Zénon was thirty years younger. In this work in which paradox abounds, the reader frequently has the sense of extremes having much in common. Although Zénon insists on rejecting unambiguous equivalences ('que pouvons-nous tirer de ces équivalences, sinon que l'esprit humain a une certaine pente?' – *ŒN*, p. 276), there is no denying that he and the prior understand each other in a way that has no parallel elsewhere in the book.

The uncertain status or significance of Zénon's position is further emphasised by an important set of responses to him which in this rich and densely woven fabric risk being overlooked. These are the responses of a gaggle of different women, all of whom are more or less characterised by their simplicity or by their closeness to Nature. To all these women (Wiwine, the dame de Frösö, Jean Myers's servant Jacqueline, Zénon's aunt by marriage) Zénon is an attractive figure to whom they feel compelled (at least in their minds) to offer themselves. It is not just Zénon's relative indifference to women that makes these erotic encounters unusual. The nature of the women themselves and the form their actions assume take us beyond the realm of the purely sexual. If they owe something to the medieval German and Flemish traditions of the grotesque, they are also marked out as examples of seemingly excessive devotion or adoration. Jacqueline, for instance, takes it upon herself to murder her master so that Zénon may inherit. What pulls us up sharply, however, are the specifically Christian terms of reference that are introduced at these moments. Of Wiwine it is said that she finds Zénon 'beau comme le sombre Christ de bois peint' (p. 70). Her attentions are then compared to 'une petite Madeleine innocente'. The insistence in nearly all these cases is on succouring Zénon. Unlike some of the other women, the dame de Frösö is beautiful, but the emphasis in the following description is elsewhere: 'Tout en elle était beau, sa haute taille, son teint clair, ses mains habiles à bander les plaies et à essuyer les sueurs des fièvres' (pp. 228–9). Zénon later uses on the prior the therapeutic skills he had learned from his Nordic hostess. ('Zénon lui massa longuement les pieds et les jambes, comme le lui avait jadis enseigné à le faire la dame de Frösö' – p. 309.) These various episodes are not Rabelaisian *clins d'œil* in the face of female sexual insatiability. Instead they confer on Zénon a symbolic status. And this in a work in which we read that Hans Bockhold, the self-styled 'Christ-Roi', 'restait un Christ, au sens où chaque homme pourrait être un Christ' (p. 102); and in which the plague-stricken Bénédicite's response to Zénon's presence at her bedside was to hum what seemed to Martha 'un bout d'air frivole mêlé à une complainte sur la visite du bon Jésus-Christ' (p. 126). Thus the idea of Zénon as a Christ-figure is placed unmistakably before us. Is it an identification to be accepted or discarded? Yourcenar would probably answer, 'both'. Zénon's death can certainly be seen as a martyrdom, raising him above the unsatisfactory nature of the world, both public and private.

All this poses more questions than can confidently be answered and seems to point to the need for the individual reader to find his own personal interpretation. This is consonant with precisely what is so remarkable about the conversations between Zénon and the prior. Their relationship remains experimental, one that is finding its way, calling its own conduct into question without disavowing it. The two interlocutors are constantly surprising themselves. Yourcenar's writing throughout promotes a sense of the elusiveness of implications and advocates a refusal to take comfort in labels. We have access merely to partial identifications, partial explanations. There is a sense that everything is an approximation. The whole has a bewildering complexity.

What cannot be gainsaid is that Zénon evolves towards an enviable maturity. We have seen how his sense of life is a preparation for death. In the conversation with Henri-Maximilien at Innsbruck he reveals: 'je m'efforce chaque jour de penser un peu plus clairement que la veille' (p. 158). And when later he has been condemned, he observes to Bartholommé in a rare resort to sarcasm: 'Je ne commettrai plus l'indécence qui consiste à essayer de montrer les choses comme elles sont' (p. 415). His career is characterised by a frankness and honesty that cause him to stand out from the rest of this large cast. For all his superiority, his recognition of his inability fully to explain the manifold mysteries that fascinate him earns our respect. He also sticks to his principles. There is a striking dismissiveness of the easy approach (even his temporary break with vegetarianism is in order to prove to himself that his stance was not due simply to a dislike of red meat). Yourcenar may call him 'naturellement ascétique' (*YO*, p. 179), but he offers the reverse of the ready-made impression that the reader is likely to have of such a being. He exhibits no obsessive contempt for more sensual pleasures. The author's inclination to criticise or reject is at all times balanced by her recognition of the need to avoid the opposite excess. As she observes with reference to the would-be rebel Martha: 'L'orpheline savait qu'en tournant le dos aux aberrations romaines ses parents n'avaient fait que s'engager plus avant dans une route qui ne va pas au ciel [. . .] L'idolâtrie était Charybde mais la révolte, la misère, le danger et l'abjection Scylla' (*ŒN*, pp. 116–17).

Thus Zénon avoids being what he could so easily have become: the portrait of a picturesque and eccentric disciple of sixteenth-century esoterism. In bringing him alive Yourcenar endows him with mental habits and standards that go well beyond the intellectual imperatives of his age. This is not at its core, any more than *Mémoires d'Hadrien* had been, an historical novel. The precise setting is ultimately of much less importance than we might have expected. Yourcenar's concern is with the mysteries of existence, the implications of the inevitability of death, and with the way we react (or might do well to consider reacting) to it. She probes the extent of our potential understanding, our epistemological limitations, and the way audacious attempts to confront such questions have a tendency to meet with repression (from society, the establishment, and those institutions charged with maintaining a monopoly of knowledge and safeguarding the status quo). That does not signify that the novel is to be considered revolutionary. Yourcenar seeks not to overthrow the social order, but to preserve the possibilities for individual freedom and above all for the exceptional and the authentically unorthodox to flourish. There remains, however, a recognition that there will always be a tension with the needs that an inevitably more conservative society ascribes to itself. Yourcenar is a realist and an aristocrat in outlook. Pervading the work is a sense of superiority born of a recognition of limitations and shortcomings.

L'Œuvre au noir is, then, a novel that is quietly subversive of its reader's routines. Interpretations are not imposed. We are pointed towards the pursuit of meanings situated in the interstices of parallels, differences and complementary attributes. There are leitmotifs and symbols that require interpretation, but they do not permit of neat conclusions and the confident identification of equivalences. Implicit throughout is the view that our perception and understanding of this world can never be more than a series of approximations.

The opening sentence of *Souvenirs pieux* informs us that 'L'être que j'appelle moi vint au monde un certain lundi 8 juin 1903, vers les 8 heures du matin, à Bruxelles . . .' The reader assumes that a detailed and intimate self-portrait will follow. Yet the volume ends almost four-hundred pages later with the statement 'Mon visage commence à se dessiner sur l'écran du temps'. That is not all. By the end of *Archives du nord*, the author has advanced no further than a picture of herself in infancy asleep on Madame Azélie's lap. Her subsequent life is condensed in a single paragraph governed by the future tense. Two-hundred years previously, Sterne's Tristram Shandy had substituted an anecdotal account of his immediate environment for the 'life and opinions' promised in his title. So Yourcenar, albeit without unduly foregrounding idiosyncrasy for its own sake, delights in the digressive nature of her narrative, which has no difficulty in accommodating, for example, lengthy passages on the friendship of Robespierre and Saint-Just or the paintings of Rubens. It continually postpones the moment at which her own biography will take up its expected position as the text's central concern.

Yourcenar's reconstruction of her family's history constantly emphasises the poverty of the material available. The past is seen as having survived merely as remnants or fragments that provoke an almost archaeological challenge. They are indeed referred to at one point as *tessons antiques*. The author's ancestors have bequeathed her little more than a trunk of bric-à-brac: painted portraits, photographs, trinkets and objets d'art, school reports, a dying patient's temperature chart. Her paternal grandfather's lengthy visit to Italy as a young man survives in the form of the souvenirs he brought back as gifts, an album of dried flowers and the letters to his family that in his old age he copied out for posterity but which in their conventionality are felt to conceal as much as they reveal. The title of the first volume clearly reflects the author's motives in writing, but at a more concrete level it refers quite specifically to the 'keepsakes' distributed in memory of the recently departed. If Yourcenar is led to wonder about the appropriateness of the biblical texts chosen for a given individual, it is only the better to highlight the conventional (and, indeed, commercial) nature of the *souvenirs pieux*, and how little they have to say to the family historian. Beyond the contents of the attic, a spent existence may now be little more than a summary on a tombstone. It is not surprising that the author admits to considerable gratitude to a maternal relative who was a prominent Belgian literary figure in the mid-nineteenth century and who provides her with the privilege of a more expansive written source.

The sources (even the oral testimonies of her father come to her in snatches over many years) have therefore to be supplemented. Yourcenar makes no secret of the way her narrative is the product of an interplay between surviving fragments and the various models she has available to her from the texts of social historians and novelists (herself included). It is striking how often an appeal is made to existing literary representations of a particular period, from a reference to the unfortunate absence in her maternal grandmother's family of a figure in the mould of Tolstoy's Dolly to an invitation to bring together in our minds for much of a particular episode her father's father (Michel-Charles) and Flaubert's Frédéric Moreau. We can none the less also find her refusing to flesh out descriptions in this way and indicating just how mechanical and automatic a process it can become. ('Je pourrais, certes, à l'aide d'un fond de cuisine littéraire, faire de chic le portrait de pauvres laboureurs égayés çà et là par une pointe de jacquerie et beaucoup de braconnage' – *AN*, p. 168.) Intellectual honesty is a characteristic of her writing, and no attempt is made to hide the extent to which the greater completeness of her portrayal leads inevitably to a reinforcement of familiar and conventional views. She apologises on more than one occasion for resorting to cliché. It takes only a little reflection to appreciate, however, that convention is an explicit theme of these volumes, as is the unremarkable nature of the subject matter. The cliché may in fact also take on a new resonance as a result of there being a perfect fit between its formulation and what has been conveyed less abstractly in the descriptions that have gone before.

Where we may have expected the narration to be self-effacing before the all-important facts of the family history, we find a project that is constantly calling attention to itself. If Marguerite is not often present as a character in the narrative, Yourcenar persistently focuses attention on her activity as researcher and writer of the text we are reading. It is not simply a question of highlighting the difficulty of obtaining access to past worlds; she openly delights on occasion in fabricating a picture for which she possesses no direct evidence ('J'aime à imaginer'), even if the result can only be a plausible period piece. She may even evoke a scenario which she admits could not have happened. (This may, of course, serve actually to heighten the distinctiveness of the milieu that is being described.) It is such procedures as these that, in part, reveal the continuity with her post-war fiction, a situation which is underlined by her recalling a moment in Hadrien's life to compensate for the lack of direct knowledge of some particularly distant forbears. It is with no sense of incongruity that she refers to the characters of *L'Œuvre au noir* alongside her own Flemish ancestors and confesses to finding attractive the idea of having Zénon as a brother.

Digression is presented as being closer to the project's central concerns than may at first be apparent ('je digresse moins qu'on ne pourrait le croire' – *SP*, p. 88). Without endowing her project with the ambitions of the author of *A la recherche du temps perdu*, Yourcenar, a self-avowed Proustian, has produced a text indelibly marked by the Proustian revolution in the evocation of the past. Her readiness to confront the apparent mediocrity of the lives of her ancestors ('la vie domestique [. . .] avec ses petites et épaisses habitudes' – *SP*, p. 308) in the absence of a series of dramatic highlights in their existence, the impression of the sheer randomness of the relics and information that have survived, and the realisation that in re-creating the past she is essentially concerned with establishing a relationship between the past and her own awareness of the present, once more place the emphasis on the actual moment of writing. This is vividly the case in *Souvenirs pieux*, where the narrative is punctuated by accounts of the author's return to Belgium in 1929, 1956 and 1971 in search of traces of her maternal family and their dwellings.

The sub-genre to which *Souvenirs pieux* and *Archives du nord* might appear to belong – the family history much beloved of amateur writers – is held up to faint ridicule. The conventions of such writing, which certain of Yourcenar's ancestors had indeed sought to practise, are felt to be at odds with the author's own motivation. Accepted notions of what constitutes a significant event and of what is appropriate to reveal to posterity are thrown into question by example. It is not that the selection of content is necessarily different, but rather a matter of the uncompromising way the material is revealed for what it is, thereby subverting, at least partially, the ethos of clan or *gens* which the genre apparently being imitated is so concerned to foster. When in *Archives du nord*, Michel echoes the influential Gidean 'familles je vous hais', this would seem to be an extreme form of an attitude that dictates much of the writer's response to her own project. Just as with much parody, however, there is undoubtedly also a positive bond with these many characters she has at best imperfectly known. The title *Souvenirs pieux* is not so much ironic as ambiguous.

In both the volumes of *Le Labyrinthe du monde* published in the 1970s, there are significant strands representing the author's particular concerns in the modern world. The experience of increased industrialisation haunts the passing references to the coalfields on which the family's fortunes were built in the nineteenth century. Our natural belief in progress is frequently held up to question, as earlier equivalents of what we might have supposed to be quintessential examples of modernity are placed before us. The broad timescale adopted is so wielded as to indicate the fragility – and indeed insignificance – of a single human existence set against the immensity of time. History generally is used to demythologise our conventional ways of looking at our own lives in the present. Ultimately, the emphasis is placed not so much on the lost world of the past as on a world that is now dying. The lives of the women, predominant in *Souvenirs pieux*, know only the events of childbirth and death. In the case of Marguerite's mother, puerperal fever unites the two. The fertility of the age in which her grandmothers lived is sensed to be addled by the periodic production of a child who is physically handicapped or 'simple d'esprit'. But with the paucity of children produced by their descendants, the biographer becomes acutely aware of the fact that so many old established families die out, just like the dwellings that had housed them.

The fact remains that it is the nineteenth century, the world of Yourcenar's grandparents and the early lives of her parents, that comes to dominate both volumes. Once again, we are aware not just of that world itself but of the curiosity the author brings to it, and of her awareness of her changed perspective: she is conscious of asking questions that would not have been thought of at the time. It is an age that fascinates her precisely for the secretiveness and furtiveness that accompany its regard for convention, though it is a source of regret to her that so few of the secrets are accessible. 'La chambre à coucher du XIXe siècle', she declares, 'est l'antre aux Mystères' (*SP*, p. 130). Although only too aware of the way the period can appear ridiculous or worse, her reconstruction, or rather deconstruction, of the age is noteworthy for its lack of impatience with those who are merely the embodiments of these conventions. A modern perspective cannot help but reveal what to our eyes seems naïveté – the apparent lack of awareness of the erotic significance of the print of 'La Cruche cassée' brought back from the Louvre as a honeymoon souvenir, for example – but this is not seen as cause for a sense of superiority. The satisfaction comes purely from seeing things for what they are, rather than veiled by the practices of convention and decency. The description in *Archives du nord* of the historic railway accident that killed virtually all the passengers other than the twenty-two-year-old Michel-Charles suddenly propels us out of the world of Frédéric Moreau with the introduction of the horrific, though doubtless medically attested, image of a naked corpse in a Priapic pose.

Woman's lot is evoked with sympathy and without sentimentality. Nevertheless, it is possible to sense the relief with which Yourcenar turns to at least some of the male family members, whose lives are moderately more eventful. If *Souvenirs pieux* is ostensibly the quest for Fernande, the mother Marguerite has never known, she is forced to admit that she knows little of the early life of this woman who went on to die young. (Typically, the author claims that the absence of her biological mother was not a traumatic experience.) The emotional centre of the book is, quite unexpectedly, the relationship between Octave and his brother Remo, a youthful suicide. Of the friendship between Robespierre and Saint-Just, Yourcenar had already observed: 'L'attachement d'un homme à un autre homme est toujours un phénomène noble' (*SP*, p. 106). In the context of Octave and Remo, it is, perhaps, in large part the absence of convention in the bond that causes it to assume a particular prestige in the biographer's eyes.

Of the two volumes, *Souvenirs pieux* possesses the more complex structure, partly as a result of being more densely populated. This volume having been used to depict the age and its conventions as much as the individuals of the family who have so little to distinguish them, the way is left open in *Archives du nord* for a simpler narrative dominated by the extensive re-creation of the lives of the author's grandfather, Michel-Charles, and her father, Michel. Though the former is not of the stuff of which remarkable men are made ('Michel-Charles n'est pas un grand homme. Je le définirais comme un homme quelconque, si l'expérience ne nous apprenait qu'il n'y a pas d'homme quelconque' – *AN*, p. 150), there is a sense in which his son Michel explains – and, it might be felt, completes – the whole project. However fragmented the conversations over several decades, the need to resort to the powers of the imagination is much less evident here than at other points in *Le Labyrinthe du monde*. Even so, we remain aware of the presence of the writer, marvelling at a relationship that has allowed the revelation of much that we might have expected to remain hidden to a daughter. There is no doubt that, for Marguerite, Michel de C[rayencour] is an exceptional being, a figure who, given the limitations of the period in which he lived, emerges in her mind as a worthy companion to Hadrien and Zénon. His attitudes and actions reveal him preceding his writer-daughter in dismantling so many of the conventions of the age. He is the rebel, the deserter (three times), the traveller, the gambler. It is only in one of his relatively brief spells as a married man that Marguerite can describe him as 'pris malgré lui dans des usages et des conventions dont il n'a ni le courage ni l'envie de se dépêtrer tout à fait' (*SP*, p. 35). This is the man whom elsewhere she describes as 'un homme infiniment libre, peut-être l'homme le plus libre que j'aie connu' (*YO*, p. 24). Above all, like Zénon, he is represented as an object of desire. From the schoolmaster-priest who places his hand on the young boy's bare knee to the various married women in whose homes he lodges, Michel exerts by his mere presence an irresistible attraction. While still in the realm of the accurate chronicle, we may sense a hint of the way the involvement of the writing self edges the representation gently towards a process of mythification.

In turning from Imperial Rome to sixteenth-century Flanders Yourcenar had already taken a decisive step towards the engagement with a personal past that becomes her more direct concern in *Le Labyrinthe du monde*. What characterises this movement more specifically, however, is the close association increasingly discernible between the autobiographical project and an acute sense of the presence of a father who, she confesses in *Les Yeux ouverts*, had not often occupied her thoughts during the previous thirty years. Moreover, Yourcenar also confided to Matthieu Galey that in creating the character of Henri-Maximilien she had had certain features of her father in mind. In other words, the composition of *L'Œuvre au noir* may perhaps be said to have set in motion the process by which Yourcenar was led to confront a figure whose importance to her and to her writing she had not previously acknowledged. At the same time, the subsequently explicit consideration of Michel de Crayencour inevitably returns us to the various powerful and attractive male figures that people her two most accomplished novels, works which belong, significantly, in date to her maturity but in inspiration to her earliest days as a writer.

The third volume of *Le Labyrinthe du monde* was published posthumously in the autumn of 1988. Although unfinished, *Quoi? L'Eternité* is approximately the length of each of the two preceding volumes. A note appended to the text, and based on conversations between the author and Yvon Bernier, outlines the scope of the portion of the work that was still unwritten at the time of her death. We learn that the final fifty or so pages would have centred upon the deaths of others: those of her father and of another figure prominent in her memories, Jeanne de Reval. These pages were also to be the occasion for establishing her attitude towards the literary works she had produced in her youth. The barest of sketches was apparently to suffice as an indication of the direction that her life had taken in the years between the two world wars.

The appearance of *Quoi? L'Eternité* confounded those of Yourcenar's readers who, with the passing of time, had been increasingly ready to conclude that the projected trilogy had reached its natural end with the completion of *Archives du nord*. The evidence to support such an assumption was by no means lacking. At the outset of the second volume of *Le Labyrinthe du monde*, Yourcenar refers to *Souvenirs pieux* and *Archives du nord* as two panels in a diptych (*AN*, p. 15). We are also told that the continuation of the narrative as far as 1914 or 1939 is dependent on the existence of sufficient time and energy. That the ambition to complete *Le Labyrinthe du monde* seems not to have been all that compelling is reinforced by the words with which *Archives du nord* ends: 'le reste est peut-être moins important qu'on ne croit.' There was indeed much to suggest Yourcenar's desire for reticence once her own life came into question.

But whether or not it was expected ever to appear, it had always been assumed that *Quoi? L'Eternité* had been conceived as the work which would contain the narrative of the author's own life and thereby form the apex of *Le Labyrinthe du monde*. In the event, it showed the author's tendency towards self-effacement taking precedence over any structural imperative. Now that attention is turned more or less exclusively to the first two decades of the twentieth century, Marguerite's life as a child is at times brought to the fore by the adult she was later to become. Yet there is no question of the process of growing up becoming the author's central concern. Direct childhood memories may constitute her major source, but the central personage remains Michel de C[rayencour]. *Quoi? L'Eternité* is in this respect more of a continuation of *Archives du nord* than expectations based on structure might have led us to suppose. The chapter that is most exclusively concerned with her own status is appropriately entitled 'Les miettes de l'enfance'. Yourcenar is clearly not concerned primarily to add to the already extensive French literature of childhood. Instead, what has remained with her is once more her understandable fascination with the irregular life of her father.

This does not mean that the volume follows the chronological progression of Michel's life. Indeed the concern with his life does not manifest itself exclusively in terms of a direct focus on his actions, thoughts and words. The central and most substantial section of *Quoi? L'Eternité* in fact pieces together the unorthodox relationship between the musician Egon de Reval and his wife Jeanne, a close friend of the mother Marguerite had never known. The presence of this account may be justified by the fact that Jeanne becomes one of the women in Michel's widower life. Yet Yourcenar feels no compulsion to restrict herself to that particular period in Jeanne's existence. The intrinsic interest of her earlier years, her original engagement to a man who ends up in psychiatric care and the closeness of her relationship with a husband who makes no secret of his commitment to fulfilling his homosexual desires, is allowed to dictate the apparently disproportionate amount of space allotted to her life at moments when Marguerite and her father are not present. Once again, *Le Labyrinthe du monde* is revealed as a work that can expand or contract with relative freedom from the constraints that are more usually associated with autobiography. Yourcenar's admiration for Jeanne's courageous and independent spirit is both unmistakable and moving. Her ability to re-create a life to which she as a girl had clearly had no access is an eloquent testimony to the depth of her ability to empathise with exceptional and unconventional figures. Much of her account of the lives of Egon and Jeanne reveals an ability to penetrate beyond surface appearances that we may more naturally associate with the novelist than with the autobiographer. Yourcenar makes no secret in this connection of the need she had felt to do more than create a patchwork out of the fragmented sources available to her. Nor does she make any apology for fleshing out the bare facts, since she is convinced that she is all the while respecting the essential truth of the situation. If at times the reader none the less feels that the experience is not dissimilar to that of reading a novel, this is not altogether surprising, since our sense that the true life story of Egon and Jeanne had been the starting point for Yourcenar's earliest novel, *Alexis*, receives explicit confirmation in the pages of *Quoi? L'Eternité*. Once again, writing for Yourcenar is to be seen more properly as rewriting.

In the final analysis, the presence in *Quoi? L'Eternité* of specific moments in Marguerite's childhood is of surprisingly little importance. The author's concern is still essentially with figures other than herself. What distinguishes *Quoi? L'Eternité* from *Souvenirs pieux* and *Archives du nord* is more the fact that the majority of the events (if they are indeed to be regarded as such) occur after Marguerite's birth in 1903. It is a comfortable pre-war world which, as the author reminds us on more than one occasion, was also the world recorded for posterity by Proust. It is, however, precisely the existence of novelists such as Proust or Balzac that frees Yourcenar from the need for exhaustive description. Instead, she is able to substitute a gloss on the significance of features of Proust's fictional composition, thereby giving her own digressive work a further dimension. Ultimately, however, *Quoi? L'Eternité* provides confirmation of the view that it is in talking of others that Yourcenar most fully reveals her own character and personality. By the end of *Le Labyrinthe du monde*, we may surely feel that we have gained an intimate acquaintance with the way she regards both herself and other human beings. What the reader is led to appreciate above all, however, are perhaps the remarkable clarity of her perceptions and the precision with which they are expressed.

There can be no doubt that Yourcenar's particular *mélange* of fiction and biography in all five works on which her reputation as a writer of importance must stand or fall represents a deep-seated personal quest. Beneath the surface differences discernible in these various narratives of a life, we may detect the same oblique attempt to discover the nature of her own propensities and responses. Nowhere is this more apparent than in parts of *Le Labyrinthe du monde*, which not only demands to be seen as an integral part of her *œuvre*, but is undoubtedly more profoundly autobiographical than the relatively infrequent appearances of Marguerite herself would suggest. Indeed, we are led to realise in retrospect that at the very moment when the autobiographical impulse appears to relinquish pride of place to a portrayal of a figure who dwarfs the author in importance, the autobiographical dimension of the writing is in fact enhanced. The pursuit of the self is revealed as indivisible from the evocation of the figure who had been her early (idiosyncratic) teacher and guide. Yourcenar's fiction is a means by which a relationship that had been dissolved at an unsatisfactorily early stage by the death of the dominant partner may be rediscovered, indeed deepened.

Yourcenar clearly experienced fiction as a privileged entry into a male domain, the pursuit of activities she associated with the world she had once shared with Michel de Crayencour. She was the companion who had survived both his wife and the other women who made transient appearances in his life. Her tepid response to contemporary feminism is wholly consistent with her representation of the lives of her fictional and biographical heroes. The translator of Virginia Woolf offers us not a quintessentially feminine view of the world but a resolutely masculine view imagined, not to say desired, by a woman.

Yourcenar's *œuvre* may, then, fairly be described as writing that is directed towards a discovery of its origin. If it remains only potentially Proustian and stops short of being an explicit consideration of its own motivation and *raison d'être*, the reader is none the less provided with a significant number of pointers towards an understanding of what writing means for this most self-effacing of authors. That her writing, as represented by her five central works, is rooted in a search for identity that spans a period of some forty or more years cannot reasonably be doubted. Yet if we are permitted a glimpse of the origin that shapes this project, it is salutary to remember that this same *œuvre* stands as a steadfast rejection of reductionism. The project owes its vibrancy to the way in which the writing is allowed to be shaped by a whole range of other concerns and ambitions. Constantly to the fore is the appreciation of the way in which writing, far from identifying an unambiguous origin, mobilises through the imagination a proliferation of potential selves and the interplay of a multiplicity of positive and negative versions of a given stance or theme. To a large extent self-discovery for Yourcenar is a matter of self-creation, just as self-definition is sought through an active set of responses to others rather than through isolated self-contemplation.

Finally, if this is writing that is rooted in a personal quest, what is likely to impress us at an early stage (but in a lasting way) is its ability to look beyond the individual self of author or character to a world of universal concerns and values. The reader of these works, which bear a superficial resemblance to the genre of the historical novel, is left feeling that differences of time, of place and of gender are, ultimately, of relative insignificance. The mass of particular details that make up an individual's experiences and which are so finely recorded by the author are revealed to us as merely the product of random accidents. Yourcenar invites her readers instead to participate in the cultivation of an art of living that is dependent first of all on a clearing of the ground. Her work is an invitation to question habit and all fixed positions, to reject extremes and to value what is complementary. There is equal distaste for facile optimism and for the perverse attractions of all-embracing despair. What Yourcenar attempts to share with her readers is a wisdom that recognises the limitations that surround us on all sides. The appreciation of paradox and a form of dialectic are held up as the only appropriate responses to our constant experience of flux and manifold uncertainty.

Bibliography

Works by Marguerite Yourcenar

Novels

Alexis ou le traité du vain combat (Au Sans Pareil, 1929)
La Nouvelle Eurydice (Grasset, 1931)
Denier du rêve (Grasset, 1934; definitive version, Plon, 1959)
Le Coup de grâce (Gallimard, 1939)
Mémoires d'Hadrien (Plon, 1951)
L'Œuvre au noir (Gallimard, 1968)

Short stories

La Mort conduit l'attelage (Grasset, 1934)
Nouvelles orientales (Gallimard, 1938; definitive edition, 1978)
Comme l'eau qui coule (Gallimard, 1982)

Autobiography

Le Labyrinthe du monde. I: *Souvenirs pieux* (Gallimard, 1974)
                    II: *Archives du nord* (Gallimard, 1977)
                 III: *Quoi? L'Eternité* (Gallimard, 1988)

Poetry

Le Jardin des chimères (Perrin, 1921)

Les Dieux ne sont pas morts (Chiberre, 1922)
Feux (Grasset, 1936; definitive edition, Plon, 1968)
Les Charités d'Alcippe et autres poèmes (Liège, La Flûte enchantée, 1956)

Theatre

Electre ou la chute des masques (Plon, 1954)
Le Mystère d'Alceste; Qui n'a pas son Minotaure? (Plon, 1963)
Théâtre, 2 vols (Gallimard, 1971). Vol. I contains *Rendre à César; La Petite Sirène; Le Dialogue dans le marécage*. Vol. 2 contains the three plays published by Plon in 1954 and 1963

Essays

Pindare (Grasset, 1932)
Les Songes et les Sorts (Grasset, 1938)
Sous bénéfice d'inventaire (Gallimard, 1962; definitive edition, 1978)
Discours de réception de Mme Marguerite Yourcenar à l'Académie royale belge de langue et de littérature françaises (Gallimard, 1971). The speech of welcome is by Carlo Bronne.
Mishima ou la Vision du vide (Gallimard, 1980)
Discours de réception de Mme Marguerite Yourcenar à l'Académie française (on Roger Caillois) (Gallimard, 1981). The reply is by Jean d'Ormesson.
Le Temps, ce grand sculpteur (Gallimard, 1983)

Marguerite Yourcenar also published translations of ancient Greek lyric poetry, negro spirituals and works by James Baldwin, Cavafy, Hortense Flexner, Henry James (*What Maisie Knew*), Mishima and Virginia Woolf (*The Waves*).

Interviews

Patrick de Rosbo, *Entretiens radiophoniques avec Marguerite Yourcenar* (Mercure de France, 1972)
Jacques Chancel, *Radioscopie avec Marguerite Yourcenar*, France Inter 11–15 June 1979 (Cassettes Radio-France)
Les Yeux ouverts. Entretiens avec Matthieu Galey (Le Centurion, 1980)

Selected critical studies

Blot, Jean, *Marguerite Yourcenar*, Ecrivains d'hier et d'aujourd'hui (Seghers, 1971; revised edition, 1980)
Hillenaar, Henk, (ed.), *Recherches sur l'œuvre de Marguerite Yourcenar* (Groningen, CRIN, 1983)
Horn, Pierre L., *Marguerite Yourcenar* (Boston, Mass., Twayne, 1985)

Jacquemin, Georges, *Marguerite Yourcenar, Qui suis-je?* (Lyons, La Manufacture, 1985)

Spencer-Noël, Geneviève, *Zénon ou le thème de l'alchimie dans 'L'Œuvre au noir' de Marguerite Yourcenar* (Nizet, 1981)

Special issues of periodicals devoted to Marguerite Yourcenar

Magazine littéraire, 153 (October 1979)

Sud, 55 (1984) (includes Michel Tournier, 'Gustave et Marguerite', on *Mémoires d'Hadrien* and Flaubert's *Salammbô*)

Bulletin de la Société internationale d'études yourcenariennes (November 1987–   )

–2–

Marguerite Duras

DAVID COWARD

Marguerite Duras has always been a rebellious spirit in love with the absolute, and her considerable and varied output over a long, productive life has taken the form of a quest for a total, transcendental love, briefly glimpsed but never grasped, carnal and spiritual, which she concedes is 'impossible'. Running in parallel with her pursuit of a personal goal is a strong political conscience which has made her impatient of all systems whether of the left or of the right, because all systems sooner or later turn into tyrannies. Restless and endlessly turning around her compulsions, she has embraced a number of fashionable intellectual attitudes without deep commitment, just as she has moved freely between fiction, theatre and the cinema. She rarely expresses herself in abstract terms – not for her the lapidary maxim or the generalised statement of wisdom – and she has published no literary manifesto setting out a philosophy or defining her artistic principles. She has, it is true, many times talked frankly to journalists, speaking with infectious enthusiasm of her work which she unfailingly interprets, sometimes in the most surprising manner, in the light of her current preoccupations.[1] Mme Duras functions – and is best read – on a level of intense emotional involvement which has become detached from its source. Her detractors have remarked that while she writes from passion recollected in a mood of loss, her work displays so little ordinary feeling that it exudes a curiously funereal aura of anaesthetised sensibility. Her many admirers, however, find her experiments with form exhilarating and her illuminations of perfect love liberating. She does not elicit moderate reactions.

Marguerite Duras was born in Indo-China in 1914, the second child of French teacher-parents in the French Colonial Service, and

---

1. In *Les Parleuses* (1974) Duras offers a largely feminist commentary on her previous work. *Les Lieux de Marguerite Duras* (1977) reflects the retrospective mood of *L'Eden cinéma*, and so on.

she lived most of her childhood and adolescence against a back-ground of poverty and tense family relationships. She left Saigon in 1931 to complete her education in Paris and never returned to the Far East, but it left its mark both on her general attitudes and on her imagination. The spectacle of colonial exploitation helped to form her radical left-wing views, while the quest for an absolute union with the springs of existence has links, if not with the 'oneness' of certain Oriental religions (which she does not claim to have stud-ied), then perhaps with the passivity, resignation and subjection of the individual which were part of everyday life for the exploited indigenous population.

After taking a degree in mathematics and law, she became a civil servant in the French Colonial Office in Paris in 1935. Three years later she married Robert Antelme, a left-wing intellectual, and began to write. During the German Occupation, she gained an entrée into existentialist and resistance circles and joined the French Communist Party from which she was excluded in about 1950 for her rejection of the party's strong Moscow allegiance. By this time she was making a name for herself as a writer of experimental fiction, but it was not until she furnished Alain Resnais with the script of *Hiroshima mon amour* (1959) that she became one of France's best-known, though not most widely read, writers. Since the early 1960s, she has chased her personal obsessions in increasingly ellipti-cal texts which she has attempted to free from the bonds of strict genre: novels which may be read as playscripts, playscripts which are filmable and journalism which reads like the condition of poetry to which all her work aspires.

These bare factual details provide a skeletal context in which Duras's books may, at least initially, be set.[2] She has claimed on a number of occasions that her work is strongly rooted in her past. In addition to the palpably autobiographical *Un Barrage contre le Pa-cifique* (1950) which was based on her family life as a girl in Indo-China, or *La Douleur* (1985) which deals with her wartime experiences, or *L'Amant* (1984) which again draws directly on her Vietnamese adolescence, she has noted that *Moderato cantabile* (1958) was a disguised 'expérience intérieure'[3] and that all her imaginative fic-tions have been an attempt to repossess her younger brother who died near Saigon in 1942 at the age of twenty-seven, 'faute de médicaments'.[4]

2. The most detailed account of Duras's life is provided by Jean Pierrot, *Marguerite Duras*, chapter 1.
3. *Les Parleuses*, pp. 59–60.
4. *Les Lieux de Marguerite Duras*, p. 46.

Sharp-eyed readers will further note the absence of fathers in her works, the presence of dominant mother figures, the occasional persona of a ne'er-do-well brother and a succession of small boys who age as Duras's own son grew older, and may be moved to speculate on additional underlying psychological pressures. But until the facts of Duras's life are better known, inferences from her biography will not contribute significantly to an understanding of her fictional universe. It is worth noting, however, that her most enduring compulsions – the need for love and the right to self-determination of the individual constrained by social and political institutions – are firmly anchored in her experience, psyche and affective being and not in any conscious intellectualisation of her desire. She has admitted that she finds writing not only a painful but also a dangerous process that has at times tested the limits of her sanity. She is an explorer of depths where she cannot be easily followed. Readers wishing to make sense of her later work may find it useful to bear in mind what preceded it: coming cold to the 'India' or 'Calcutta' cycle, say, or the brief but dense texts published after 1980 can otherwise be a disorienting experience.

The few critics who noticed *Les Impudents* (1943) and *La Vie tranquille* (1944) when they appeared in occupied Paris remarked on their 'existentialist' qualities and placed them 'dans la perspective ouverte par les romans de Sartre et de Camus'.[5] Certainly Duras's bookless Vietnamese home and non-literary training, combined with the overwhelming circumstances of the war, gave her early allegiances a decidedly modern flavour. Her flat, understated style, the incitement to revolt against the enclosing world of bourgeois values, the possibility of choosing freedom ('il suffit de vouloir', her early characters say) all carry over into *Le Marin de Gibraltar* (1952) the first part of which, with its Meursault-like protagonist, was written before 1945. Some reviewers detected traces of Mauriac in her depiction of intense family relationships, though by the time of *Un Barrage contre le Pacifique* (1950) influences on her were as various as Gide, Rousseau and Kafka, the American novelists Hemingway, Faulkner and Erskine Caldwell and English writers such as Virginia Woolf and Ivy Compton-Burnett. If *Un Barrage contre le Pacifique* mobilised and to some extent exorcised her Vietnamese past, *Le Marin de Gibraltar* was a quest not merely for identity but for a revolt which opened onto an uncertain future.

While these first four novels state the essence of the Durassian

---

5. See Renée Ballon's review of *La Vie tranquille* in *Confluences*, 7 (September 1945), 782–5.

creed – that the fullness of the individual is to be realised through union with total desire – their formal qualities tied them uneasily to the conventions of psychological and narrative realism. *Les Petits Chevaux de Tarquinia* (1953) marked a change of manner which led to Duras's being described in the literary press as one of the more exciting exponents of 'le nouveau réalisme'. In the books which followed, the simplification of plot and character is accompanied by a new spareness of form. The time of the action is compressed into a few days, sometimes hours. The place is indeterminate, a park bench perhaps or a holiday beach or coastal town halfway between the confining land and the free, open sea, a frontier which undermines routine and favours change. The action is reduced to a static situation which evolves through repetitious enactments, suggested parallels and fusions of events and characters. The narrative voice speaks with a mixture of diffidence and authority while the elusive, elliptical dialogue creates a mood of intense expectation which is never allowed to reach a satisfying climax in the traditional literary sense of an ending.

Conveyed through symbols (the weather, the sea) and orchestrated with haunting incantations, the routine lives of Duras's usually middle-class women characters are interrupted by a glimpse of total love which is both a form of death and the sign of a rebirth into a freer, liberated existence: the ideal state for Francine in *La Vie tranquille* and for all who followed her was to be as water in the sea. This love is perceived in a privileged moment which may be public, as in *Hiroshima mon amour*, or private, as in *Dix heures et demie du soir en été* (1960). Its colouring may be political, as in *Le Square* (1955), or personal, as in *Moderato cantabile* (1958).

Yet, as Duras makes clear, the private and the public, the personal and the political, are all one: the freedom she speaks of is an 'impossible', 'utopian' union of the individual with natural, social and emotional reality. It is a process that involves forgetting what has been and proceeding beyond the fear of change to a state of harmony between the self and the world. The transfer is achieved in an atmosphere of violence, real or vicariously experienced. It may involve criminal acts or simply take the form of a brutal rejection of the past. The process does not bring happiness or wisdom or joy and is called 'folie', a difficult term which Duras uses to designate the post-revelatory, intuitive, passive knowledge that one is free to be what one has become. To be 'mad' is to know that one is finite when love and justice are irremediably infinite; that everything which stands as an obstacle to love – family, class and convention – is expendable; that the state – totalitarian or fascist – must be eternally challenged since the state is the eternal constrainer of individual and group liberties. It is a demanding and daunting creed.

However 'difficult' her books before *L'Après-midi de Monsieur Andesmas* (1962) appeared to contemporary reviewers, they were, in comparison with her later work, discursive and overripe. Since the early 1960s Duras's preoccupations have become increasingly obsessive, and her technique has undergone several transformations in her search for simplicity. She has several times discounted everything she wrote before *Moderato cantabile* (1958), the summit of her early manner. Yet with hindsight it was with *Le Ravissement de Lol V. Stein* in 1964 that the quest for liberating 'madness' acquired a new intensity and a new mythology. Here, Duras found in her own past the emancipated woman she had been seeking: Anne-Marie Stretter.

As a girl in Vietnam Marguerite Duras had been aware of the scandal surrounding the wife of a colonial administrator, a cool, elegant, self-composed woman of forty who could be observed driving around Vinh-Long in a chauffeured car. Nothing in her manner suggested that she was in any way concerned with the rumour, which Duras continued to believe was true, that a young man had killed himself for love of her. The two women never met – the Elisabeth Striedter of reality died in 1978 aged ninety-one[6] – but Duras came to think of her as the ideal of the 'modèle féminin'.

Anne-Marie Stretter is aware of the horrors of existence – poverty, hunger and disease – and behaves with instinctive promiscuity. In so doing, she is part of that world while remaining fully herself. Her egoism and indifference to the suffering she sees and feels are only apparent, for she makes no distinction between the personal tragedy of unhappy love and the political tragedy of unhappy humanity. She is a kind of impassive contemplative for whom the pain of the unloved lover is qualitatively the same as the incurable ills of the East. Yet, though her place in Duras's world is dominant, Anne-Marie Stretter is not the only exemplar of the emancipated woman. A second major archetype is the Vietnamese peasant (equally a figure from Duras's past and first encountered in *Un Barrage contre le Pacifique* where she abandons the child she cannot feed) who also immerses herself in the sufferings of the world, as both victim and collaborator. Just as, in *Hiroshima mon amour*, the private horror of Nevers is equated with the public horror of the holocaust, Anne-Marie Stretter and the beggar-woman are two faces of the same freedom and the same despair. They exist like drops of

6. See *Les Yeux verts* (1980), pp. 17 and 19. On Anne-Marie Stretter, Jean Pierrot's discussion (*Marguerite Duras*, pp. 233–6) is invaluable.

water in the sea and constitute unchanging reference points in a landscape of impossible desires. Duras never attempts to provide psychological or philosophical explanations of their serenity: she simply states it as a fact, a final condition to which all her characters aspire.

Anne-Marie Stretter makes her first, brief appearance – as a supporting 'femme fatale', a first reading might suggest – in *Le Ravissement de Lol V. Stein*. Lol is abandoned at her engagement ball by Michael Richardson who dances with the fascinating Anne-Marie Stretter. We learn subsequently that she abandons him and that he sells up and removes to Calcutta. Lol is neither angry nor jealous, for she is 'entranced' by the total love she senses between them. Unable to cope, though, with this revelation of the absolute, she becomes withdrawn and goes through a nervous breakdown from which she eventually recovers. She marries, raises a family and lives the kind of routine life against which Anne Desbaresdes had rebelled in *Moderato cantabile*. One day, ten years after the ball, she overhears a snatch of conversation between two lovers, and this chance encounter reactivates her desire. She renews her acquaintance with Tatiana Karl in whose love for Jacques Hold she detects the same perfection she recognised on the night of the ball. Her attempts to participate in absolute love prove unsatisfying, and the novel closes with Lol lying in a field, mysteriously and voyeuristically at one with a pair of lovers in a nearby hotel. We suspect that they are Tatiana and Jacques, but their identity is unimportant since they have become the love which is as eternal as the uncontrollable sea which is never far away.

Duras's narrative contains enough detail to allow the reader to interpret Lol's actions and moods as a mental breakdown – Lacan himself has expressed his admiration for the clinical accuracy of the portrait[7] – yet the power of the novel does not lie in psychological realism. Lol's obsession may be strong enough in a classic sense to turn others into part of the fabric of her desire, but she is never troubled, even at the moment when she is cruelly abandoned, by anything so ordinary as jealousy. It is rather that the crisis of the ball gives her an immediate revelation of a transcendental actuality – the pure love between Michael Richardson and Anne-Marie Stretter – which she too must share if she is to feel whole, in which she must lose her identity if she is ever to be herself. Lol's journey is

---

7. Jacques Lacan, 'Hommage fait à Marguerite Duras du *Ravissement de Lol V. Stein*', in Marguerite Duras et al., *Marguerite Duras*, Editions Albatros, Collection Ça/Cinéma, 1979 (nouvelle édition augmentée), pp. 131–9.

mystical and, structurally, is close to the saint's merging of the self with God, though it should be stressed that the transcendence involved has nothing whatsoever to do with religion, which has no role in Duras's world.[8] Lol seeks to be as serene, as self-contained, as free as the sea which we hear and observe constantly. If Anne Desbaresdes had to conquer her fear of the dangerous sea, Lol surrenders to its call, giving her access to love which is as detached from earthly contact as Duras's strange tale is removed from realistic fiction. The price Lol pays is her reason. But what, Duras asks, has reason brought if not destruction, systematic cruelty and political tyranny? 'Madness' becomes a new sanity, and however sluggishly Lol moves through a narrative made puzzling by unclear cross-referencing, multiple narrators, and unexplained symbols, her unreason is shown to be not a flight from reality but a positive form of liberation.

Similar demands upon the reader's imagination are made by *Le Vice-consul* (1966), one of Duras's most finished and disturbing novels. The immediate link with the odyssey of Lol V. Stein is provided by the presence of Anne-Marie Stretter and Michael Richard (*sic*), though later works in the cycle will make the connection much more strongly. States of mind are preferred to psychological analyses, just as the setting is mythical: Calcutta is not on the Ganges nor has it ever been the location of the French Embassy. In narrative terms there is no plot but three strands which fuse in a bathetic climax.

The novel opens with a long account of the wanderings of the Vietnamese beggar-woman who, disowned by her family, marches over a period of ten years from Laos to Calcutta.

The second theme concerns the French vice-consul at Lahore, a naturally rebellious and even unsympathetic man who has never known love. He has come in disgrace to Calcutta, where Stretter, as ambassador, has to reassign him to new duties. His reputation and scandalous behaviour – we learn in an aside that he fired indiscriminately into a crowd of lepers at Lahore – make him an outsider at the embassy reception which occupies a third of the book. Though the point is never made clearly, his anti-social and even cruel action was both a metaphysical protest against the arbitrariness of existence and a more specifically political response to the overwhelming poverty and disease which surround him.

The third strand of the novel is constituted by Anne-Marie, the ambassador's wife, who discharges all the duties of her position

---

8. It is probably in this sense that we should understand why Anne-Marie Stretter will later be described as a 'chrétienne sans Dieu' (*India Song*, p. 46).

while conducting numerous adulterous affairs as distractions from the despair which she feels in her own life. As the situation evolves, the vice-consul becomes obsessed with her, and she in turn finds in his personal and political wretchedness a reflection of her own: she understands his longings in the same way that we come to see her anaesthetised indifference as the personal equivalent of the public misery of suffering India which the beggar-woman represents. After passing through a moment of intense but quite impossible desire, the vice-consul accepts another posting and leaves Anne-Marie Stretter to continue her hopeless existence and the beggar-woman to her grimly resigned struggle for survival.

This bald – and doubtless contestable – outline of what 'happens' in *Le Vice-consul* barely suggests the complexity of a novel whose richness lies in its allusive, suggestive, poetic manner: the calm narrative voice, the symbolic notations and the spare, understated dialogue. Even so, *Le Vice-consul* far from fully expresses the 'laconisme' which Duras had set as her goal since before *Moderato cantabile*. What she meant by this term was a refusal to explain what she showed: she carefully records actions, gestures, words and looks without analysing them or giving the reader overt guidance in the matter of their interpretation. Her 'théorie des blancs' involved omitting whole stages of a situation, whole exchanges of a dialogue or even whole actions – like the vice-consul's crucial act at Lahore – which become so many 'récits absents' to be reconstructed by the reader. The privileged position given to the unseen and the half-said is the means whereby our need for logical explanations and comforting generalisations is subverted: we too must become 'mad' if we are to enter into her fictions.

Duras's technical boldness and her consequent demands upon the reader increased markedly after *Le Vice-consul* and are particularly visible in a series of works, conceived for different mediums, which all dwell on the characters and situations first explored, in less concentrated forms, in *Le Ravissement de Lol V. Stein* and the first Calcutta novel. The former gave rise to *L'Amour* (1971), an atmospheric tale which strips the original of the anecdotal and relocates the de-concretised action in a barely evoked seaside town halfway between the constraining land and the liberating sea. In this deserted place, which contains the possibilities of change, the wandering 'voyageur' is turned from suicide by an apprehension of self-harmony provided by 'la femme' – incidental details reveal that she is Lol – who has found peace with another man who is known simply as 'le fou'.

A related film, *La Femme du Gange* (1972), retains the general mood and situation but evokes the character of Anne-Marie Stretter more directly. For if Duras had not quite done with Lol, neither had she exhausted the possibilities of her Calcutta story. *India Song*, published in 1973 and filmed in 1975, is not an adaptation of *Le Vice-consul* but a complete recasting of the book. The action remains the same – though we learn now that Anne-Marie Stretter drowns herself and that the vice-consul disappears, never to be heard of again – but the tone and the presentation are much more powerful. *India Song* is a statuesque film of great beauty which uses the medium of cinema as inventively as any film-maker has done since the days of the pioneers. What we see does not correspond to what we hear, and the tale is told by disembodied voices and lingering images which constitute a kind of audio-visual patchwork which, for the willing spectator, reassembles into a poetic design. The closing sequences will be of especial interest to readers of *Le Vice-consul*, for it becomes clear that, having spent long years in an attempt to lose herself in her sexual affairs, Anne-Marie arrives at a point where she knows that her pretences are finished. For her, as for the vice-consul, their meeting is a moment of knowledge after which there can be only despair and death.

But even this brilliant treatment of her material did not satisfy Duras who, a year later, made *Son nom de Venise dans Calcutta désert* with the same sound-track and a new set of images. Her text is here spoken to long panning shots of the abandoned Trianon Palace Hotel. The slowly unfolding glimpses of crumbling interiors and weathered façades, expressive of past grandeurs and devoid of any human presence, add an aching sense of loss which gives a new, sombre colouring to the mood of the narrative. With each reading or viewing, the same landscape peopled by the same figures reappears in new ways, variously lit and with altered perspective.

These six interlinked treatments of the same primary materials are not simply six progressively ambitious attempts to convey the same vision: they constitute one vision conveyed in six different ways. Together, the 'India' texts (or perhaps more accurately the 'Lol cycle') create an extraordinary three-dimensional impression. Images on the screen evoke echoes from the novels until the odysseys of Lol, the vice-consul, Anne-Marie Stretter and the beggar-woman fuse and acquire depth from our feeling that what we see or hear or read is somehow part of our own experience: we understand the woman in *La Femme du Gange* when we remember who and what Lol Stein was. It is not that we identify with their predicaments but rather that, with each telling, we enter further into their lives which thereby become more poignant and more tragic.

Duras's reworkings were not consciously conceived as a cycle, nor did she embark on them because she was particularly dissatisfied with previous performances. She was simply aware of other ways her stories might have been told, other facets which might have been polished. She had known from the start of her writing career that her desires were 'impossible'. To love one person is not to love others, for loving can express only one face of love. In the same way, a story told is a denial of all other stories which might have been told, a repudiation of all other ways in which any story might have been told. In a sense, these multiple versions must be seen as a deliberate attempt to overcome the 'impossible' in literature, for with each reworking Duras concentrates upon some aspect of the situation which she believed had been left unexploited.

A significant proportion of her output since 1964 has indeed been devoted to giving new forms to previously published work. The matter of *La Musica*, a fairly traditional psychological playlet first performed in 1965, filmed in 1967 and reworked as *La Musica Deuxième* (1985), was the starting point for the hurriedly written 'gageure boulevardière' *Suzanna Andler*, which in turn became a film entitled *Baxter, Vera Baxter* (1976), which Duras disliked, and the revised play- or film-script *Vera Baxter, ou les plages de l'Atlantique* (1980). Over a period of fifteen years the links in both form and content between the initial conception and its most recent manifestation have become so distant that it is quite clear that far more than adaptation is involved: each version is an autonomous rendering of other ways of telling the tale which either were implicit in the material or else emerged in tune with Duras's changing preoccupations.

A more specific, because less diffuse, example of the process is provided by the transmutation of *Les Viaducs de la Seine-et-Oise*, successfully staged in 1960, into a novel (1967) and a play (1968) each called *L'Amante anglaise*. The starting point was a newspaper report of an unusual murder. In 1954, parts of a dismembered corpse were found in railway freight trucks in goods-yards in various parts of France. A police inquiry concluded that they must have been dropped from the only bridge under which all the trains in question had passed. The murderers proved to be a retired couple of good character who had killed a handicapped relative who had lived with them for almost thirty years. The killers were jailed but were unable to offer any motive for their action. In 1960 Duras's first attempt at the subject resulted in a philosophical thriller of sorts – murder as a rejection of established values and as an act of self-liberation – which was consistent with her current view of crime as a trigger for the revolt which precedes the freeing of the self: both *Moderato cantabile* and *Dix heures et demie du soir en été* involve vicarious *crimes passionnels*. In 1967 *L'Amante anglaise* (a punning title – *La Menthe anglaise*, *L'Amante en glaise* – suggestive of multiple interpretations) cast the situation as a novel made up of transcriptions of three tape-recorded interviews conducted by a man who is perhaps a prison psychiatrist or simply an author gathering material for a book.

Claire Lannes confesses that she alone committed the murder and in so doing displays a total absence of moral responsibility. While her indifference is perfectly consistent with the withdrawn inversion of the Claire Ragond of *Les Viaducs*, it is given an edge by Duras's often stated dislike of the paternalism of De Gaulle's increasingly autocratic Fifth Republic. And where Claire Ragond was mentally confused, Claire Lannes exhibits much clearer signs of mental derangement and to this extent reflects Duras's declining interest in crime-as-trigger and her new preoccupation with the depiction of alienation (in Lol V. Stein most obviously) as the essential prerequisite for emancipation.

Another significant development is to be seen in Claire Lannes's insistence that she was never so happy as when she lived at Cahors as a young woman. Before 1964, with the exception of the heroine in *Hiroshima mon amour*, where present and past coincide, the Durassian heroine struggles towards a freedom which is located beyond the moment of crisis which must first be lived through. With *Le Ravissement de Lol V. Stein*, the moment of crisis (Lol's betrayal by Michael Richardson) occurs early in the book, which then proceeds to show how the heroine seeks to rejoin her past. In other words, by the mid-1960s, Duras was consistently exploring the themes of memory and forgetting. Lol is merely the first of many characters who feel compelled to relive their past the better to forget it, for true fulfilment of the self lies beyond remembering.

But *L'Amante anglaise* is significant, too, in a formal sense. The fragmentary exposition, the overlapping interviews, each slightly different, take it as close to the *nouveau roman* in its classic phase – that of Robbe-Grillet's *La Jalousie*, for instance – as Duras had ever come. A similar structure – a multi-faceted view of the same data presented from different perspectives – may be perceived in the clusters of related works, the 'Lol cycle' most obviously. Yet Duras's writings have no more been conscious attempts to maintain the momentum of the new novel than her rewritings were attempts to repair deficiencies in books already published. She denies ever having been 'un écrivain de chapelle' and remains what she has always been, an intuitive writer who follows where her compulsions lead.

It is clear that at times her compulsions have led her into blind alleys and that she has more than once seemed in danger of repeating herself. One such moment occurred in the early 1960s when her energies were dissipated on a variety of projects, and it was not until *Le Ravissement* that she was able to find new territories to explore. Another flat period may be noticed in her affair with the theatre between 1965 and 1968 when she staged a number of plays in quite different moods, ranging from the unexpectedly Ionesco-ish *Les Eaux et forêts* (1965) to *Le Shaga* (1968), an experimental work which invents a gibberish language – 'le shaga' of the title – to indicate the distance separating educated French from the language of the people. But at a time when Duras appeared to be losing her way in avant-garde theatre productions, the upheaval of 1968 gave her a new firmness of purpose.

Some of Duras's plays, like *Yes, peut-être* (January 1968) with its pacifist message and advocacy of change, or *Un Homme est venu me voir* (written in 1967) which carried a strong attack on Russian totalitarianism, indicate the strength of her political mood in the closing phase of De Gaulle's ten-year rule. Like many others she welcomed the events of May '68. She participated in committees and discussions, and she signed collective statements. She also wrote one of her most accomplished novels, *Détruire, dit-elle* (1969) which she turned into a film. The action is set in the grounds of what might be an out-of-season hotel or perhaps a psychiatric clinic. Elisabeth Alione is a conventional, married bourgeoise, vaguely uneasy in her settled life. She becomes the object of the persuasive, persistent and at times brutal talk of two men who, between them, set out to 'destroy' her complacency and overcome her fear of the nearby forest which, like the sea, is a recognisable symbol of natural liberty. The meaning is clear: the 'impossible revolution' can become possible if we choose to abandon our imprisoning conventions and our fear of change. In other words, the process of emancipation, hitherto played out in terms of sexual love, is now extended to cover a wider, political freedom.

Duras advances no specific political programme and her position is anarchist-revolutionary. She took up the student slogan, 'nous sommes tous des Juifs allemands', and used it as a warning that all members of society are victims of the oppressive state. To revolt means saying no to ready-made political ideas and to any kind of doctrinaire collectivism. Her wish was to preserve individual identity within a collective human framework – the political equivalent of being that drop of water in the ocean. But very quickly, Duras's optimism vanished as the promised new order lost its revolutionary impetus. With *Abahn Sabana David* (1970), she delivered a novel which made the general point that all systems are undesirable and argued more specifically that party communism leads to terror and capitalism to fascism. What remains, she suggests, is a spirit of non-doctrinaire communism which takes no particular form and promotes freedom, toleration, love, joy and madness, those ingredients of human nature which are more valuable than the rigid social structures of the left or the bourgeois values of work, money, tradition and family which are no less powerful, if more insidious, forms of restraint. In the novel little hope is held out for the Jews who represent Duras's ideal, though a faint ray of optimism illuminates its otherwise bleak landscape as we infer that the struggle will continue.

If most French people turned their backs on the 'Revolution of 1968', Duras kept faith with its spirit. Unlike Sartre (whose courage she admired but whose ideas she found doctrinaire), she made few overt political statements, though in 1971 she took part in a sit-in at the offices of the Conseil national du Patronat français (the French equivalent of the Confederation of British Industry) to protest about the living conditions of immigrant workers. She maintained her momentum with *Nathalie Granger*, a film shot in 1972. Here she projects the philosophy of revolt into a specifically feminist context. Nathalie is a little girl of ten whose behaviour is so violent that her headmistress recommends that she be sent to a special school. At the very least she should be made to continue with her hated piano lessons which will help to discipline her. The Granger household is a female domain, calm, orderly and so serene that male influences are neutralised; the ineffectual washing-machine salesman drops his masculine bluster and, 'destroyed' as Elisabeth Alione had been, leaves with a truer notion of himself and his relation to his surroundings. Against these events the radio reports the progress of a police hunt for two teenage murderers whose senseless violence is not far removed from that of Nathalie, who symbolises the disobedience which is the essence of revolt. Always inclined to view personal acts of violence as a positive gesture against conventional values which deny the free expression of the self – an attitude which attracted much adverse publicity when in an article in *Libération* (22 July 1985) she declared a mother accused of infanticide to be politically innocent even if technically guilty of murder – Duras ensures that Nathalie's revolt succeeds. She will not be sent to a special school nor will she be forced to continue her piano lessons, which are here as clearly representative of bourgeois indoctrination as they had been in *Moderato cantabile*.

The same incitement to revolt underscores *Le Camion*, which was entered for the Cannes Film Festival in 1977. A lorry-driver picks up a hitch-hiker, played by Duras herself, a 'déclassée' who forces him to see that the oppression of the right is indistinguishable from the tyranny of the left and that membership of a communist trade union or of the French Communist Party means signing away his right to say no. *Le Camion* is another affirmation of the obligation on each individual to seek the freedom without which there is neither personal happiness nor collective harmony. It was on the same grounds that Duras later deplored the Russian invasion of Afghanistan as a denial of the right of self-determination and that she rejoiced when Polish workers struck against the monolithic power of Soviet collectivism. In an article in *Libération*[9] in August 1980, she observes that more people would have understood the true nature of the Polish revolt if French men and women had not ceased to think in revolutionary terms.

Duras's libertarian and anti-tyrannical stance has never changed. It is implicit in *Le Square* (1955), which she has always considered an essentially political statement. The force of her convictions clearly stems from the fact that she has lived through terrible times. Her memories of French colonial rule in Indo-China, her experience of Paris during the Occupation, her knowledge of German concentration camps (where her husband nearly died), the Hiroshima holocaust, the immovable orthodoxy of the French Communist Party, the brutalities of the Algerian war, Russian imperialism in Hungary, Poland and Afghanistan, American involvement in Vietnam and Central America – all of this affected her deeply, and her highly personal reactions help to explain why Duras remains bitterly opposed to political doctrines of all colours. All doctrines are rooted in violence because all dogmas require followers, willing or unwilling. Given the events of the twentieth century which she has always observed with passion, it is understandable that all her political statements are statements of opposition and that her own sympathies are decidedly left-wing to the extent that she unfailingly champions the individual against the state and against all conformist and depersonalising values. Once this is conceded, the consistency of her views emerges clearly. It is but one step from the revolt and emancipation of Lol to the revolt and freedom of Elisabeth Alione, Nathalie Granger and the lorry-driver. Duras admits that what she wants for people is quite 'impossible' but adds that this does not prevent what she wants from being right.

9. See *L'Eté 80*, pp. 60–1.

In 1971 she gave up one 'impossible' struggle when she decided to abandon the novel. Her reasons for doing so were highly personal. Writing this novel in this way (rather than another novel or the same novel in a different way) now seemed to her to involve quite arbitrary and meaningless choices. Moreover, even the most self-effacing novelist, however committed to objective story-telling, inevitably shows this scene or that action and in the process limits the free responses of the reader, who has no option but to react to what he is arbitrarily offered. Ultimately, therefore, the writer operates a form of authorial *dirigisme* which is incompatible with Duras's libertarianism. In addition to these theoretical concerns she admitted that the strain of solitary creation was becoming harder to bear and that she found working in the theatre or on a film set much more congenial.

In a sense, the move was long overdue. From the mid-1950s onwards her tales had been cast in increasingly theatrical and even cinematographic forms: *Le Square*, for instance, was performed as a play more or less as it was written. The experimental impetus of the plays staged between 1965 and 1968 settled in the 1970s into a more regular pattern. Some of her performance ventures were dictated by circumstance. It was as a vehicle for Madeleine Renaud, an old friend, that she turned her 1954 story, *Des Journées entières dans les arbres* into a naturalistic play, which she later filmed, in 1976. Madeleine Renaud also starred in *L'Eden cinéma* (1977), a highly condensed, formal and emotionally charged re-writing of the auto-biographical *Un Barrage contre le Pacifique*. In 1979 *Le Navire Night* dramatised a strange love story (also filmed) about a rich heiress with leukaemia who makes nocturnal phone calls to a man who falls in love with her voice. It is another atmospheric piece which transmits the feel of an 'impossible' love betrayed by the act of telling.

In these plays Duras's taste for anti-theatre is translated into an almost total absence of action. The drama is carried by the text which is spoken unemotionally by static actors (who may, for instance, remain seated throughout) on an undecorated stage. As may be imagined, the demands made upon the audience are intense, and no one who refuses to make a considerable imaginative investment in the performance is likely to be satisfied. Indeed, Duras makes no secret of what she expects of her public, who are required to match her 20 per cent of creativity with 80 per cent of their own. She has said, for example, that the lorry of *Le Camion* is empty at the beginning of the film, and it is for the spectator to load it with ideas and feelings as it moves across the screen towards the destination it will never reach.

But however intriguing the plays of the 1970s, they pale beside the series of films into which Duras put the best of her invention and passion. Of course she was not without experience of the cinema industry. Indeed, much of her fame in the 1960s derived from the script she had written for Alain Resnais's production of *Hiroshima mon amour*. Moreover, she had written other scenarios in collaboration with Gérard Jarlot – *Moderato cantabile* (1960) and *Une aussi longue absence* (1961) – and a number of her books had been filmed: *Un Barrage contre le Pacifique* by René Clément, *Dix heures et demie du soir en été* by Jules Dassin and *Le Marin de Gibraltar* by Tony Richardson.

None of these screen versions satisfied her because they compromised her vision and pandered to the commercial cinema's patronising and unadventurous ideas of what the public wanted. Believing that she could do better, she co-directed her first feature, *La Musica*, in 1967. She disliked the result but enjoyed the collective activity of film-making. More significantly, she began to ponder the aesthetic possibilities of a medium which seemed ideally suited to express her preoccupations. Cinema offered intimacy and immediacy. It contained the potential for showing in vivid, graphic terms what was with difficulty described in words. On film, she hoped to say more fully, more poetically, what she had hitherto set down on the coldness of the printed page. And not least, cinema, the diversion of the young, would give her access to a new audience who were of an age to respond to her promise of revolt and liberation.

Her first film as writer/director, *Détruire, dit-elle* (1969), rapidly acquired a cult status as one of the key works of the 'Revolution' of May 1968. Part of its success lay in its rather ostentatious non-commercialism. Privately financed, it was made in two weeks for £25,000 and qualifies as 'cinéma pauvre'. In 1971, in the same conditions, she shot *Jaune le soleil*, which, for reasons that are unclear, was never released. It presents the case of a man sentenced to death by two parties who are unnamed but roughly represent capitalism and Soviet imperialism. In comparison *Nathalie Granger*, shot the following year at Duras's house at Neauphle-le-Château just outside Paris, is a much more naturalistic film which boasts events which amount to a linear 'story', and the character of the washing-machine salesman injects a realistic note of tragi-comedy that is rare in the Duras canon.

La Femme du Gange (1972) is as static and mysterious as the novel *L'Amour*, to which it is related, yet it is notable for the first significant use of the 'voice-off'. 'Le off', as Duras refers to it, is a technique which allows lines to be spoken over the image by characters who do not appear on screen, have no apparent role in the action, deliver no commentary on what we see but simply 'traversent le texte'. The 'voice-off' is designed to open the film and create multi-dimensional echoes which reverberate around the action as it unfolds. The dislocation of words and images, with its ¬llusiveness and strange ritualism, was for Duras not merely a dynamic means of liberating her characters but a technique which freed the cinema from its reliance on the well-worn devices of rapid-cutting, the close-up and the flashback which she simply ignores. Her discovery of the 'voice-off' finds its fullest expression in *India Song* (1975) which had been commissioned by Peter Brook for the National Theatre. Plans to stage it, however, came to nothing, but the text was recorded in the Paris studios of ORTF.

For the reasons suggested earlier, *India Song*, and its other face *Son nom de Venise dans Calcutta désert*, represent Duras's most accomplished and sophisticated work for the cinema: here are two sober, elegant moods which slowly uncurl to reveal the familiar patterns of love, madness and emancipation, and they work on the principle that the spectator cannot possess what he has never discovered for himself.

Duras has always been both temperamentally and politically opposed to the rationale of commercial cinema and prefers to be considered a practitioner of 'le cinéma artisanal'. She works on a small, intimate scale partly because finance is always a problem for the film-maker but also because she regards big-budget movies as an 'obscenity' in a world where millions are starving. The Centre National de la Cinématographie provided her with modest backing for certain ventures; none of her films cost more than *India Song*, and most considerably less. They were made quickly, usually in a week or ten days, and only the technicians were paid: stars like Jeanne Moreau, Gérard Depardieu, Delphine Seyrig and Michael Lonsdale simply gave their time or accepted a small percentage of receipts.

Unaware or at least suspicious of what the industry normally considers practicable and desirable in a film, Duras proceeded to break most of the rules. Her camera lingers for minutes on end until the spectator finally 'sees' what is being shown, while the unidentified voices disorient audiences and prepare them to accept new ways of apprehending reality. Through a mixture of boldness and intuition, Duras achieves a sepulchrally-paced, hallucinatory exteriorisation of her vision. She always works from a written, sometimes published, text, yet freely admits to a considerable amount of improvisation on the set. When, for example, with shooting time already booked for *Le Camion*, she learned that two actresses had withdrawn from the project for contractual reasons, Duras simply dispensed with the film she had conceived and instead directed an unrehearsed 'happening' in which she and the lorry-driver read the text of the film which would have been made. *Le Camion* is therefore not so much the definitive screen presentation of what Duras had envisaged when she wrote the scenario but a trigger which releases another film which each spectator may imagine for himself.

The accident of *Le Camion* highlighted the old problem of finding a total form to express a total vision. Her hold on genre had never been strong, and since her abandonment of the novel in 1971 she had cast her written works in no particular mode. *India Song* was published under the omnibus classification 'texte-théâtre-film', which means that it may be read as it stands or performed or imagined as cinema. The 'arbitrary' film of *Le Camion* ('ç'aurait été un film', she told journalists) now raised the issue of how images may best be used to exploit words. The two visually quite different films derived from the soundtrack of *India Song* were clearly only two of the many more which might have been made. Duras came to wonder whether any screen narrative can ever be more than arbitrary. In other words, cinema was becoming as 'impossible' as the novel had been. In 1979, she made a number of short films in which a ruminative text is spoken (by Duras herself) to a series of long, slow tracking shots of Paris and the Seine. Three of these texts, each called *Aurélia Steiner* (two were filmed), are 'possible' expressions of the mood of 1968: we are all German Jews, displaced, dispossessed and constantly seeking the love and freedom which are betrayed by the collectivity.

Her three Aurélias (just three of the many who might have been given a voice) call us from Melbourne, Vancouver and Paris just as the prehistoric handprints evoked in *Les Mains négatives* gesture to us through time. There is no doubting the sincerity or the passionate assurance of the message they give. The problem was to know how best, if at all, that message might be conveyed in moving pictures. One solution, already tentatively tried in her experimental short films, was to show nothing. Perhaps the perfect image for her written texts, always read unemphatically by Duras herself, would be a blank, exposed film onto which the spectator might project his own pictures and thereby regain control of his inner eye. The idea of a 'cinéma intérieur' is subversive though hardly new. Underground film-makers have sometimes tried it, and it is the central justification of radio drama, a form which Duras has never seriously contemplated. In certain of the films which she has made subsequently (some of which have been pieced together from out-takes left over from earlier productions), she has made some use of the blank screen, as in *L'Homme Atlantique* (1982) where the absence of images is linked to passages in the text which evoke the author's private life. But though she has filmed a number of her more recent published texts, sometimes by way of giving them an alternative form, her preoccupations have moved on, and she has to some extent lost faith with 'impossible' cinema.

By 1980 Duras appeared once again to have worked herself into a corner. She had become disenchanted with the feminism of the 1970s, and her affair with the cinema was fading. Her passion for 'impossible' love and the 'impossible' revolution remained bright and vital, but the formal problems of communicating that passion seemed insuperable. Yet the compulsion to write has forced solutions to emerge, and the 1980s have proved to be as inventive, as surprising and as aesthetically radical as any period in her career. She has continued to re-tailor previously published works – like *La Musica Deuxième* (1985) – and she has occasionally returned to the manner of *L'Amour*. *Savannah Bay*, performed in 1982, shows the older Madeleine in a state of 'ravissement' leading a young woman to an apprehension of pure love on a Durassian beach. The familiar battery of symbols is summoned (blue for infinity, the sea for oneness with the absolute, the shore as a non-specific zone of possible becoming between bondage and freedom) to create a world where time and space are confused and characters and events merge into each other. *Savannah Bay* is Duras at her fluid, evocative best.

At no point, however, does she simply repeat herself. For anyone wishing for an idea of how much her manner has changed from the classic mode of the late 1950s, there is no more illuminating text than the thirty-page *L'Homme assis dans le couloir* (1980), which is *Moderato cantabile* laid bare. The scene is described in the conditional perfect – 'L'homme aurait été assis dans l'ombre du couloir' – as though to remove what follows from concrete reality. What we are shown is the brutal union of the man and an unnamed woman in sex and death. What is new here is the frank sensuality and an even more systematic deconstruction of the actual. In *Agatha* (1981), which exists as a written text, a play and a film, the autobiographical relationship of Duras with her younger brother is turned into a statement that desire of any kind is the essence of absolute love. *La Maladie de la mort* (1982) presents an unnamed man who pays an anonymous woman for sexual services but proves to be incurable since he suffers from terminal lovelessness.

In these short, much-worked texts, which are delivered by a narrator who is sometimes 'je' and sometimes absent and are directed either to 'vous' or to no one in particular, physical settings are indeterminate, and the characters are deprived of any personal traits. The evolving but circular situation is set in a room, in a hotel, near a beach. The man and the woman relate to each other on a plane of sexual desire which is also the essence of absolute love. Unable to recognise each other, they are strangers from themselves. They cannot remember their past but are full of a sense of loss which they struggle to replace in a new union. Music, and references to the mood of the sea and to the innocence of children relate their quest to an undefined and undefinable state of purity in the same way that the beach is now in Normandy and now in the Far East, or that the characters melt into each other. Duras offers us mystical visions of a state of pure being, a final harmony between the self and the world. There is no exaltation here, merely measured, imageless prose and rhythmic, hypnotic, slowly evolving repetitions of apparently banal details. Memory has been forgotten and the commonplace world is irrelevant. Duras does not hold out the promise of joy or even peace, merely a state in which a sense of unredeemable deprivation and the certainty of never-becoming are temporarily suspended. From these texts, a solution to the problem of finding a mode of expression emerges. Duras has gravitated to a kind of ritualistic, understated poetry which only just contains the force of her passion.

But even this does not exhaust the catalogue of experiments with form which she has tried. In 1984 she published a straightforward account of her Vietnamese adolescence, *L'Amant*, which recalls with disarming frankness her affair with a Chinese businessman and defines the impact made upon her by the liberated woman whom we recognise as Anne-Marie Stretter. The elements of her writing remain the same – the deconstruction of time, the notations of place, time and the weather as reflections of mood – but they are much diluted. The result is a new lyricism which has brought her a vast new audience. Her books had never sold more than 30,000 copies or so, though *L'Eté 1980*, a collection of newspaper articles, sold over 70,000 copies when it appeared in 1980. *L'Amant* has had world sales of 1½ million and was awarded the 1984 Prix Goncourt.

In 1985 Duras brought out *La Douleur*, which contains part of what appears to be her harrowing wartime journal together with a number of quite brilliant conventional short stories dealing with the same period. For a moment, it seemed that she had given up the unequal struggle for the ultimate form of expression, and that the more direct communication with her audience which she had achieved in her traditionally styled bestsellers would be enough to satisfy her. But this was to reckon without the obsessiveness of her need to say what she feels. *Les Yeux bleus cheveux noirs* (1986) was a triumphal affirmation that no literary ideals had been compromised. It is a story designed to be read as though it were a play in performance. A man and a woman on the verge of desire work through the substitutions of vicarious love to the brief moment where forgetting and remembering meet. In a claustrophobic atmosphere of suppressed violence and torpid eroticism, they enact the rituals of symbolic death and madness. It is a book of polished surfaces and submerged passion, intense and disturbing, which obeys its own rhythms. Some of the obscurities are explained in *La Pute de la côte normande* (1986), a kind of postface published separately, where Duras admits with total honesty that the book squeezed itself mysteriously out of a crisis in her relationship with her companion, Yann Andréa.[10] 'Dans le livre, j'ai dix-huit ans, j'aime un homme qui hait mon désir, mon corps.' It is a confession which reveals that Marguerite Duras, who has never stopped exploring her own history, remains what she has always been: a writer of instinct, stonily, obsessively, even self-destructively chained to the task of reaching beyond the material world of self and society towards the impossible absolute.

She readily confesses that her writing derives less from a conscious urge to create or to make statements than from moods which are in some way exorcised by being expressed yet never quite lost. At the centre of her re-created world is a prism which reflects the same light in different colours and in always changing directions. *La Vie matérielle* (1987), an edited collection of conversations with Jérôme Beaujour, is a gently ruminative assortment of memories, opinion and topical comment (some of it very sharp). She speaks frankly of her drinking problem, of her surprisingly warm view of family life and of her writing, which she has come to believe is not a process of inventing but of 'discovering' and 'seeing' what already exists.

This preoccupation with the nature of literary creation is at the heart of *Emily L.* (1987), a novel of sober and measured elegance which remained in the best-seller lists for some months. The narrator and her companion observe an English couple in a bar at Quilleboeuf and reconstruct (or 'discover') the story of the unrealisable love which has both kept them apart and drawn them together throughout their long life. They are followed (or are led: it does not matter which) through time and space to the point where their story coincides with that of those who watch them. Emily L. is a return to Lol just as the man she has loved is a calmer but no less desperate version of the vice-consul or even of the questing heroine of *Le Marin*

10. On this relationship, see Yann Andréa, *M.D.*, Editions de Minuit, 1983.

de Gibraltar. More accessible and less anguished than *Les Yeux bleus cheveux noirs*, but underscored by a sense of the narrator's vulnerability, *Emily L.* is a compelling story told with elegiac lyricism of great beauty. The search for the 'impossible' goes on.

If Duras's vision of that 'utopian' absolute (the word is hers) has not changed greatly since the publication of *Le Ravissement de Lol V. Stein*, from which so much of her later work derives, then it has become more sharply focused and been stated with increasing urgency. Her compulsion to transmit what she sees with her inner eye explains why she has experimented so vitally with forms of expression. Her early rejection of nineteenth-century models of fictional creation now appears as a mere first step to later audacities. She has at different times abandoned traditional forms of theatre and cinema and from 1971 long repudiated the novel itself. Crossing the boundaries of genre, she has composed texts which are simultaneously novel, play and film, and she has exploded her material into self-sufficient fragments which, when taken together, prove to be so many reflections of the same object. Yet however far she may at times have strayed from what is normally considered to be 'literature', she remains committed to the written word. In her view the imagination is never better stimulated than in the act of reading. It may be that her texts should be classed as a form of poetry. But Duras is uninterested in labels. She is concerned with ensuring that we look at what she, as a visionary of liberation, has been seeing for over forty years.

Bibliography

Works by Marguerite Duras
(* denotes film)

Les Impudents (Plon, 1943)
La Vie tranquille (Gallimard, 1944)
Un Barrage contre le Pacifique (Gallimard, 1950)
Le Marin de Gibraltar (Gallimard, 1952)
Les Petits Chevaux de Tarquinia (Gallimard, 1953)
Des Journées entières dans les arbres (Gallimard, 1954)
Le Square (Gallimard, 1955)

Moderato cantabile (Editions de Minuit, 1958)

Les Viaducs de la Seine-et-Oise (Gallimard, 1960)

Dix heures et demie du soir en été (Gallimard, 1960)

Hiroshima mon amour (Gallimard, 1960)

Une aussi longue absence (in collaboration with Gérard Jarlot) (Gallimard, 1961)

L'Après-midi de Monsieur Andesmas (Gallimard, 1962)

Le Ravissement de Lol V. Stein (Gallimard, 1964)

Théâtre I: Les Eaux et forêts, Le Square, La Musica (Gallimard, 1965)

Le Vice-consul (Gallimard, 1966)

*La Musica (co-directed with Paul Seban), 1967

L'Amante anglaise - novel (Gallimard, 1967)

L'Amante anglaise - play (Cahiers du Théâtre national populaire, 1968)

Théâtre II: Suzanna Andler, Des Journées entières dans les arbres, Yes, peut-être, Le Shaga, Un Homme est venu me voir (Gallimard, 1968)

Détruire, dit-elle (Editions de Minuit, 1969)

*Détruire, dit-elle, 1969, Distributed by S.E.P.A.

Abahn Sabana David (Gallimard, 1970)

L'Amour (Gallimard, 1971)

*Jaune le soleil, 1971 (Never released)

*Nathalie Granger, 1972, Distributed by Les Films Molière

*La Femme du Gange, 1972 (Never released)

India Song, texte-théâtre-film (Gallimard, 1973)

Nathalie Granger, suivie de la Femme du Gange (Gallimard, 1973)

*India Song, 1975, Distributed by Les Films Armorial

*Baxter, Vera Baxter, 1976, Distributed by N.E.F. Diffusion

*Son nom de Venise dans Calcutta désert, 1976, Distributed by Cinéma 9

*Des Journées entières dans les arbres, 1976, Distributed by Gaumont

*Le Camion, 1977, Distributed by Les Films Molière

Le Camion, suivi de Entretiens avec Michelle Porte (Editions de Minuit, 1977)

L'Eden cinéma (Mercure de France, 1977)

*Le Navire Night, 1978, Distributed by Les Films du Losange

*Césarée, 1979, Distributed by Les Films du Losange

*Les Mains négatives, 1979, Distributed by Les Films du Losange

*Aurélia Steiner (known as *Aurélia Melbourne*), 1979, Distributed by Les Films Paris-Audiovisuel

*Aurélia Steiner (known as *Aurélia Vancouver*), 1979, Distributed by Les Films du Losange

Le Navire Night – Césarée – Les Mains négatives – Aurélia Steiner – Aurélia Steiner – Aurélia Steiner (Mercure de France, 1979)

Vera Baxter, ou les plages de l'Atlantique (Editions Albatros, 1980)

L'Homme assis dans le couloir (Editions de Minuit, 1980)

Les Yeux verts, Cahiers du Cinéma, nos. 312–313, June 1980; revised edition (Editions de l'Etoile, 1983)

L'Eté 80 (collected journalism) (Editions de Minuit, 1980)

Outside. Papiers d'un jour (collected journalism) (Albin Michel, 1981)
Agatha (Editions de Minuit, 1981)
*Agatha et les lectures illimitées, 1981, Distributed by Hors Champ Diffusion
L'Homme Atlantique (Editions de Minuit, 1982)
*L'Homme Atlantique, 1982, Distributed by Hors Champ Diffusion
Savannah Bay (Editions de Minuit, 1982; revised edition, 1983)
La Maladie de la mort (Editions de Minuit, 1982) Filmed as *Das Mal des Todes*
   by the Austrian, Peter Handke, in 1985
Théâtre III (Gallimard, 1984) Contains versions of foreign plays written for
   the commercial theatre and for television
L'Amant (Editions de Minuit, 1984)
*Dialogue de Rome, 1984
(Uncollected articles published intermittently in *L'Autre Journal* between its
   first number in December 1984 and its demise in 1986)
La Douleur (P.O.L., 1985)
*Les Enfants, 1985, Distributed by Les Films sans frontières
La Musica Deuxième (Gallimard, 1985)
Les Yeux bleus cheveux noirs (Editions de Minuit, 1986)
La Pute de la côte normande (Editions de Minuit, 1986)
Emily L. (Editions de Minuit, 1987)

Interviews

Among the many interviews given by Duras, of special interest are her
   conversations with Dominique Noguez which accompany the edition of
   her *Œuvres cinématographiques* (distributed by the Bureau d'Animation cul-
   turelle of the Ministère des Relations extérieures, 1984). See also:
Les Parleuses (Editions de Minuit, 1974) Contains full transcript of taped
   conversations with Xavière Gauthier conducted between May and July
   1973
Les Lieux de Marguerite Duras (Editions de Minuit, 1977) Conversations with
   Michelle Porte
Marguerite Duras à Montréal. Textes réunis et présentés par Suzanne Lamy et André
   Roy (Montréal, Editions Spirale, 1981)
La Vie matérielle (P.O.L., 1987) Conversations with Jérôme Beaujour

Selected Critical Studies

Borgomano, Madeleine, *L'Ecriture filmique de Marguerite Duras* (Editions
   Albatros, 1985)
Coward, David, *Marguerite Duras: 'Moderato cantabile'*, Critical Guides to
   French Literature (Grant & Cutler, 1981)
Magazine Littéraire, 158, March 1980 (special issue devoted to Marguerite
   Duras)
Murphy, Carol J., *Alienation and Absence in the Novels of Marguerite Duras*

(Lexington, Kentucky, French Forum, 1982)

Pierrot, Jean, *Marguerite Duras* (Corti, 1986)

Skutta, Franciska, *Aspects de la narration dans les romans de Marguerite Duras* (Debrecen, 1981)

Tison-Braun, Micheline, *Marguerite Duras* (Amsterdam, Rodopi, 1985)

Willis, Sharon, *Marguerite Duras: Writing on the Body* (Urbana, University of Illinois Press, 1987)

–3–

Michel Tournier

DAVID GASCOIGNE

André Gide a dit qu'il n'écrivait pas pour être lu mais pour être relu. Il voulait dire par là qu'il entendait être lu au moins deux fois. J'écris moi aussi pour être relu, mais, moins exigeant que Gide, je ne demande qu'une seule lecture. Mes livres doivent être reconnus – relus – dès la première lecture.

Michel Tournier, Le Vent Paraclet (p. 189)[1]

In the late 1960s the situation and future of the French novel appeared to many to be fraught with doubt. On the one hand avant-garde writers, some inspired by the theory and practice of the *nouveau roman*, published demanding texts for a literary élite, eschewing a wider audience; on the other a steady stream of unashamedly popular novels continued, few of which were regarded as worthy of serious attention by the literary intelligentsia. No contemporary novelist was widely recognised as having decisively bridged that gap.

Michel Tournier's arrival on this stage was timely, and his rise to literary stardom was meteoric. His first novel, *Vendredi ou les limbes du Pacifique* (1967), was awarded the Grand Prix du Roman de l'Académie Française in 1967, and his second, *Le Roi des Aulnes* (1970), received the ultimate accolade of the Prix Goncourt. On the basis, essentially, of these two novels, backed by a successful career in publishing and the media, he found himself henceforth an influential member of the Goncourt jury.

The Académie Goncourt, accused by some of being too much under the influence of the major publishing houses, likes to see itself as reflecting the taste of the wider educated public rather than just of professional *literati*. Tournier himself seldom refers in articles or interviews to the *nouveau roman*: its main exponents do not feature in *Le Vol du vampire* (1982), his collection of literary notes and essays.

---

1. Page references in the essay are to the Folio (Gallimard) editions of Tournier's works.

There are aspects of his work, admittedly – his interest in semiology and cultural systems, his intellectual debt to Lévi-Strauss – which align him with Barthes. In contrast, however, his avowed literary values and critical vocabulary, placing weight on the 'depth' of good writing and the creation of richly detailed characters to whom readers can relate, are of a kind which *nouveau roman* theorists strove to discredit. Tournier's fiction, likewise, has appealed less to the literary avant-garde, who have tended to dismiss his technique as nineteenth-century, than to those delighted to rediscover a fiction which, like the major 'existentialist' novels of Gide, Sartre, Malraux and Camus, was prepared to engage directly with ideology and philosophical ideas.

The *phénomène Tournier* can be seen, in retrospect, not simply as the emergence of a major talent. It was also the response to a need, and the product of professional self-marketing. As he indicates in the opening pages of *Le Vol du vampire*, Tournier sees himself unapologetically as an artisan, a writer who writes not idealistically or in the abstract but to be published, sold and read as widely as possible. *Le Vol du vampire* is itself one example of the careful husbandry of the prudent writer, gathering together occasional pieces, prefaces and articles to make up a more substantial product. The volume published as *Petites proses* in 1986 is an arguably less satisfactory example of the same reassembling of previous fragments. *Le Coq de bruyère* (1978) brings together a group of stories, some for children, some previously published. It would be easy to see here simply the desire to squeeze the maximum profit from a single piece of writing (but what is wrong with that?). What is more interesting is that, when reproduced in a different context, writing can be seen to have fresh significance. The juxtaposition of stories in *Le Coq de bruyère* and of reflections on different writers and themes in *Le Vol du vampire* set up certain insistent resonances. This resituation of material is comparable to the exhibition of paintings or photographs: the same picture, displayed between different neighbours in a different light, takes on a new and unforeseen meaning.

The presentation of already published material in new guises takes an interesting form in the novels that Tournier has rewritten in a simpler version more suitable for children.[2] The text of *Vendredi ou les limbes du Pacifique* was shorn of passages of explicit metaphysical reflection; this shorter, seemingly more artless text was then entitled

---

2. See the articles by Michael Worton, 'Michel Tournier and the masterful art of re-writing', *PN Review*, 41, vol. 11, no. 3 (1984), 24–5, and 'Ecrire et ré-écrire: le projet de Tournier', *Sud*, 61 (1986), 52–69.

Vendredi ou la vie sauvage (1971). His fourth novel, *Gaspard, Melchior et Balthazar* (1980), underwent a similar process to become *Les Rois Mages* (1983). These 'children's versions' have been extremely successful, and *Vendredi ou la vie sauvage* in particular is very widely used as a school text. They are not, however, necessarily to be considered as vulgarisations. Tournier is passionately interested in the education of the young and places enormous importance on the task of writing for children. He sees the requirement of writing a text which is less intellectualised, more primal, as a real challenge to a writer. One of his aims has been to cultivate a narrative technique in which the abstract significances of the story are implicit within the telling of the tale rather than made explicit in authorial reflection or commentary. He is wont to observe of himself that, given his training as a philosopher, he needed above all to develop a sense of precisely observed and richly experienced reality (what he calls 'le côté Zola') to counterbalance and give substance to his penchant for metaphysics.[3] This evolution away from 'philosophising' and towards a more naïve, self-contained and economical style of narrative is apparent in his work since *Les Météores* (1975): *Gilles et Jeanne* (1983) and *La Goutte d'or* (1986) have disappointed readers looking for the baroque complexity and richness of texture of the earlier works. When Tournier speaks of the influence of Flaubert, it is the author of the *Trois Contes* rather than that of *La Tentation de Saint-Antoine* that he has in mind.

Tournier the writer is a re-writer. He not only republishes or rewrites his own works, seeking new audiences, new effects, new meanings: he also rewrites other, pre-existing stories. He draws self-consciously and eclectically on a European heritage of literature, legend and myth. *Le Roi des Aulnes* takes its title from Goethe's poem *Erlkönig* ('Erl-king', familiar in its musical setting by Schubert) whose text is quoted and provocatively exploited in the narrative. *Gaspard, Melchior et Balthazar* is a reworking of the biblical story (and the legends which have accrued around it) of the Magi. *Gilles et Jeanne* recounts the lives, likewise overlaid with legend, of Gilles de Rais and Joan of Arc. Tournier explicitly offers these and other texts as rewritings of earlier stories, rewritings which suggest a new, provocative and even scandalous reading of texts or tales which have faded into the tapestry of our culture and whose ability to surprise needs to be rediscovered.

---

3. See for instance *Le Vent Paraclet*, p. 179.

'Un mythe est une histoire que tout le monde connaît déjà' (*Le Vent Paraclet*, p. 189). It is a token of Tournier's confidence that the story he chose to re-tell in his first published novel was one which has achieved this mythic status in world literature, that of Robinson Crusoe. Tournier's chosen title, *Vendredi ou les limbes du Pacifique*,[4] is already an indication that the re-telling will involve a substantial change of perspective from that of Defoe's original version. Despite the fact that the story is still being told mainly from Robinson's point of view, it is Defoe's Man Friday (present only in the second half of *Vendredi*) who has been elevated to the 'title role'. This already suggests a displacement, away from the European centre towards the representation of Pacific (as well as pacific?) culture.

The placing of the island in the Pacific Ocean is itself a change from Defoe's Caribbean setting: Tournier reverts to the site of Alexander Selkirk's original autobiographical narrative which Defoe exploited and amplified. (The episode in chapter 9 relating to Andoar the goat also has its source in Selkirk rather than Defoe.) Moreover, Tournier unobtrusively moves the series of events forward by a century, placing Robinson's shipwreck in 1759, not 1659 as in Defoe, thereby making his whole narrative anachronistic in relationship to Defoe's novel, published in 1719. By this shift Tournier is offering a quite different context of reference to the history and thought of the Enlightenment period, against which his narrative can be read. Many strands from the intense intellectual debate of that age are echoed here: the ethics of colonialism and the slave trade, the relativity of cultures and the revaluation of 'primitive' peoples, the myth of Tahiti and the South Seas, the relative status of nature and civilisation, the function of government and the principles of constitution and law, Rousseau's search for self-definition and felicity in solitude. Tournier's novel has been criticised by some for an excessively overt philosophical content, but this notion of philosophical fiction was also an accepted eighteenth-century mode of literary production.[5]

Defoe's novel is very much a point of departure: Tournier's itinerary will be strikingly different. Initially he appears to stay quite

4. The shortened title *Vendredi* will be used henceforth when referring to *Vendredi ou les limbes du Pacifique*.

5. Some of these points of comparison are amplified in Anthony Purdy, 'From Defoe's *Crusoe* to Tournier's *Vendredi*: the metamorphosis of a myth', *Canadian Review of Comparative Literature*, 11 (1984), 216–35. See also Margaret Sankey, 'Meaning through intertextuality: isomorphism of Defoe's *Robinson Crusoe* and Tournier's *Vendredi ou les limbes du Pacifique*', *Australian Journal of French Studies*, vol. 18, no. 1 (1981), 77–88, and Erhard Reckwitz, *Die Robinsonade. Themen und Formen einer literarischen Gattung* (Amsterdam, 1976).

close to Defoe's narrative: he gives Robinson the same York merchant background, a strong acquaintance with the Bible and the same puritanical turn of mind and practical skill. New elements Tournier brings to the story include a twentieth-century view of the psychology of solitude and a central concern with sexuality which is wholly absent from Defoe. While Defoe's Crusoe changes little as a result of his ordeal, Tournier's Robinson is transformed by the absence of those pressures which have hitherto shaped his awareness: social consensus and interpersonal exchange. In Tournier's version, a new Robinson emerges from the inherited chrysalis of his former socialised self and its now inappropriate values. By the same token Tournier's narrative emerges into an independent life of its own, out of the cocoon of the Defoe text on which it has nourished itself and which it now outgrows.

A prologue to the narrative proper, which has no equivalent in Defoe, announces from the outset the difference in orientation. Robinson has joined the captain of the *Virginie*, Pieter Van Deyssel, in his cabin to ride out the storm that will eventually prove fatal to the vessel. Van Deyssel, who has a whimsically philosophical turn of mind, reads Robinson's fortune in the tarot cards. By this device Tournier intriguingly provides the reader at the start with an obscurely coded version of the course that Robinson's development and destiny will take. The code is not that of the rewards and punishments of Divine Providence as perceived by Defoe's hero: it is rather of an arcane and non-Christian nature. Robinson does not attend closely to Van Deyssel's words: he is distracted by the tempest and the tossing of the boat. Van Deyssel is divining the future, whereas Robinson is preoccupied by the present, and a tension is thus set up from the start between the physical and the metaphysical, between the demands of the present and the mysterious maturation of future changes and events. When the helmsman sees the rocks on which they will be dashed and shouts 'terre', Robinson at first hears 'Jupiter', echoing Van Deyssel's invocation of ancient gods. It is at this moment of collision between the metaphysical discourse of prediction ('Jupiter') and the brutal reality of the present ('terre') that the ship is wrecked, and Robinson is expelled from the closed space of the boat to begin his life on the island.

The main text opens with Robinson regaining consciousness on the beach, after being washed up by the sea. He has been metaphorically re-born into a new life, exiled from the comforting environment of human society like the baby from its mother's body. For the first two chapters he thinks of little but escape, devoting all his hours to the building of a substantial boat, *L'Evasion*. When this enterprise fails because of an elementary oversight, he succumbs to the ever-present temptation of the mud-pool in which he immerses himself, abdicating responsibility and self-respect. After a crisis of hallucination in which he ends up floundering in the sea, trying to reach an imaginary galleon in the bay, he is washed up on the beach for a second time.

This second 're-birth' inaugurates a new phase, in which he commits himself to maintaining his human dignity by re-establishing the values that have always sustained it: hard work, discipline, self-denial, the rigorous ordering of time, space and environment, thrift and the accumulation of wealth through the exploitation of the available resources. By chapter 4 his commitment to rebuilding the social structures of Europe in an alien land has led him to colonial delusions of grandeur: he names himself governor of the island, general of the armed forces and priest of the temple and establishes a constitution and penal code to externalise the code of discipline he feels he requires.

As these tasks, roles and rituals become increasingly elaborate and onerous, it becomes apparent, even to Robinson himself, that they are a provisional shell within which a new Robinson is slowly developing. His ambition to make bread, for instance, betrays this doubleness of self. On one level Robinson sees this as a sacramental act, an epitome of religious observance. On a quite different level the image of kneading dough evokes a childhood memory of a baker at work which is powerfully suggestive: the dough is 'ce grand corps sans tête, tiède et lascif, qui s'abandonnait au fond du pétrin aux étreintes d'un homme à demi nu' (p. 81). This image of a headless, docile, sensuous body emerges elsewhere in the text, in connection with the island. Robinson, having first called the island Désolation, now re-christens it Speranza – and once more a double resonance is present. Speranza (the Italian for hope) is one of the three theological virtues, but it is also the name of 'une ardente Italienne' (p. 45) whom Robinson once knew at York. A pious gesture is again overlaid by a 'très profane souvenir' (p. 45) of an object of sexual desire. The map he draws of Speranza island bears a strange resemblance to 'un corps féminin sans tête, [. . .] dans une attitude [. . .] de soumission, de peur ou de simple abandon' (p. 46).

Such moments suggest that Robinson's spiritual pretensions are indissolubly wedded to sensual dreams, but his Puritan inheritance cannot yet accommodate and make sense of this link. An important step comes in chapter 5, when Robinson stops his water-clock, thereby suspending the complex order of his 'administered island', and descends naked into a womb-like cavity beneath the grotto at the centre of the island. Again the vocabulary suggests a religious initiation – the grotto is compared to a cathedral, the cavity to a crypt – yet he is also aware that it is an orifice in the 'undeniably feminine' body of Speranza, and the memories which flood back to him are of his mother. His surrender of clothing (decency) and of the faculty of sight (order) in the darkness is rewarded by an experience of supra-sensual awareness of the island, a mystic expansion of self to encompass its whole space. From being the body of a mother, Speranza will now become that of a lover, receiving Robinson's passionate embraces. Chapter 6, the culmination of the first half of the book, celebrates this love affair with ecstatic quotations from the Song of Songs – the voice of the Bible becomes, at last, the voice of desire and gratification, not that of prohibition.

It is at this half-way point, at the beginning of chapter 7, that Vendredi arrives on the scene. A group of natives land by boat and, as Robinson watches from a concealed position, one of them is denounced by the sorceress of the tribe and condemned to death as the scapegoat for some tribal misfortune. By a fluke, the chosen victim escapes his murderous pursuers, who give up the chase and leave. In his own eyes, however, Vendredi is dead: his soul is departed, and Robinson is master of his body. Vendredi's arrival on Speranza is, like Robinson's, a kind of re-birth, an ejection from his society and an entry into a new life. This interpretation has already been anticipated by Van Deyssel's reference to the birth of Venus, who arose from the waves: Vendredi, the name Robinson gives the newcomer, derives, as we are told, from *Veneris dies*, the day of Venus.

Robinson seeks to recruit Vendredi to the roles prescribed by his colonial system – as slave in his economy, subject in his kingdom, worshipper in his religion, pupil ready for his schooling. This regime satisfies the needs of the 'old Robinson', but not those of the new one, who craves love and companionship more than submission and fear. The euphoric dialogue between Robinson and Speranza is also complicated by the presence of this third party: the island seems to respond to Vendredi, and Robinson becomes jealous of the black man's spontaneous, unforced relationship to his environment. When, at the end of chapter 8, he discovers Vendredi making love to the island in his own favourite hollow, his rage is fuelled both by the fury of the jealous lover and by the atavistic fear of the European of the sexual potency of the black man. Vendredi, in his panic at the retribution about to descend on him, inadvertently detonates the barrels of explosive that Robinson has stored in the grotto when he throws away the lighted pipe of tobacco he is illicitly smoking.

This incident highlights an interpretative model which has been implied from the beginning, based on the traditional idea of the four elements of earth, air, fire and water and their symbolic relationship to human temperament. Robinson is consistently represented as a man of earth and fire – attracted to the mud pool and the subterranean grotto, storing gunpowder and lighting a pillar of flame to attract passing vessels. It is in the seemingly trivial observation of Robinson's and Vendredi's different pleasures in pipe-smoking that Tournier most clearly points up the 'elemental' difference between the two. For Robinson, the pleasure is in the glowing pipe-bowl, 'l'enveloppe terrestre d'un petit soleil souterrain, une manière de volcan portatif et domestiqué' (p. 182); for Vendredi the joy is in watching the whorls of smoke in the still air of the grotto. Vendredi's presiding element is air: he climbs high in the trees, sleeps in a hammock, fires elaborate arrows into the sky, flies kites. Robinson's pipe-bowl suggests containment, Vendredi's smoke diffusion into space. The gunpowder explosion not only literally devastates the fabric of Robinson's 'administration' by demolishing his buildings: it is the logical expression of a cataclysm of earth and fire, breaking the bands of a containment which can no longer be sustained. It is the eruption of that destructive inner fire of violence, hatred and self-hatred to which Robinson is prone.

This point represents yet another symbolic re-birth – Robinson sheds his burnt clothes and emerges from the shattered shell of his complex of buildings into a wholly new relationship with the island. Vendredi's instinctive resistance to assimilation into the colonialist order has brought about its collapse, and it is now he who becomes the leader and teacher. The presence and example of Vendredi form the catalyst which enables Robinson to accept his own body, his sexual and sensual needs, and to integrate them into a new metaphysical awareness. Vendredi directs Robinson's gaze upwards to the sun, so that the element of fire to which he is attracted can be in the image of the radiant, life-giving sun rather than of the enclosed, explosive volcano. When Vendredi hunts and kills the wild he-goat Andoar, he turns the skin into a kite and the skull and gut into an aeolian harp. Andoar, the earth-bound beast, becomes the plaything of the wind and the musician of air, and in this metamorphosis Robinson sees a parable of his own transformation at Vendredi's hands.

Chapter 10, like chapter 6, is a chapter of euphoria: fresh log-book entries celebrate Robinson's new sense of oneness with the natural world and his wonder at the beauty of Vendredi's body. Like chapter 6, this high point heralds a decisive new arrival – this time it is the *Whitebird*, a British merchant ship which brings with it the chance for Robinson to end his long years of exile. It is an index of how much he has changed that he is now dismayed by the shallow and uncaring attitude of his compatriots and finds himself reluctant to re-enter the mainstream of history and linear time from which he has so completely escaped. He decides to remain, but in chapter 11 he discovers to his distress that Vendredi has joined the ship and departed, seduced by the aerial magic of the high-rigged schooner (and perhaps even by its name). It is as though Robinson, having passed the test of commitment to his new way of life, must now undergo a final rite of passage to prove his independence of Vendredi. The compensating reward for this final ordeal comes when an Estonian cabin-boy, Jaan, who has deserted the ship, emerges in a final symbolic birth from the rocks of the shattered grotto to become Robinson's adoptive child, or perhaps even a reincarnation of Robinson, in the eternal cycle of time in which Robinson now exists. The twelve chapters of the book, like the twelve hours of the clock-face, have now elapsed, and the hand can start the same journey again.

The final pages of the text describe Robinson and the child standing on a pinnacle, bathed in the light of the rising sun. The passage suggests a mystic initiation and transfiguration as the shafts of light consecrate the pair in an apotheosis of strength and metallic beauty. Tournier gives us here a pagan rewriting of the Transfiguration of Christ who, having brought three disciples up 'into a high mountain apart [. . .] was transfigured before them: and his face did shine as the sun, and his raiment was white as the light' (Matthew 17: 1, 2). There are many quotations in Tournier's text from the Old Testament, but no explicit reference to the New. This is in part because Robinson's biblical readings are largely associated with his earlier phase of development, when he feels the need for a strict, repressive law rather than for the ethos of love, charity and forgiveness. The shift to such values as these is, however, implicit in Tournier's text: the emergence of the new Robinson is analogous to that of the new Adam wrought by the coming of Christ. Tournier's text can be read as a pseudo-Bible for a religious order that aims to encompass an acceptance of physical pleasure and sensuality, a transcendence of self, a sense of wonder at the natural world and an intuition of supernatural wisdom. The specific yet oblique relationship of Tournier's ideology to orthodox Christianity is suggested by the word 'limbes' in the title of the novel. The doctrine of Limbo has no biblical basis but it was defined by Catholic teaching as the dwelling-place of two kinds of souls: the *Limbus patrum*, refuge of the righteous of the Old Testament, who pre-dated Christ's redemption and also of noble heathens, and the *Limbus infantum*, for unbaptised children. The view of the nature of Limbo became more benign over the centuries: from being an antechamber to hell, it was later seen by some as a natural paradise, just short of the celestial vision. The same progression, from 'Désolation' to natural paradise, takes place in Robinson's view of his Limbo, and it is here that Tournier places his symbolic couple: the *pater*, the would-be man of Old Testament righteousness, now turned noble heathen, and the *infans*, the unbaptised child.

In his dialogue with Defoe's text, as well as with other Robinson narratives such as Jules Verne's *L'Ile mystérieuse* (1874) and Buñuel's film *Robinson Crusoe* (1954),[6] Tournier has formulated a critique of European values: we may remember that the year in which Tournier's Robinson is shipwrecked is the year of the publication of Voltaire's *Candide*, which offers a fascinating comparison in the manner and the targets of its criticism. More than this, however, Tournier's first novel points towards a religious sensibility which draws on Christianity while subjecting it to strange transformations. Both these dimensions – the critique of culture and the thrust towards a renewed spiritual consciousness – are richly explored in Tournier's subsequent works.

The narrative of Tournier's second novel, *Le Roi des Aulnes*, follows the career of one man, Abel Tiffauges, between 1938 and 1945, with flashbacks to his formative school experiences at the Collège Saint-Christophe at Beauvais. In 1938 Tiffauges is a modest garage-owner in Paris: by 1945, after a period as prisoner of war, he ends up effectively in charge of an SS training establishment for boys (a 'Napola') in East Prussia, until the arrival of Soviet forces. Bizarre though this progression is, the reader is not simply invited to wonder at its more sensational aspect. What gives the narrative a particular tone is the fact that Tiffauges, whose point of view orients the text as a whole, sees this progression not as a fortuitous by-product of turbulent times but as embodying a special coherence and significance. He sees himself as a particular instrument of destiny and the path he follows as marked out by patterns which infinitely transcend his individual life. The long opening section headed 'Ecrits sinistres' is in the form of a diary written with his left (or 'sinister') hand, and it is appropriately heavy with omens. From the very opening paragraph, the diarist declares his special link with destiny: 'Je crois

6. See *Le Vent Paraclet*, ch. 4. This volume of 'autobiographie intellectuelle' offers a wealth of illuminating observations on the first three novels, as well as on the author's sources and working methods.

[. . .] à cette connivence secrète qui mêle en profondeur mon aventure personnelle au cours des choses, et lui permet de l'incliner dans son sens' (p. 13).

A second article of faith, as important as the first, is also offered on the opening page: 'Je crois aussi que je suis issu de la nuit des temps [. . .] Moi, j'étais là déjà, il y a mille ans, il y a cent mille ans. Quand la terre n'était encore qu'une boule de feu tournoyant dans un ciel d'hélium, l'âme qui la faisait flamber, qui la faisait tourner, c'était la mienne' (p. 13). Tiffauges sees himself as of the race of ogres or titans, as the incarnation of a timeless archetype whose being is untouched by history. Ogres are sterile; therefore their characteristics are not transmitted through procreation: 'Vieux comme le monde, immortel comme lui, je ne puis avoir qu'un père et une mère putatifs, et des enfants d'adoption' (p. 14). When he is taken from France into Nazi Germany he senses that he is entering his 'chosen land', the zone most propitious to the unfolding of his destiny. When he encounters Nazi ideology, as expounded for instance by the fanatical eugenicist Dr Blättchen, his disquiet is intense. Blättchen's thesis is that heredity, the inheritance of blood, is all and that environment and the cultural context count for nothing in the value of the individual. Tiffauges is aware that Blättchen's bloodthirsty enthusiasm for the extermination of the racially inferior could readily apply to the likes of him. Yet the reader may also observe that Tiffauges himself claims special status by virtue of belonging to 'la race ogresse', marked by particular physical and behavioural characteristics. His non-genetic concept of 'race' is different from Blättchen's, and the characteristics of the ogre race bear little resemblance to those of Blättchen's Teutonic ideal. Nevertheless Tiffauges, like Blättchen, disdains any responsibility to history for the consequences of his actions in the present and claims a metaphysical vocation which feeds on the residue of ancient fears and legends. Time does not represent progress and change for Tiffauges: it is simply the recurrent representation of the same prototypes, that Nietzschean 'Eternal Return' which he sees as embodied in Nazism. 'L'hitlérisme est réfractaire à toute idée de progrès, de création, de découverte et d'invention d'un avenir vierge' (p. 413).

Tiffauges comments penetratingly on Nazism's rejection of time as progress: 'Sa vertu n'est pas de rupture, mais de restauration: culte de la race, des ancêtres, du sang, des morts, de la terre . . .' (pp. 413–14). Yet the critical force of these words is blunted by Tiffauges's own insistence on his privileged status as exemplar of the prototype 'ogre' and his consequent acceptance of brutality and bloodshed as a necessary part of his ordained vocation.

The 'putative father' he mentions on the opening page is Nestor, his friend and mentor at the Collège Saint-Christophe, of the same physical type as himself. Nestor is a formidable counterweight to the normal authority structure of the school, which it seems he can influence at will. He is also a source of mysterious and lapidary wisdom to his younger protégé. Nestor too seems ageless, and after his death in a fire at the school, Abel feels that the spirit and the force of Nestor have passed into him: 'D'une certaine façon il revit en moi, je suis Nestor' (p. 204). Tiffauges's use in his diary of the ambiguous nickname 'Mabel' ('ma belle'?), by which Nestor used to address him, suggests that Nestor's voice has been internalised and is leading him towards a clearer vision of his destiny: 'C'est lui également qui détient le secret de l'obscure complicité unissant mon destin et le cours général des choses . . .' (pp. 116–7).

Tiffauges recognises himself not just in Nestor, but in other figures: the murderer Weidmann, whose execution he attends, appears as a kind of twin, and the equally notorious Rasputin as a kind of maligned predecessor. He senses an atavistic affinity too with more ancient forebears: with the man whose body is exhumed from the Prussian peat where it had lain buried for two-thousand years, and in particular with the legendary, threatening figure of the Erl-King. These references to the 'family' of figures to which he feels he belongs move further and further away from present reality as he goes on, starting with Weidmann and culminating in the Erl-King, whose origins are lost in the mists of ancient superstition. This represents the increasing ascendancy of race over history, of symbol over fact, as well as a reversal of the progress of time which he perceives in other aspects too – from being a car mechanic, he becomes a driver of wood-fuelled vehicles and finally a horseman, as the penury of the war imposes ever more primitive solutions.

The most ancient figure, that of the Erl-King, represents a culmination not only of the theme of ogre, but also of the notion of 'la phorie', which is intricately and extensively developed in the novel. Tiffauges feels an intense euphoria when he carries a boy-child in his arms: Tournier exploits the ambiguity of the French expression 'porter un enfant' (to bear a child) to suggest that this is the expression of the paternal (or maternal) vocation of the sterile giant. This action however is morally ambiguous: if it is an act of submission to the child, it is a sacred act of service like that of St Christopher, patron saint of the college at Beauvais. If it is an act of domination against the child's will, it is an abduction, like that of the child by the Erl-King in Goethe's famous poem. This latter, perverse aspect, which characterises Tiffauges's hunting down of recruits for the Napola, is the malign counterpart of the gesture of tender concern with which, much earlier, he gathers up the injured apprentice in his garage. The predatory Erl-King and the distraught father of Goethe's narration are twin faces of the same coin, Tournier suggests: the bad father and the good, ogre and saint. Tiffauges's pilgrimage, as he moves from France to Prussia, and from the present, against the tide of history, back to an age of primeval forces, brings this primal polarity starkly into focus – absolute evil, in the form of the mass sadism and inhuman brutality of the death camps, can only be answered by an equally radical commitment to a gesture of sacrifice, as Tiffauges moves from the ruins of the Napola carrying a frail Jewish child on his shoulders.

As a member of the 'race ogresse', Tiffauges is in his own eyes beyond the reach of history – but this does not exhaust his relationship to it. If we return to that first statement about his origins in the spinning ball of fire that became the earth, we note his statement that 'l'âme qui la faisait flamber, qui la faisait tourner, c'était la mienne' (p. 13). He appropriates the divine title of the Supreme Being, the Principle of Creation, and as the book continues, this translates by its own logic into the conviction that the world revolves around his destiny. The fire at the college and the eruption of the second world war are, to him, timely interventions to release him from a state of impasse and advance his life into its next allotted phase. Catastrophe strikes not only to rescue the besieged hero but also to chasten his enemies: Tiffauges views the panic-stricken exodus of the civilian population in 1940 as the natural retribution exacted on a society misguided enough to execute Weidmann and persecute himself. Five years later the distress of the German population will be seen even more forcefully as a necessary preparation for the moment when he can assume total power in the Napola. 'Ci-gît le grand corps sans défense de la Prusse, toujours vivant et chaud, mais étalant ses parties molles et vulnérables sous mes bottes. Il n'en fallait pas moins pour soumettre ce pays et ses enfants aux exigences de mon impérieuse tendresse' (pp. 533–4).

Tiffauges's task, as he sees it, is not that of choosing the direction of his life, for that is done for him: it is to understand the elements of his destiny. His task is not the achievement of power, although that is vouchsafed to him: it is the acquisition of knowledge, of insight. If his whole environment is arranged in accordance with the shape of his personal fate, then it follows that every event and every perception is potentially significant to him. Anything that enters his field of awareness is liable to be viewed as part of a giant code which it is his task to unravel, a piece in the 'grand puzzle que je compose patiemment' (p. 140), in 'mon système'(p. 457).

Systems of knowledge and of interpretation are a source of endless fascination for Tiffauges and doubtless for Tournier himself with his philosophical training, and the book contains some displays of unusual erudition. Goering, we gather, is an expert on animal-droppings, Professor Essig on deer antlers and different ways of evaluating them, Bertold on types of pigeons, Pressman on horse-manship and dressage, Professor Keil on the ancient peat-bog men and their culture, Professor Blättchen on racial classification and physiology and the Kommandeur on heraldry. These techniques of analysis and classification are not innocent, however. Those to do with animals are all designed to assist or glorify the hunter or the trainer: they are concerned with bloodshed or with discipline. Tiffauges learns from all these experts, and by the same token he must learn also the whole range of insignia of different ranks in the SS: discipline and bloodshed are implicit here too. The expert deductions drawn from the bodies of humans past (Keil) or present (Blättchen) are not disinterested: each is fired with the desire to reinforce the national-racial superiority required by Nazism. Even heraldry, the least material of these sciences, whose subject matter is signs and symbols, is a powerful source of ritual and mystic fervour for the Third Reich.

Quite late in the novel Tiffauges reflects on two different images of the process of knowing and understanding, the key and the grid: 'Je comprends mieux maintenant la différence entre la *clé* qui ne nous livre qu'un sens particulier de l'essence, et la *grille* qui en prend totalement possession, et l'offre illuminée à notre intuition' (p. 495). The feature of a classification grid is that, to be effective, it needs to include all examples: it must constitute a field within which every item under scrutiny can be enclosed. Descartes's rule 'Faire partout des dénombrements si entiers et des revues si générales que je fusse assuré de ne rien omettre', quoted by Tiffauges (p. 147), is by nature totalitarian. A few pages later (p. 152) Tiffauges plays on the literal and metaphorical sense of 'grille', after taking photos of children through the railings (*grilles*) round the school playground. The photographs themselves represent rectangular 'cages' within which the children are enclosed, ready to be arranged in any order chosen by the owner. This symbolic act of enclosure and domination becomes real at the Napola, when Tiffauges gathers boys from the countryside into the fortress of Kaltenborn and presides over dor-mitory and parade ground. Tiffauges, like Nestor, revels in the 'density of atmosphere' generated by such enclosed spaces. A se-quence of examples of 'le monde clos sur lui-même' structures the novel, from the Collège Saint-Christophe via the prisoner-of-war camp and the Rominten estate to Kaltenborn and the shadow of the horrific enclosed world of Auschwitz behind the final pages. The notion of '*concentration* camp' acquires particular force as a malign manifestation of this notion of enclosure and density. Tournier's power here is to make manifest the potent link between spatial organisation and knowledge, between the external discipline and violence of a regime and the structures it imposes in its decoding of experience. The notion of 'grille' does indeed, as Tiffauges darkly perceives, go well beyond a 'simple jeu de mots' (p. 152). We have here an insight into the relationship between knowledge and power, *le savoir* and *le pouvoir*, which finds fascinating parallels, for instance, in the writings of Michel Foucault.

Tiffauges's search for *le savoir* and his conviction that in his life every encounter is potentially pregnant with meaning lead him to pay particular attention to the texts he reads or hears. In the same way that he constructs a notional 'family' of ancestors and twins, ancient and modern, he assembles an anthology of texts in which he sees reflections of his own destiny. Tiffauges is of course short-sighted, but he compensates for this with a sharpness of hearing: the whole novel puts stress on the rich significance of sound in his life. The texts he absorbs are often read aloud: Nestor recites to him stretches of the only novel he reads, *Le Piège d'or*, by Curwood, including appropriately a vivid description of the *sound* of a man-wolf howling (p. 63). From Nestor too comes the tale of the Baron des Adrets (pp. 80–1). An anecdote from Montaigne features in a sermon by the Father Superior. To each of these texts Tiffauges attaches a private significance. Later in the novel Tournier establishes a counterpoint of textual quotation between the Bible and Nazi songs. In a period of apocalyptic bloodshed the murder of Abel, the massacre of the Innocents, the plagues of Egypt, the lamentations of Job and the cosmic visions of the book of Revelation all offer resonant harmonics to the narrative. Against this biblical fresco of guilt and judgement are set the confident battle-chants of the SS cadets which punctuate the long fifth section of the novel. This counterpoint finally resolves into the singsong recitation by Ephraim of the passage from the book of Job about Behemoth, a huge, strong, yet gentle creature. After the playground noise that Tiffauges records and studies, and the 'voix métalliques' (p. 490) of the cadets, the voice of a single boy, representing all those in the text, finally offers a consoling biblical image of Tiffauges's phoric vocation.[7]

7. *Le Roi des Aulnes* was written, Tournier tells us, to the obsessive accompaniment of

The image may be consoling, but when Ephraim gives Tiffauges the title of 'Cheval d'Israël', it is not without humour and a hint of mockery. Any assessment of the characterisation of Tiffauges in the narrative must take account of the strain of critical irony which is implicit, not least in the naïvety to which the *écrits sinistres* bear witness. One instance of Tournier's careful development of a motif is the imagery used to characterise Tiffauges's euphoria as he holds a boy's body in his arms: 'Les neuf chœurs des anges m'environnaient d'une gloire invisible et radieuse. L'air était plein d'encens et d'accords de harpes. Un fleuve de douceur coulait majestueusement dans mes veines' (pp. 130–1); 'quel fleuve de miel coulait majestueusement en moi!' (p. 143); 'mes épaules touchent le ciel, ma tête est environnée d'archanges musiciens qui chantent ma gloire. Les roses mystiques épanchent pour moi leur plus frais parfum' (p. 173).

The first effect is one of cliché; the unalloyed imagery of popular piety is presented with the same effect of disconcerting and ambiguous detachment as by Flaubert at the end of 'La légende de St Julien l'Hospitalier' in his *Trois Contes*. The third quotation, however, marks a shift by suggesting specifically that he is himself the object of the celestial praise: the image of Tiffauges, like Eliot's hippopotamus 'ascending from the damp savannas' to where 'quiring angels round him sing / The praise of God, in loud hosannas' is intentionally incongruous, but the spiritual arrogance which it expresses is also disquieting, in the context of the novel. As the climax of the narrative approaches Tiffauges himself argues that this imagery, however derivative ('d'une inspiration fade, vaguement sulpicienne'), is nevertheless a genuine expression of 'les fastes de mon apothéose' (p. 517). Twenty pages later, as he stands holding the body of Hellmut, a cadet decapitated by the flame from a hand-held rocket-launcher, the heaven into which he feels uplifted is 'un ciel noir qu'ébranlait de seconde en seconde la pulsation des canons de l'Apocalypse' (p. 539).

Tournier is accomplishing two things here. He is provoking, through his own textual representation, a reflection on the weight and functioning of images, on the ambiguities of semiology which are a central preoccupation of the novel. He is also, as Gide is in *L'Immoraliste*, setting the reader at odds with the point of view of a central character pursuing his own vision of self-fulfilment into realms of irresponsibility and brutality. The irony here cannot but

---

Stockhausen's *Gesang der Jünglinge* (Chant des jeunes Hébreux) about the young Israelites thrown into the fiery furnace by Nebuchadnezzar, which ends with the multi-track recording of a single boy's voice. See *Le Vent Paraclet*, pp. 126–8.

draw attention to the element of delusional self-aggrandisement in Tiffauges's perception of things. It is a trademark of Tournier's work that it can be viewed simultaneously as preposterous and serious. Through Tiffauges we are offered a deeply eccentric relationship to history and to culture: yet this may be as useful and revealing a model as any other for exploring the causality of a period marked by a collective irrationality and an insane brutality which threatened and scarred western civilisation.

Les Météores (1975) remains, in terms of scale and construction, Tournier's most ambitious novel to date. While both the earlier novels followed the evolution of an individual, the focus here is divided from the beginning. Though the structure may appear on first reading to be less tightly controlled than before, a closer look suggests that the novel does have a definite overall architecture.

Of the twenty-two chapters, the first fourteen are divided equally between two parallel centres of interest. On the one hand we follow the childhood and development of the identical twins Jean and Paul, so similar that only their mother Maria-Barbara can tell them apart. Tournier describes vividly many of the features of the psychology and behaviour of twins, which he clearly researched carefully. Though the relationship represents on one level an apparently perfect unity which no other kind of couple can rival, it also generates tension: Paul wishes to retain the exclusive and hermetic bond which separates them from all others, while Jean experiences the twin-cell as a prison out of which he must ultimately break.

The parallel narrative strand is concerned with the twins' uncle, Alexandre, a flamboyant homosexual, who inherits the family business of waste disposal, represented by enormous rubbish dumps serving a number of French cities as well as Casablanca. Alexandre is characterised, by contrast with the twins, as a '*sans-pareil*'; being unique, lacking an 'other half', his keen sexual desire and predatory nature set him wandering in search of partners. His sarcastic observations on heterosexuality are wholly in tune with a cynical vision of civilisation seen from the point of view of its waste products.

Each of these interleaved sequences of seven chapters prepares for and culminates in a catastrophe. In chapter 13, the last of the Alexandre sequence, he sets forth to meet the colourful death to which he aspires: as a hunter, sword in hand, defying the odds in the dockland back-streets of Casablanca. In chapter 14, the last of the 'twins' sequence, the bond between the two brothers snaps when Paul dupes Jean's fiancée Sophie into sleeping with him, an action which provokes first Sophie, then Jean himself, to depart, never to return.

That explosion of the twin-cell and the irreversible dispersal of those involved was prepared for also by the account of an earlier disaster in chapter 12: the arrest and deportation of Maria-Barbara in 1943 for Resistance activity and the consequent wretched decline of her grief-stricken husband Edouard (the twins' father).

After these three points of dramatic crisis, there follows a third and final sequence of seven chapters (15–21) which recount Paul's journeys round the globe in the footsteps of his brother Jean. This sequence in a sense represents a synthesis of the earlier stories: the opposition which governed them, between twinship and the *sans-pareil*, has broken down. Paul, the 'bereaved' twin, now takes on the wandering vocation of his uncle Alexandre, eternally in pursuit of the partner. In the new pattern which emerges, Paul becomes the point of convergence of the 'lost' twin and of the uncle he never knew, the field of force in which the different visions of the twin and the non-twin can find their balance. Within this sequence Paul's journeys follow a definite pattern. He first visits Venice, a city characterised by its reflecting and deflecting mirrors, 'un miroir *dérapant*, distrayant, un miroir centrifuge' (p. 431), which incites to departure and travel. Thereafter he journeys south to Africa, north to Iceland, then round the world to Japan (east) and Canada (west). Finally, in the seventh chapter of the sequence (21), he comes to Berlin at the very moment when the wall is being built. As the architecture of the text by now requires, disaster strikes once more: Paul is crushed in a collapsing escape tunnel under the wall, and half his body is paralysed.

In *Les Météores* Tournier has explored and skilfully interwoven two areas of investigation: that of twinship and the (homosexual) couple on the one hand, and on the other the nature of space and time: topology, chronology and meteorology. What links these apparently disparate concerns is a preoccupation with the notion of openness and closure, which we have already noticed in *Le Roi des Aulnes* and its multiple systems of knowledge. The twin-cell represents a closed space, not only shut off from intercourse with others but aspiring to eternity. As Jean perceives, 'la cellule gémellaire [. . .] c'est la négation du temps, de l'histoire' (p. 274): Paul, like Abel Tiffauges, sees himself (and his brother) as born to the privilege of timeless-ness, of a-history, and like Abel he will go to Germany to pay a heavy price for his baptism into the terrible conflicts of contemporary history. When the twin-cell breaks up and the distance between the brothers is extended, Paul is obliged to take account of this open space. If Jean can be a world away, then Paul as the self-appointed guardian of the ethos of twinship must be able to stretch that space to include the world and make sense of it. His 'reading' of geography and culture as he travels is often in terms of his obsession with twinship. In his eyes Venice is, like him, bereaved by the loss of its Eastern twin Constantinople. Deflected by the mirror of Venice, which reflects too painfully his own grief, Paul visits the four compass points. These too can be read as pairs of twins. In Africa he finds a garden fed by an oasis spring, lovingly created in the wilderness by Deborah, and now devastated by the elements: a vulnerable closed space broken open and laid waste. In Iceland he finds another wilderness and other gardens in glass houses, drawing sustenance from underground geysers. 'Ces deux jardins manifestent la victoire précaire et fleurie des profondeurs sur la face de la terre' (p. 511). Japan and Canada (east and west) form another couple, this time marked more by opposition than by similarity. The Japanese, short of space, excel in the miniature, in the exquisite encapsulation of eternity on a tiny scale. Canada, by comparison, represents macro-space, scarcely tamed by the surveyors and the railway. The Berlin to which Paul returns is the most vivid image of the agony of twinship. If Venice is, in its self-conscious finery, akin to the spirit of Alexandre, inciting to restless departure, then Berlin, as its wall is built, is the image of Jean-Paul, of an organism suffering grievous schism into twin cells henceforth divided: a city and a country slashed in half.

The Berlin chapter (21) begins with the description of Heinz, a man blown up in the war, half his body torn away. The right-hand side which remains seems unnaturally flourishing, as though it has drawn on all the vitality of its shattered other half. On one level, this is a caricatural image of the two Germanies, but its importance extends further. Paul reflects that, to preserve the notion of twinship, he must draw into himself the substance of the lost Jean. Paul's final injuries reproduce those of Heinz, as though the loss of his twin must be symbolically inscribed on his body before it can be accepted. The final chapter (22: 'L'Âme déployée'), which can be seen as an epilogue to the three sequences of seven, shows a new, spiritual consciousness being born in Paul after his ordeal. In the metaphysical, poetic logic of the narrative, the 'space' of the twin-cell has now become infinitely, cosmically extended. Paul has travelled north, south, east and west; he has descended to be crushed in the underground tunnel in Berlin, and now, to complete the sphere, his gaze travels upwards to the sky, amidst wind and cloud. The final, terrible closed space of the tunnel has given way to the infinity of space, the closed timelessness of the twin-cell has been replaced by an openness to seasons and to weather (les météores).

The reader is given, too, the opportunity for a religious reading of Paul's destiny. Alexandre's old friend, Thomas Koussek, who becomes a priest, tells Alexandre at some length in chapter 5 of his beliefs as they had developed. He has become convinced that Christ was a twin to Koussek's namesake Thomas Didymus (alias Doubting Thomas). Koussek had a carnal fixation on the body of Christ, which led him to a spiritual crisis. This he transcended at last through the realisation that the death of Christ was only a preparation for the coming of the Holy Spirit. The true spiritual gift was the coming of the 'ruah', the 'vent paraclet'. (*Le Vent Paraclet* is the title Tournier later used for his autobiography and had at one point considered for this novel.) After the Old Testament and the Gospels, the third testament, says Koussek, is the Acts of the Apostles, inspired by the Holy Spirit. The greatest of these apostles, we may recall, was named Paul: and it is the third sequence of chapters here which takes him to the far corners of the known world, like the apostles in their journeys. 'L'Esprit-Saint est vent, tempête, souffle, il a un corps météorologique, les météores sont sacrés' (p. 158). We are invited to accept that Paul, rooted bodily to the earth by his infirmity but soaring aloft in spirit, is an image of euphoric salvation. 'Car je suis désormais un drapeau claquant dans le vent, et si son bord droit est prisonnier du bois de la hampe, son bord gauche est libre et vibre [. . .] dans la véhémence des météores' (p. 624). His bodily right half (Paul) is present: his mutilated, absent half (Jean) is the aperture leading into infinite space: like the flag, half fixed, half free, Paul would seem to have realised the perfect synthesis of openness and closure.

The title of *Gaspard, Melchior et Balthazar* (1980) is to some extent misleading. Tournier quotes as an appendix to his text the verses from St Matthew's gospel (2:1–16) which contain all the Bible tells us of the Magi, but he is not content merely to illustrate the traditional story of the three kings. For one thing he invents a fourth, Prince Taor, who arrives too late for the nativity. For another Tournier's text accommodates the stories of two further kings: one a real historical figure (Herod) and one a figment of the storyteller's art (Barbedor). The story of three kings becomes that of six, to whom must be added a seventh: Christ, king of kings, whose birth and sacrifice furnish the two culminating points of the narrative.

The notion of quest is, naturally, central: each of the kings is in search of something different. The black king, Gaspard, is afflicted with unrequited love for a fickle, fair-skinned slave, Biltine: when his astrologer shows him the portentous comet, it is for him a head with blonde hair streaming behind. Balthazar is an art-lover and collector of beautiful antique objects. His immediate cause of suffering is the destruction of his treasured museum by fanatical religious iconoclasts hostile to any effigies of the human form; to him the star is a butterfly-angel, bearing his own portrait as its emblem. Prince Melchior's journey is involuntary. Heir to a kingdom, he is, on the death of his father, displaced by his uncle in a ruthless and internecine palace revolution and reduced to flight and paupery. The salvation each king seeks is in the image of what he has suffered: for Gaspard it is a new, fulfilling love, for Balthazar a new art which can link the human and the transcendental, while for Melchior it is a politics cleansed of hatred and violence. The spectacle of the nativity gives to each according to his needs. Gaspard's vision is of a love which would be wholly selfless, content to rejoice simply in the happiness and well-being of the loved one: Christian love. Balthazar's experience is of a moment of ordinary human life illuminated in its ordinariness by an eternal significance; this intersection of real and supernatural truths is for him the basis of a revolution in art, Christianised and humanised.

Melchior, the victim of dynastic conflict, listens with the others to two contrasted stories which bear on the topic: Herod, at his banquet, regales them with the horrific story of how political necessity, as he sees it, has led him to murder his nearest and dearest. Herod's storyteller, responding to his sovereign's anxieties over the succession, then tells the tale of King Barbedor, who in a magic metamorphosis becomes himself the young heir who will succeed to the throne. Melchior's problem is to find a coincidence between the harmonious, supernatural solution vouchsafed to Barbedor and the violent discord wrought in real life by his own uncle and by Herod, for what may be seen as the most compelling of political reasons. Melchior is inspired to plan an ideal community, a City of God, 'une communauté d'hommes libres dont la seule loi commune sera la loi d'amour . . .' (p. 218).

The quest of the supernumerary Prince Taor is of another order. Not for him the ideals of love, art or politics. A born gourmet, he sets out to find the recipe for a sweetmeat which has captivated him – Turkish delight. In Tournier's narratives the incongruous or trivial is often the doorway through which the reader is led towards the most surprising and profound conclusions. Like Paul in *Les Météores* on his journey round the world, Taor is always too late to find him whom he seeks: yet, as for Paul, the discrepancy in time is part of a destiny that marks him out for a special martyrdom and a special grace. The Holy Family has left on its flight into Egypt. The sweetmeats he cannot now lay at the feet of the sought-for 'Divin Confiseur' he offers instead as a sumptuous feast for the children of Bethlehem. This feast coincides with the massacre of the Innocents, taking place not far away. Taor, horrified, nevertheless has an intuition of a significant relationship between the two events, massacre and feast. Like his three predecessors, he is experiencing treachery and violence and seeks a way of relating this to a compensating spirit of human generosity. For Taor, that spirit is expressed by the act of taking food together with others in innocent companionship. Abel Tiffauges, too, we recall, saw himself in a benign aspect as *pater nutritor* to his charges, and just as Abel finally gives his body to the service of a child victim, Taor agrees to take the place of a debtor condemned to slavery in the salt mines so that the man can be restored to his weeping wife and four children. The motif of sacrifice, invariably related to absorption into the earth, is common to Tiffauges sinking into the marsh, to Paul crushed in the tunnel, and to Taor, the lover of sugar, buried deep in the hell of a salt mine for thirty-three years (a period which corresponds to the span of Christ's life on earth).

The principal structure of this text is one which is frequently apparent in Tournier: that of the synthesis of opposites. Each of the earlier kings sought, in art, politics or love, a coincidence of real and ideal, an antidote to division and conflict. Taor seeks the food of paradise, which, as the Rabbi Rizza tells him, satisfied both carnal and spiritual hunger, making the physiological divine and the divine incarnate. He hears of Jesus as a prophet who feeds the multitude on a hillside with loaves and fishes and changes water into wine at a wedding; on his release he hastens to seek him. Once more he arrives too late, but partakes of the bread and the wine left on the table after the Last Supper. The last (of the kings) shall be first (to partake of the Eucharist).

Another less explicit but equally characteristic process of synthesis can also be discerned. In the stories of the three kings named in the title, heterosexual and homosexual elements are relatively balanced. On the heterosexual side, Gaspard is in love with Biltine, while Balthazar, the art lover, is infatuated with the picture of his wife Malvina, which their daughter Miranda comes to resemble. On the homosexual side, Balthazar created a group of cultivated and handsome young men, 'les Narcisses', whose *mores* are those of the Greek culture he so much admires and to whom the young Melchior in his turn is strongly attracted. Taor, the gastronome and lover of sweets, is like a child whose chief satisfaction is oral, and it is logical that he should feast with children and be affected by the affliction of the debtor's offspring. He experiences the alternatives of homosexuality and heterosexuality in their more grotesque and exaggerated forms. He takes on his journey his favourite elephant, a white female called Yasmina. Yasmina's coquettish gestures towards him are described in caricaturally humanised terms, especially at the moment of farewell (p. 209) when she has been adopted as a resident deity by a tribe who took the royal party prisoner. In the salt mines of Sodom, the sarcasm and acerbic intelligence of the homosexual community, devoid of any warmth or human concern, is again caricaturally presented. By implication Taor is aspiring to an ideal synthesis of the languor and sentiment of Yasmina and the sharpness of perception and intellect of the Sodomites, perhaps a re-creation of childhood generosity and vivacity beyond restrictive adult codes.

The reader is also left to construct a relationship between the apotheosis of the fourth king and those of the other three. It is the notion of sacrifice, symbolised in the Last Supper, we may conclude, which makes the realisation of the other ideals, of love, community and art, possible. The final conventional images of apotheosis, which seemed self-consciously ironic when used to describe Tiffauges's feelings of phoric exaltation, are more of a piece with a narrative whose tone is generally that of fable rather than realist narrative. That these elements are so explicitly Christian may come as a surprise after the more pantheistic euphoria evoked in the final pages of *Vendredi* and *Les Météores*: perhaps these two notions themselves, pantheism and Christianity, should be seen as the terms of a proposed synthesis which Tournier's whole *œuvre* is striving to enact.

Gilles et Jeanne (1983) is described on its title page as a *récit*, not a *roman*. Tournier, like Gide, obviously makes a clear distinction between *récit* and *roman*. Gide saw the *récit* as essentially an economical, unified narrative of modest proportions with a single, consistent focus, whereas the novel is essentially complex, multiple, with a number of sub-plots or dispersed centres of interest. As a *récit*, *Gilles et Jeanne* offers a concise and more or less chronological account of the lives of the eponymous characters, Joan of Arc and Gilles de Rais: the question it poses concerns the relationship between these two lives. It is a question we have seen posed before, in the more complex narratives of *Les Météores* and *Gaspard, Melchior et Balthazar*, where the reader is invited to reflect on the structural link between the different lives presented. In this text the element of contrast seems dominant: Jeanne's career is one of inspirational success, born of piety and indomitable bravery, which then plunges after her capture to the ignominy and horror of death at the stake. Gilles's life is given its decisive direction by his contact with Jeanne: he worships her in life and is devastated by her death. Thereafter the path he follows leads to madness, sadism and mass murder, before his final confession, condemnation and burning. The same inglorious death by fire ends both lives, but for Jeanne it is at the end of a life that has soared on high before being brought low, whereas Gilles has plumbed the lowest depths of evil before emerging to regain the common ground of moral responsibility through recognising his guilt and claiming death as a necessary atonement.

Gilles's itinerary is thus presented as an 'inversion maligne', a diabolical reflection of Jeanne's passage to eventual martyrdom. This basic contrast is however subverted by ambivalence. Gilles perceives Jeanne as a double being, 'Jeanne bifrons', to whom he chants a double litany: 'Jeanne la sainte, Jeanne la chaste, Jeanne la victorieuse sous l'étendard de saint Michel! Jeanne, le monstre en forme de femme, condamnée au feu pour sorcellerie, hérésie, schismatisme, changement de sexe, blasphème et apostasie [. . .]' (p. 48). This moral paradox in the image of Jeanne is amplified in other references to Lucifer, the most beautiful and beloved of all God's angels, and to the voices both she and Gilles hear (angels or demons?). It is particularly apparent in the consistent evocation of the ambiguous element of fire: the fire with which Gilles burns his victims' bodies, the consuming punitive fire of the stake and the inner fire which he perceives in Jeanne: 'Il y a un feu en toi. Je le crois de Dieu, mais il est peut-être d'enfer' (p. 31). This ambivalence of the moral sign is constantly stressed. If good and evil always co-exist, then for Gilles even Jeanne's sainthood must conjure up its opposite, her condemnation as a devil-worshipper. In the conviction that every moral sign is only given full value by the presence of its opposite, Gilles will pay the greatest homage he can to his beloved Jeanne by making his own life the inversion, and thus the completion and valorisation, of her own. Therein lies his justification, and he boldly wagers that this supreme dialectic will ensure that his evil will attract in the end a compensating elevation to holiness.

After the trauma of the death of Jeanne, the second turning point in Gilles's career is the arrival on the scene of one Francesco Prelati. Prelati is an advocate of the new Renaissance culture who has been brought to Brittany from Florence by Gilles's confessor Blanchet. Blanchet sought someone to save Gilles, but Prelati will instead encourage him in the ways of alchemy, devil-worship and child-murder. In Florence, Blanchet had noticed that alongside the brilliance of the Medici court were to be seen more corpses, cemeteries and gallows than he had ever before witnessed. Prelati explains that one must accept death as the necessary counterpart of life, its 'moitié d'ombre', and the modern art he admires depends not just on the antique perception of external human beauty but also on the inner secrets of the human body laid bare by the dissector's knife: 'amour plus anatomie'. The voice that speaks of the interdependence of opposites is Tournier's own, and it speaks through the whole text. It is when the new humanism of Italy in the person of Prelati encounters the bestiality (as he sees it) of the north that Gilles's final evolution is set in motion. Prelati initiates Gilles into alchemy. Alchemy, the fusion of opposite elements through fire into gold (the gold which Prelati praises as the substance of goodness itself), is symbolic too of the human chemistry involved. Prelati is the catalyst of Gilles's transmutation.

The setting of the scandalous alongside the revered is wholly characteristic of Tournier. Not content with the *image d'Epinal* of St Joan, any more than he was with that of the Magi, he sets alongside the figure of Jeanne, as its necessary corollary, the story of a pathological child-murderer. The two must be read in conjunction, and it is the conjunction which is of interest to him, for it defines a space in which absolute concepts of purity and perversion cannot be entertained, a human space in which each is implicated in the other.

This ambivalence pervades the intertextual elements of the writing also. There are many references to the life of Christ, and notably (again) to the nativity. The first intimation of Jeanne's entry into the narrative is the sentence: 'C'est alors qu'on annonce une étrange visite' (p. 10). Jeanne claims to be 'envoyée de Dieu' (p. 13): Gilles sees in her 'une sainte nimbée de lumière' (p. 14), in fact 'un ange' (p. 15). Like Gabriel, she has come to proclaim a king. In the shadow play of the gospel story which is a kind of back-projection to the drama, Jeanne's role is not just that of annunciatory angel. The stress on her virginity links her to Mary, and that reference is strengthened further by the implicit evocation of Claudel's play *L'Annonce faite à Marie*. Gilles's family name is de Craon; in Claudel's play Pierre de Craon is the leper who worships the saintly Violaine and who, when she kisses him and contracts the disease, becomes the instrument of her martyrdom and beneficiary of her grace. Claudel's play also contains a symbolic re-enactment of the nativity and references to Joan of Arc, and it is Tournier's awareness of this other, fervent, twentieth-century text which lends a Claudelian overtone to such lines as 'mais je t'aime surtout pour cette pureté qui est en toi et que rien ne peut ternir' (p. 32).

Jeanne's role reflects at one moment Gabriel's, at another Mary's, and at others that of Christ. Gilles kisses her wound and declares 'J'ai communié de ton sang' (p. 33); his futile attempt to release her by force of arms may suggest the disciple Peter's unsheathing of the sword (John 18:10) just as his distress and flight after her death echo the disarray of the disciples after the crucifixion. Like Peter, he will choose to share the same fate as the one he reveres: he will be burned between his two fellow malefactors, a reflection – or parody – of Calvary. Gilles's re-enactment of biblical roles is also shifting: if he is a disciple like Peter, he is also, more directly, a new Herod, perpetrating his own massacre of the Innocents (the subject of a fresco he has painted in his castle). As in Taor's story, the massacre is seen as the dark shadow of the nativity: the intolerable paradox of nativity and massacre is re-expressed in the tension between Gilles and Jeanne and their destinies.

Gilles et Jeanne was dismissed on publication by some critics as an impoverished re-presentation of themes that Tournier had already richly developed. It is true that, arguably, no single thematic ingredient is new, but the text brings some of them into new perspective. The theme of sainthood and the diabolical, not directly treated since *Le Roi des Aulnes* with its twin archetypes of St Christopher and the Erl-King, is here viewed through the more limpid narrative texture characteristic of *Gaspard, Melchior et Balthazar*, and any lack of startling innovation in the foreground may be compensated by the subtle play of intertextuality which gives this text its shifting resonances and an intriguing dimension of ambivalence in the reading.

One of the questions left unanswered at the end of *Vendredi* relates to Vendredi's likely fate after he leaves the island on board the *Whitebird*. The prospects for a black man ill-prepared for a world where slavery is still prevalent are not promising. There was clearly an opening for a sequel here, about the hazards and revelations which await the naïve non-European trying to make sense of European urban life and to find a role which gives him value within this hostile environment. *La Goutte d'or* (1986) is, in a sense, this sequel: it tells the tale of Idriss who comes from a desert village to Paris and, after many vicissitudes, achieves a *modus vivendi*. It is a twin, or mirror-image, narrative to *Vendredi*; Idriss is a counter-Robinson, moving from the Third World to the First, and likewise undergoing a crash-course in cultural re-education.

Exile is a powerful stimulus to the awareness of cultural relativity. What Balthazar called 'le privilège de l'éloignement' (*Gaspard, Melchior et Balthazar*, p. 69) gives Idriss, like Tournier's other hero-travellers, a sharp and often painful insight not only into the culture he is entering but into that of the Saharan village he has left. He has not gone far – just to Béni Abbès – before he is caught up in a party visiting a museum of Saharan life and is disconcerted to see an exhibition of the familiar objects and customs he has grown up with at Tabelbala. For the first time he sees his own culture from the outside, through the curious scrutiny of the visitors and the conde-scending commentary of the guide. When he reaches France he will be astonished by the advertising images of the Sahara and desert life.

The theme of the attractive and yet deceptive image is a dominant one, and it provides the incitement to his departure from Tabelbala. A French woman gets out of a Land Rover and takes his photo-graph, explaining that she will send him a copy from Paris when it is developed. Idriss is left with the memory of a provocatively dressed blonde and a superstitious sense of excitement at the idea of his picture returning to France. His attitude is shaped by a community which regards photographs with awe and distrust as thefts of the self, talismans which, left to themselves, can have perilous conse-quences for the person depicted. The image abducted by the blonde photographer is thus literally attractive, in that it draws Idriss to France, just as the holiday posters of the Sahara Idriss sees in Marseilles seek to lure tourists in the opposite direction.

Idriss's pretext for leaving – to find his picture again – is, like Taor's quest for Turkish delight, seemingly absurd, but it is the thread that will lead to a much more far-reaching evolution. A number of episodes illustrate the sinister, corrosive power of the image. When Salah Brahim, the delivery man, teases him by pre-tending that his picture has arrived by post and then produces one of a donkey, Idriss's self-esteem takes a severe blow. Subsequent attacks by the power of the image on his sense of individual identity are more insidious. His passport photograph is of someone else, yet it is accepted. A wealthy woman deranged by the loss of her family tries to recruit him as a substitute for her son Ismail, whose photo-graph adorns his tomb. The image is here in danger of conferring a false identity, not confirming a real one. As the jeweller he meets on the ferry observes, 'L'image est douée d'une force mauvaise. Elle n'est pas la servante dévouée et fidèle que tu voudrais. [. . .] Elle aspire de toute sa mauvaiseté à te réduire en esclavage' (p. 100).

Tournier gives us two amusing portraits of professional image-makers: Mustapha, 'artiste photographe', who with his plausible patter persuades visiting tourists to strike heroic attitudes in front of a painted back-drop in his studio, and his Parisian opposite number, Achille Mage, who directs television commercials. Each trades in the cheap currency of exotic fantasy, but Tournier's portraits are affectionate as well as satirical: their 'art' is perhaps not wholly unrelated to that of the novelist, who also seeks, with whatever materials come to hand, to give substance to the myths that inhabit our culture. One feature of the photograph or the television picture, however, is that, in privileging the visual, it amputates other senses: Idriss experiences Paris as a nightmare world of shop windows and peep-shows, all visual promise and no substance, exploitative and alienating.

The theme of the image is linked to Tournier's even more familiar preoccupation with the twin. This link was established in *Les Météores*: when Jean looked in the mirror, what he saw was not himself but his twin, Paul. The obedient reflection becomes a double with a life of its own. As we saw, Paul is dependent on the unity of self and double as a source of reassurance, whereas Jean perceives the double as a threat to the freedom and independence of his self. The photograph, compared to the twin, seems innocuously insubstantial, merely visual, yet it exhibits a similar power to reinforce or to erode the sense of self. Between the flat photograph and the living replica of the twin there is an intermediary range of images, lifeless yet three-dimensional: sculptures and mannequins. In a supermarket Idriss meets Etienne Milan negotiating the purchase of some obsolete mannequins. It transpires that Milan has a whole collection of mannequin figures of boys, images of himself at the same age, which he can dismantle, re-assemble and re-arrange. His habit of photographing his mannequins alongside real children in a natural outdoor setting manifests the creative yet disturbing dialectic of image and reality, 'une contamination réciproque' (p. 181) whereby the setting makes the dolls look real, but the dolls may also make the landscape look artificial. 'C'est absolument la réalité sapée à sa base par l'image' (p. 181). Idriss himself experiences this annexation of reality by the image when he is persuaded to have a cast made of his body so that polyester mannequins can be manufactured in his likeness. As the casting is removed it pulls off his eyelashes and eyebrows. When the shop manager proposes that he should be made up to resemble the mannequins and placed alongside them in the window, making mechanical movements, eyes permanently open, it is apparent that the images are after more than his eyelashes and eyebrows: they threaten his very humanity. 'Thou shalt have no graven image . . .' – we are back, by a different route, to the disagreement between Balthazar and the iconoclasts.

As in *Gaspard, Melchior et Balthazar*, the inclusion of two self-contained fables, like that of Barbedor, point up the theme of the ambivalent power of the image. In one, King Barberousse finds that the royal portrait made of him frees him from an inherited sense of shame at his red hair. In the contrasting story, 'La reine blonde', the portrait of a beautiful queen exerts a fascination so powerful as to destroy those who look on it. Its power is only disarmed when a young man trained in calligraphy disentangles the lines of the portrait and identifies the inscription of the epigrams which compose it. This story is central to the teaching of the master calligrapher Abd Al Ghafari who undertakes to teach Idriss his art. The antidote, for Idriss, to the tyranny of the western image is the reproduction of Arabic script, at once beautiful and wise, through an act which involves both a physiological and an intellectual discipline: the semiology, the narrative tells us, of the eternal space of the desert.

Tournier contrasts the treachery of the image with the plenitude of the sign in calligraphy, and 'le signe pur, la forme absolue' (p. 31) is represented by the 'goutte d'or' itself, a jewel worn by the belly dancer Zett Zobaïda. Idriss finds this jewel lying on the ground after her dance, and it becomes a talisman of his childhood and his freedom. In Marseilles he leaves behind all three – childhood, freedom and jewel – and the 'goutte d'or' is not seen again until the final pages, when it appears in a window of an exclusive jeweller in the Place Vendôme. After his period of enslavement to the image in his role as passive mannequin or impotent voyeur, he now reasserts his strength and freedom. He is wielding a pneumatic drill to penetrate beneath the surface of the earth, and this image of virile potency is reinforced when the jeweller's window cracks, and the jewel is accessible once more. Beneath the road, behind the window, the third dimension is restored, and the spell of the image is broken.

Every Tournier novel is at heart a *Bildungsroman*. The stories of Robinson, Tiffauges and Idriss fill and unify the novels which concern them; in the other texts, Paul, Gilles and Taor emerge in the later stages of the narrative to command our whole attention. In every case except that of Gilles, the hero (the central character is always male) undergoes a significant *dépaysement*, undertaking a journey which leads him away from his homeland to unforeseen adventures abroad in pursuit of what he perceives obscurely as destiny or salvation. A traditional feature of such quest narratives is that the hero encounters one or more mentors, who counsel him on the path he should follow. In Tournier's *œuvre* one can identify a number of subsidiary characters – the heterodox priest Thomas Koussek, the Renaissance man Francesco Prelati, the calligrapher Abd Al Ghafari – who fulfil that role. So too do Vendredi and Nestor, but the function of these two is more than just that of mentor. Nestor can be seen as Abel's 'putative' father, and for Robinson, Vendredi is 'toute l'humanité rassemblée en un seul individu, mon fils et mon père, mon frère et mon voisin . . .' (p. 224). The death of Nestor and the unannounced departure of Vendredi are crucial turning-points, after which the hero must continue his path alone and assume responsibility for his own destiny. The experience of loss and bereavement is also a pivotal one in each of the other texts. Paul is abandoned by Jean, and in addition is never given the chance to know his uncle Alexandre. Gilles is traumatised by the burning of Jeanne, and Idriss sees his friend Ibrahim buried and crushed in a collapsing well in the opening chapters of *La Goutte d'or*. For Taor the bereavement is more indirect, but no less powerful in its influence: it is caused by the massacre of the Innocents, which itself prefigures the Crucifixion, which will follow after the end of the story. This exemplary experience of pain and grief suffered by all the characters represents the ordeal which is by convention a necessary feature of the quest if the hero is to earn salvation.

In each case Tournier's hero absorbs into his own life the values bequeathed by the lost partner. Robinson strives to emulate the example of Vendredi. Abel perceives his fate as being directed by the voice of Nestor. Idriss becomes nomadic like Ibrahim, and Paul too becomes an errant globetrotter, footloose like his uncle Alexandre and, literally, following the footsteps of his twin brother to share vicariously the sequence of his experiences. Gilles aspires by another path to the sainthood of Jeanne, and dies with her name on his lips. Taor imitates Christ in that he too, in his way, redeems the massacre of the Innocents by the gift of his own life and body.

At the last, each hero is granted his apotheosis, either in the ecstatic affirmation of life (Robinson, Paul, Idriss) or in sacrifice and martyrdom (Abel, Gilles, Taor). This apotheosis is characterised by a conjunction of the finite and the infinite, the physical and the metaphysical. Robinson and Jaan standing on the pinnacle are poised between the earth beneath their feet and the sun-god as it rises in the heavens: Abel and Paul, likewise earthbound, gaze upwards to the stars or to the air and the winds. After *Les Météores* this moment of 'sublimation' (the last word in that novel) is represented less literally, but the notion of spanning the earthly and the heavenly is still present. Gilles's end presents the paradoxical juxtaposition of sin and salvation, of the evil criminal over whose death rings out an 'appel céleste' (p. 152). The Eucharist vouchsafed to Taor represents another such paradoxical moment, at which the base substances of unleavened bread and red wine can suddenly acquire transcendental significance, and the human act of eating can summon angels. This double presence of the transcendent and the real is separated out at the end of *La Goutte d'or*, where for Idriss two moments of apotheosis complement each other: he discovers the metaphysical art of calligraphy and its dialogue with God, and he is thereby strengthened to confront the alien affluence of the Place Vendôme with a new, exuberant confidence, armed with his pneumatic drill.

The model that emerges, therefore, when one superimposes Tournier's texts one onto another, is an epic one. His heroes, seemingly marked out for a special destiny, undergo an ordeal of loss and grief, are educated by those around them and finally achieve a culminating realisation of their destiny which confers on them by implication some superior wisdom. Tournier is interested in the *transformation* of the hero, and as the epic model and supernatural references suggest, he is not content with an empirical, psychological explanation of the hero's development. He offers his reader a bewildering variety of metaphysical keys – religious, mythological, cultural – with which to unlock the secrets of his hero's destiny. The story of Robinson is, as we have seen, prefaced by its adumbration through the tarot cards. There is an element of textual game-playing here certainly, but more central is the suggestion that Robinson's future development is foreseeable: it is not narrowly predetermined, but it is subject to a kind of organic inevitability. Tournier is fond of the image of natural metamorphosis. Robinson senses 'la métamorphose qui travaillait le plus secret de lui-même. [. . .] La larve avait pressenti dans une brève extase qu'elle volerait un jour' (p. 94). Gilles's more sinister evolution after Jeanne's death is predicted through the same image: 'Il va devenir chenille dans son cocon. Puis la métamorphose maligne accomplie, il en sortira, et c'est un ange infernal qui déploiera ses ailes' (p. 45).

In the imaginary obituary notice for himself published in *Petites proses* (1986) (p. 245), Tournier describes himself as a 'naturaliste mystique', that is, a writer obsessed by the co-presence of the physical and the metaphysical. 'Amour plus anatomie' is Prelati's description of Renaissance art, and it will serve for Tournier's description of art also. The blending of the language of science and passion is as apparent in the writing of Tournier as in that of Proust or Valéry. Robinson contemplates Vendredi's body with a sense both of scientific curiosity and of passionate wonder (pp. 216, 222), and it is this combination of an acute perception of physique and profound sensual gratification that marks the passages when Alexandre and Abel gaze at the bodies of their young recruits. Tournier's writing moves with versatility between the play of interpretative codes and the expression of the fundamental human appetites, producing at its best a heady synthesis of the two.

The fact that the desire which energises Tournier's text is often that of the male for another male body is only one of the more obvious ways in which he subverts the dominant cultural norms. His texts are inspired by the view from the margin, through the eyes of the exile, the immigrant, the criminal, of characters driven by a non-standard sexuality or a personal obsession which often invites the name of 'perversion'. For most readers, then, the Tournier text will impose a displacement of their vision, as they are invited to view a familiar set of European social and heterosexual norms from an off-centre position. The Tournier text is seductive, leading far from the straight and narrow, inviting unthinkable empathies with paedophiles and sadists as well as with more innocent eccentrics. Of Nestor, sitting in the corner of his classroom, Abel Tiffauges writes: 'Sa masse formidable semblait faire basculer toute la pièce du côté de ce coin, au fond, à gauche, où elle se tassait. Pour moi c'était bien là en effet le foyer central de toute la classe, bien plus en tout cas que l'estrade où se succédaient de dérisoires et éphémères orateurs' (p. 53). This formidable, seductive magnetism which operates a displacement of the centre is an image of the functioning of the Tournier text. His heroes travel from a home base into exile – from York to the Pacific, from the Sahara to Paris and so on – and that distance enables them to see more clearly the culture that has shaped their being. Likewise, the magnetism of the Tournier text displaces the reader and thereby places familiar cultural patterns at a quizzical, critical distance. Words are redefined, often in terms of a surprising etymology, to rediscover a disruptive truth beneath the accepted gloss. The thoroughgoing monomania of an Abel Tiffauges or an Alexandre Surin can engender a whole new reading of our culture, in which the sharp freshness of the perception may give pause even to those with no sympathy for the character's obsessions. It is Alexandre, in *Les Météores*, who places writers among the ranks of 'les délinquants par l'esprit [. . .], lesquels dérangent l'ordre établi dans l'exacte mesure où ils sont créateurs' (p. 118).

Several of Tournier's heroes are themselves writers. Robinson keeps a 'log-book', Abel writes his *écrits sinistres*, and in both cases the writing is ultimately 'délinquant' in its effect, assisting and focusing the disruption of the established order. This private discourse is a means by which they can become themselves the 'foyer central' of their lives, instead of remaining passively obedient to the 'dérisoires et éphémères orateurs' on the podium, to the threadbare rhetoric of an authoritarian culture. Idriss, Tournier's latest hero to date, finds redemption precisely in writing, both in the sublime Arabic calligraphy which gives value to his own culture and (in a grotesque counterpart) in the figures of desire and liberation inscribed by his pneumatic drill on the blank surfaces of Paris.

By writing, Tournier's heroes, especially in the first three novels, can enter into a dialogue with the 'readings' of reality which they have inherited or which are proposed to them; writing allows them to develop their own 'reading' of experience on which they can found their life. Tournier constantly stresses how a sign is read differently by different individuals. The Japanese Zen garden described in *Les Météores* (p. 526) signifies one thing to the samurai, another to the philosopher and something different again to the betrayed lover. A few pages later Urs Kraus's portraits are shown as subject to the same variety of subjective interpretations: 'c'est au spectateur qu'il incombe de développer telle ou telle âme ayant affinité avec la sienne' (p. 535). When Gilles, Prelati and Blanchet gaze at the stormy sea, 'chacun entendait à sa façon ce que disait la clameur océane' (p. 92). Each of the Magi interprets the comet in the light of his own preoccupations. Masterly works of art (Zen garden or portrait painting) share with the signs of nature (comet or sea-storm) the sense of containing a multiplicity of potential truths, of which the 'reader' at the moment of perception can choose the most appropriate. This is how Tournier himself treats the major primal scenes from the Bible – the creation of Adam and Eve, the nativity, the massacre of the Innocents – to which he returns more than once, offering 'readings' appropriate to his context and the character concerned. Tournier re-reads and wilfully misreads these stories to extract from them a new, undiscovered sense. In *Les Météores* Alexandre writes of Thomas Koussek that '[il] avait détourné de leur sens la plupart des prières et des cérémonies dont nous étions abreuvés – mais avaient-elles bien un sens en elles-mêmes, n'atten-daient-elles pas, libres et disponibles, la douce violence d'un être de génie pour les plier à son système?' (pp. 49–50).

Tournier's texts are re-readings and re-writings of our culture. They manifest an acute and constant awareness of intertextuality. Moreover this explicit, intertextual self-consciousness extends to the inter-relationship between them. Tournier is given to self-quotation and cross-reference. To illustrate this from just one novel, the twins in *Les Météores* meet Abel Tiffauges, hero of *Le Roi des Aulnes*. The text of *Les Météores* also contains a reference to Robinson Crusoe (p. 336), and a little later a footnote explicitly refers the reader to *Vendredi* (p. 421). There is mention too of 'la merveilleuse aventure des Rois Mages' (p. 322), which anticipates the subject of his next novel. These intertextual references within his own *œuvre*, reinforced by many other echoes at the level of vocabulary and ideas, function to blur the limits of any one text *vis-à-vis* its fellows and undermine its status as a distinct, self-contained unit. A cumulative reading of a number of Tournier's texts is seduced into being a comparative reading. The reader is encouraged to see a particular description or idea less as a particular moment in a particular text and more as part of a wider and freer dialogue between elements in different texts. Tournier's texts speak of the hero's escape from closure into openness. The *œuvre* itself enacts that shift: each work holds the gaze of the reader by its unique character, but also deflects it, like the mirrors of Venice, by its self-conscious intertextuality. The texts thus seek to achieve that porosity, that sense of openness and exchange, which Tournier articulates as a humane ideal. Abel Tiffauges sees his destiny not in its closed uniqueness but as a moment in a dynasty of fellow-beings which transcends history. Tournier's ambition as a writer is no less spectacular – it is that his texts too should, through their dialogue with each other and with many of the seminal texts of our culture, be read *sub specie aeternitatis*, that they should thereby escape from the historical confines of their creator's life to join a more fundamental family of texts. There is no modesty in Tournier's choice of family, of putative progenitors and would-be twins, for his own texts. Natural heir or imposter? Whichever he be, we can be in little doubt that Tournier the writer is claiming a right royal pedigree.

Bibliography

Works by Michel Tournier
(All works published by Gallimard)

Fiction

Vendredi ou les limbes du Pacifique (1967)
Le Roi des Aulnes (1970)
Vendredi ou la vie sauvage (1971)
Les Météores (1975)
Le Coq de bruyère (1978)
Gaspard, Melchior et Balthazar (1980)
Les Rois Mages (1983)
Gilles et Jeanne (1983)
La Goutte d'or (1986)

Non-fiction

Le Vent Paraclet (1977)
Des Clefs et des serrures: images et proses (1979)
Le Vol du vampire (1982)
Journal de voyage au Canada (1984) (with E. Boubat)
Le Vagabond immobile (1984) (with J.-M. Toubeau)
Petites proses (1986)

Selected Critical Studies

Bevan, D.G., *Michel Tournier* (Amsterdam, Rodopi, 1986)

Cloonan, William, *Michel Tournier* (Boston, Mass., Twayne, 1985)

Davis, Colin, *Michel Tournier: philosophy and fiction* (Oxford, Clarendon Press, 1988)

Jay, Salim, *Idriss, Michel Tournier et les autres* (Editions de la différence, 1986) (on *La Goutte d'or*)

Koster, Serge, *Tournier* (Veyrier, 1986)

Maclean, K.M., 'Human relations in the novels of Tournier: polarity and transcendance', *Forum for Modern Language Studies*, 23. 3 (1987), 241–52

Sbiroli, Lynn Salkin, *Michel Tournier: la séduction du jeu* (Geneva and Paris, Slatkine, 1987) (on *Vendredi ou les limbes du Pacifique*)

Shattuck, Roger, 'Why not the best?', *New York Review of Books*, vol. XXX, no. 7 (28 April 1983), 8–15

York, R.A., 'Thematic construction in *Le Roi des Aulnes*', *Orbis Litterarum*, 36. 1 (1981), 76–91

Special issues of periodicals devoted to Michel Tournier

Sud (hors série) (1980)
Sud no. 61 (1986)
Magazine littéraire no. 138 (June 1978)
                no. 226 (January 1986)

-4-

Philippe Sollers and *Tel Quel*

LESLIE HILL

From its foundation in 1960 until its dissolution in 1983 the quar-
terly literary review *Tel Quel* was indisputably one of the most
influential of Parisian intellectual and theoretical journals. During
the twenty-three years of its existence, though its editorial policy
underwent a number of significant and, at times, controversial
changes, as too, of course, did the composition of its editorial board,
Tel Quel remained a major focus of attention for contemporary
writing and literary theory. From the outset, *Tel Quel* was an
ambitious undertaking, and committed itself immediately to publishing new and experimental writing as well as promoting a critical
context within which literary innovation could be treated more
seriously. 'Les idéologues', declared *Tel Quel* in its opening editorial,
'ont suffisamment régné sur l'expression pour que celle-ci se per-
mette enfin de leur fausser compagnie, de ne plus s'occuper que
d'elle-même, de sa fatalité et de ses règles particulières.' What was
signalled by this assertion of autonomy and by the journal's defence
of what the editorial called the 'passion de la littérature' and 'la
qualité littéraire' was, as early issues made clear, the rejection of the
'littérature engagée' of Sartre's *Les Temps modernes*, which was still a
potent force on the Left Bank (but showed less and less interest in
literature itself), as well as the conservative values of the literary
establishment. What *Tel Quel* sought to embrace instead was the
alternative idiom of the avant-garde, and to this end published, in its
early issues, in addition to work by its own members, texts by
writers such as Ponge, Robbe-Grillet, Michaux, Antonin Artaud
and Georges Bataille.

Tel Quel was not a literary review in the narrow sense of the term.
Indeed, it published a broad mixture of material, including experimental fictional and poetic texts, essays dealing with philosophical,
cultural and political issues and discussions of the links between
avant-garde writing and structuralist literary theory, psychoanalysis
and, in the later 1960s and early 1970s, revolutionary Marxist

aesthetics. Together with the series of books published by the Editions du Seuil under the *Tel Quel* imprint, the magazine was instrumental in establishing the reputations of a whole range of prominent intellectual figures, including theorists such as Roland Barthes, Gérard Genette, Julia Kristeva and Jacques Derrida. It also served as an important platform for the new writing of several younger novelists and poets, such as, for instance, the novelist and essayist Philippe Sollers, who, as the editor of the Editions du Seuil's *Tel Quel* series and since 1983 also the editor of *Tel Quel*'s successor, the journal *L'Infini*, is the writer most closely identified with *Tel Quel* throughout the various phases of its existence.

Some measure of *Tel Quel*'s success in extending the audience for experimental writing and for radical post-structuralist literary theory can be gauged from the way in which the journal was largely responsible for bringing about a fundamental shift in the prevailing literary and theoretical climate in France. By the late 1960s and early 1970s, when the influence of the *Tel Quel* group was at its height, the word *Tel Quel* became Parisian shorthand for a potent blend of linguistic theory, psychoanalysis and Marxism together with a philosophical critique of Western metaphysics. Admittedly, in the later 1970s, *Tel Quel*'s theoretical and political position was to change, and the journal abandoned, for instance, its commitment to Marxism, as well as considerably redefining its conception of the literary avant-garde. The journal did not, as some have tended to claim, change its ideas out of a wilful attempt to stay ahead in the market-place of intellectual fashion but in response to deep-seated stresses appearing in French intellectual life and society and, by the same token, in the relationship of the avant-garde to its audience. The history of the *Tel Quel* group and of the fiction it produced provides a unique insight into the position and role of literature in France from the 1960s to the early 1980s.

One major, and enduring, emphasis of the literary and theoretical work with which *Tel Quel* soon became synonymous lay in the elaboration of a new and radical concept of writing, of *écriture*, as it became known in the work of Roland Barthes and Jacques Derrida. The word was originally introduced by Barthes in his 1953 book *Le Degré zéro de l'écriture* as a means of rejecting the traditional separation between form and content in the literary text and unifying them as integral parts of a single entity, which was writing. For Barthes, in the literary domain, form was content, and to write was to explore linguistic forms without subordinating that process of discovery to the conveying of ready-made meanings. In this way, the term 'écriture' was used to designate all literary or fictional writing which refused to respect philosophical values such as the clarity and distinctness of ideas or truthfulness to reality, preferring to explore the specific potential of literature itself. Previously in France, the literary mode had been scorned by philosophy for its imprecision, its fanciful pursuit of the fictitious and its dependence on rhetoric and language. Now it was precisely that maverick freedom and linguistic inventiveness of the literary which was seen by *Tel Quel* to call into question traditional norms and metaphysical assumptions about literature, the nature of the real, of human identity and society. The literary, from this perspective, held the key for a dramatically different, more radical understanding of the world.

In broader terms the word 'écriture' also referred to writing as such, as opposed to speech. In his book *De la grammatologie*, Derrida argued, in an influential formulation, that in the Western philosophical tradition, writing had been treated – with damaging effect – as a mere tool in the service of spoken language. Speech, the spoken word, the voice, Derrida argued, had always been seen in philosophy as the purest embodiment of language, as a repository of authentic presence, of unadulterated meaning, spiritual wholeness and transcendental value. Writing, on the other hand, was associated with the negative characteristics found in language. Writing, it was claimed by the metaphysical tradition, could be misunderstood, or might be forged, or could simply be an unreliable copy of another text and lacked the security of the express intent of the author as voiced by the author himself.

Now language, Saussure had established at the turn of the century in his *Cours de linguistique générale*, was not a list of names (as, for instance, the Bible had it, with Adam naming the beasts one by one) but functioned rather as a relational system of differences between signifying marks, spoken phonemes or written characters which no single individual could dominate or appropriate. As a result, Derrida argued, it was misleading to associate language with the authenticity and clarity of the voice. Language could never deliver stable and identifiable meanings since it was a complex fabric of relationships which could never be tied down permanently in any one way. Ambiguity, for instance, was inherent in language, and not an unfortunate accident of relative unimportance. The traditional view of writing, which rejected it as being an unreliable, inauthentic and entirely dubious imposter, stealing the place which rightly belonged to the voice, was not, according to Derrida, just misleadingly biased. It served to conceal, he continued, the extent to which speech itself was reliant on writing, on writing understood in the broadest possible terms. This meant writing as the relational interplay between elements of meaning, not only the writing of words but also drawing, inscribing, tracing, marking. Writing in Derrida's sense was not an inferior double of spoken words but the condition of the existence of language, the prerequisite of language.

It is not difficult to see the import of this revaluation of the philosophical concept of writing for literature itself. Indeed, following from these arguments, one of the aims of *Tel Quel* by the end of the 1960s was to reverse the received hierarchy of speech and writing and liberate writing from the repressive dominance of the model of spoken language (which placed a premium on the clarity of ideas and efficiency in communication). As a result *Tel Quel* welcomed the abstractness, the trickery, the anarchic unsubmissiveness of writing as fundamental traits to be affirmed rather than condemned. In common with other modernist avant-garde movements, *Tel Quel*'s main purpose was to free literature from notions such as representation, mimetic reproduction or imitation. Within the context of the *Tel Quel* group, writing came to be seen as praxis (in neo-Marxist terms), a 'pratique signifiante' (as Julia Kristeva formulated it) fundamentally transgressive of inherited metaphysical, social and literary norms and having the capacity to call into question notions of literary genre and concepts of transparent or univocal meaning, as well as other, more deep-seated structures of subjectivity or social behaviour. Avant-garde literature thus had the means, and the potential, to challenge the very basis of the social order itself.

Much of the energy of *Tel Quel* went into this rethinking of the status and importance of literature. The campaign was waged on a number of different fronts. In the theoretical domain *Tel Quel* was active in promoting a number of the ideas associated at the time with the structuralist analysis of literary texts. The *Tel Quel* series of books published some of the most influential theoretical works of the period. In 1965, for instance, it published an important collection, edited by Tzvetan Todorov, of texts by the Russian Formalists, who had been the first to apply linguistic insights to the study of literary texts in the 1920s. Similarly, the series published the major part of the literary-critical and theoretical work of Roland Barthes, including such important books as *S/Z*, his detailed line-by-line account of Balzac's short story 'Sarrasine', and *Le Plaisir du texte*, which openly took issue with the idea of a scientifically based structuralist approach to literature. In addition, *Tel Quel* brought out several important early essays by Derrida, whose *L'Ecriture et la différence* and *La Dissémination* were published in the *Tel Quel* series, and whose essays on Mallarmé, Georges Bataille, and Antonin Artaud were first printed in the journal. As a result of all these texts it was, paradoxically, *Tel Quel*, which many had begun to see as the standard-bearer of structuralist literary analysis in France, that became most closely identified with the challenge to structuralism. It fell, however, to Julia Kristeva, who joined the editorial board in 1970, to articulate and elaborate the key theoretical concerns of the *Tel Quel* group in the literary and textual domain. This she did in a series of books such as *Séméiotiké*, *Polylogue* and her doctoral thesis of 1974, *La Révolution du langage poétique*, which formulated in rigorous and influential fashion *Tel Quel*'s position concerning the modern, revolutionary, poetic or literary text.

The second strategy in *Tel Quel*'s rethinking of the meaning and place of literature lay in the re-invention, or re-discovery, of a new radical anti-tradition in literature. This was represented by writers who by pursuing writing, as Barthes put it, intransitively, for itself and not in the service of pre-established norms, were able to demonstrate the disruptive energy embodied in writing. The names that *Tel Quel* put forward and returned to repeatedly in this connection were those of Sade, Mallarmé, Lautréamont, Artaud and Bataille. These were all writers, it was argued, whose work had hitherto been seen as marginal by the literary establishment or by literary theorists but who, by challenging accepted norms, explored the very limits of the literary mode in its relation to human experience. What these authors had in common, *Tel Quel* argued, was a shared commitment to the transgressive potential of literature, a readiness to make writing itself into an exploration of experiences which are at the limit of intelligibility or of inherited modes of understanding, but which, by going beyond established taboos, in fact penetrated to the very centre of human experience. The concept of the 'texte-limite' was introduced to describe how writing, in the case of, say, Bataille's exploration of the experience of excess, in novel, poem, ecstatic meditation and philosophical essay, undermined accepted borders with explosive consequences and broke cultural taboos to uncover new and uncharted territory.

Though *Tel Quel* acquired its notoriety through the development of these theoretical views, it is important to recognise the prime importance given within the journal itself to literary texts. The majority of the members of the editorial board of *Tel Quel* were practising writers, poets or novelists. These included Sollers, Jean-Louis Baudry, Marcelin Pleynet, Denis Roche (who departed in 1973), Jean Ricardou and Jean Thibaudeau (both of whom were to leave in disagreement at the endorsement of Maoism in 1971), as well as a host of others who were briefly associated in earlier years, or who, like Maurice Roche, Pierre Guyotat and Jacques Henric, were closely linked to *Tel Quel* without ever being involved in editorial responsibilities. As Julia Kristeva remarks in her paper recalling the *Tel Quel* years, 'Mémoire', which appeared in the first issue of the magazine *L'Infini*, one of the distinctive traits of *Tel Quel* as a journal of the avant-garde was this bringing together of theoretical exploration and the practice of writing in a close and reciprocal dialogue.

Clearly, when it was set up, *Tel Quel* was not alone in its endorsement of the literary avant-garde. From the start it shared its rejection of 'committed literature' and its interest in formal experiment with the *nouveau roman* of Claude Simon and Alain Robbe-Grillet (whose work Barthes had enthusiastically welcomed back in the early 1950s). Naturally enough the policy adopted by the fledgling review in 1960 was one of support for the *nouveau roman*. At the same time it sought to generalise and extend in more systematic and adventurous ways what the *nouveau roman* had undertaken. While early numbers of the journal published material by Robbe-Grillet and Simon, it also more readily placed emphasis on texts by Ponge, Artaud and Bataille. Significantly, a piece by Sollers which appeared in the second number of *Tel Quel* ('Sept propositions sur Alain Robbe-Grillet'), though speaking warmly of Robbe-Grillet's *Dans le labyrinthe*, still managed to be more about Ponge than about Robbe-Grillet, and this was symptomatic of what the relations between the two groups were to be: more of rivalry than of collaboration. Throughout the 1960s a prominent figure in the relations between the *nouveau roman* and the *Tel Quel* group was Jean Ricardou, at the time an influential though isolated member of the *Tel Quel* editorial board, who directed much of his energy as a critic and novelist towards radicalising the *nouveau roman* by encouraging it to adopt more complex and more Byzantine formal and self-reflexive techniques, like those explored in his own novel of 1965 *La Prise de Constantinople*, the back cover of which, in an aptly self-questioning and self-reflexive pirouette, carried the title *La Prose de Constantinople*. In 1971, however, Ricardou left *Tel Quel* to carry on his career as fiction-writer and theoretical godfather to the now well-established *nouveau nouveau roman*.

It is true that some of the first novels published in the *Tel Quel* series bear some resemblance to the work of Robbe-Grillet and share an interest in the self-reflexive description of objects and in dramatising the act of writing metaphorically. At the same time the fictional self-consciousness of the early novels of Sollers and Jean-Louis Baudry explore territory far removed from that of the fiction that Robbe-Grillet was writing at the time. Sollers's third novel (and the first to be issued in the *Tel Quel* series) was a case in point. Entitled *Drame* and published in 1964, it was, somewhat like Robbe-Grillet's *Dans le labyrinthe*, an attempt to treat, in narrative form, the process of generation, or emergence, of fiction as such and of itself as a novel. But there the similarity ends. Robbe-Grillet's novel tackles the issue indirectly, by transposing the act of writing metaphorically into a dual story-line in which two parallel series of events mirror each other. One series deals with the actions of a soldier marching up and down uniform city streets (alluding to the lines of the printed page), disappearing back and forth into a painting of a café, as though to remind the reader that he is already a two-dimensional representation and not a flesh-and-blood living character, while the other series of (implied) actions are those of a writer perusing his desk, noting its surface (which is covered in dust just as the streets the soldier is marching down are blanketed with snow) and soldiering on across it in the quest for meaning.

In *Drame*, however, Sollers explores the process of writing more directly and shuns the idea of an artfully constructed external plot with characters, objects and events. *Drame* is a novel in which the underlying plot is continually being suspended, interrupted or abandoned; it proves difficult for the reader to summarise the narrative in the usual way or even to identify what it is. Indeed, it soon becomes clear that what is being described cannot be captured within the realm of story at all. The novel contains numerous story elements in the shape of small incidents and fragments of events, dreams, memories and imaginings, drawn apparently from the life of the unnamed protagonist, but these are treated as hypothetical snatches from a story which is still in the process of being written and in which the hero is merely an actor with no control over the script. The book is made up of sixty-four short, page-long segments or 'chants' (an allusion to Lautréamont's *Chants de Maldoror* and to the poetic rather than the novelistic tradition). Segments written in the third person, recounting the thoughts and emotions of an unnamed writer as he readies himself to write, alternate with passages in the first person, which are put in quotation marks and are introduced with the phrase 'il écrit:'. These give a version of a text being written by the writer-hero. Sollers's own prose, unlike Robbe-Grillet's, is both discursive and lyrical and manifestly conscious of all the figurative resources of language. It is reflexive both in the sense of seeking to illuminate its own process of creation and in the sense of being concerned, rather like a meditation, with its own limits and possibilities. Here, to give an example, is part of a 'chant' describing what is taking place, as Sollers phrases it, 'derrière les yeux et le front' (*Drame*, p. 11) of his protagonist:

Il pourrait évidemment résumer ou exagérer la situation: un homme, une ville, une femme – ce qui arrive, ce qui se fait –, procéder à une narration elliptique qui aurait l'avantage de profiter de mille détails concrets en même temps que d'éléments personnels. Il pourrait recourir à une fable commode: présentation spectaculaire sur fond de légende, digressions de plus en plus ambiguës, menées souterraines, démentis, détours [. . .] (C'est ainsi probablement qu'on écrit un livre. Mais il s'agit bien d'écrire un livre.) Ce n'est pas la fausse évidence des premières constatations, ni une invention privilégiée qui peut maintenir la question à ses yeux. Ce qu'il faut défendre: une sorte de netteté exubérante, maintenant, tout près, gravitant sur et sous la page, tournant avec sa face nocturne à l'intérieur du mouvement qui le fait parler, l'anime, l'irrigue, lui permet de respirer, le double et conduit sa main. Plus vite. On ne choisit pas. On n'arrange rien. Opération chimique, plutôt: décoller, isoler [. . .] Problème: comment faire passer ici un immeuble de vingt étages et par la même occasion une grande apparition rouge vif et encore un train lancé dans la plaine et ce paysage à rivière suspendu par la main d'un peintre et la multitude des livres tout à coup et son visage effrayé et les couloirs du sommeil et l'oubli crispé à chaque moment – conscience effacée, noyée – et le geste qui trace et dégage à mesure cette violence libre éclairant rapidement le trajet? Comment être là? Comment accepter l'aventure? Arrêté, il n'insiste pas, il attend. Sentant fuir et se dissoudre la véritable histoire, le drame implicite qu'il était sur le point d'esquisser, qui déjà s'édifiait et se chantait imperceptiblement en lui par grandes zones transparentes, en marchant le long des quais, le soir, sous le ciel rouge et noir, dans le désordre et le bruit de la poussière chaude, l'odeur d'essence brûlée occupant les rues. Cependant – (pp. 60–2)

There are a number of traits here which are characteristic of Sollers's writing at this time and of the fiction produced by *Tel Quel* in the 1960s. In those texts, writing is not about adventures, it is itself that adventure. The idea of representing the real by the use of mimetic techniques of illusion gives way to the desire to dramatise the act of writing as a radical experience in which the relationship between subjectivity, language and the world are reshaped in new and provocative ways. Traditional narrative structure (even of the sort being parodied and manipulated by Robbe-Grillet in his novels) is therefore abandoned. Sollers, in *Drame*, for instance, is less concerned with the formal aspects of narrative structure than with isolating and capturing, in narrative, that elusive moment of generation or emergence of writing, when meanings are at their most inchoate and words have not yet lost their dynamic, multivalent potential. The paradox lies in the attempt to use the framework of a novel to dramatise a process which is usually concealed within fiction, and much of the interest of *Drame* lies in the way the conventions of narrative are adapted and reworked in order to fit the needs of Sollers's experimental dismantling of representational literary assumptions.

Most of the fiction written at the time by the *Tel Quel* group takes, then, as its major preoccupation the activity and practice of writing itself. In this respect most of the novels produced by *Tel Quel* are self-reflexive or self-conscious. They tend, however, not to use plot and character to mirror the literary text (in the way that a *nouveau roman*, for instance, will invent metaphors to alert the reader to the formal properties or artificial status of the book), but rather to reflect in more overt and meditative fashion on the process of writing itself. It would be wrong to say, however, that as a result (as traditional critics sometimes complain) the concerns of *Drame*, say, are narrowly parochial and cut off from the world at large. Sollers's endeavour is certainly ascetic and the result of sustained and intense concentration on the sole act of writing. The outcome, however, is not self-indulgence but a text of striking energy and seductive power. Indeed, in *Drame*, writing becomes charged with a quite peculiar intensity ('cette violence libre', as Sollers puts it here), and one of the most frequent metaphors to arise in *Drame* and other work from *Tel Quel* is that of life itself as a mode of writing. Living, like writing, is a perpetual confrontation with signs and with the need to decipher, interpret and re-invent the signs in which human life is immersed. In numerous passages *Drame* compares the world to a surface covered with words and symbols, a shifting palimpsest covered this way and that with enigmatic messages. The city, for instance, writes the novel's hero, is like a 'grande page qui n'en finit pas de se surcharger et de s'obscurcir' (p. 49). To explore the process of writing is thus to investigate the borders and complexities, the arabesques and obscurities, of human experience itself. And, by that token, it is to abandon the illusion that either life or writing fiction can be self-evident or unproblematic.

Despite its self-consciousness, *Drame* is not an overly cerebral novel. However powerful the creative imagination, notes the hero, experience is limited by the human body. 'Ce que je dis', he writes, 'en dépend, n'oublie pas cela' (p. 20), and some of *Drame*'s most striking moments come from this intermingling of the register of the corporeal with that of the mental. Elsewhere Sollers goes on to explore in detail the border zones between waking and sleeping, remembering and dreaming, life and death, reality and fiction. The elusive 'source' of writing, we read, is a kind of 'vibration [. . .] de plus en plus forte: le corps entier, mais un corps pensé plutôt que perçu, semble [. . .] osciller sur place' (p. 52). This idea of writing as a kind of pulsating rhythm which cannot be located either in the body or in the mind alone, but rather in the complex intermediary space between, is a recurrent theme (and one treated at length in Sollers's early prose pieces collected in *L'Intermédiaire*). Besides giving writing a dynamic energy of its own, which has little to do with literature as a representation of the real, it highlights the extent to which writing in fiction has often to do with tracing and investigating limits. Indeed, if writing, in Derrida's sense, is understood to be the medium in which distinctions or differences are articulated, then one of the particular functions of fictional writing would seem to be to question established distinctions and to reinvent or redraw those differences. For *Tel Quel*, the power of the avant-garde literary text, as was noted earlier, lies in its capacity to challenge the separations and taboos which structure everyday experience.

At one point, mid-way through the novel, writing – the writing of *Drame* – is described as being like an 'histoire suspendue où rien ne semblerait arriver et qui pourtant serait le comble d'une activité interne répondant, répliquant à l'agitation comme aux vastes tableaux réguliers du dehors' (p. 73), and clearly, *Drame* strives to write such a story. 'La difficulté, cependant', we are told on the previous page, 'vient de ces interruptions continuelles, imprévisibles, de ces rappels, méandres, détours apparemment inutiles, de ces piétinements – et, soudain, de ces accélérations impossibles à suivre, heurts, mélanges, rafles – et, de nouveau: apaisements, communications ambiguës' (p. 72). In writing *Drame*, Sollers attempts to stage the act of writing in its disorderly movement and, as a result, the text has to cope without the traditional support of a continuous, linear plot (even of the type Robbe-Grillet sets up, in *Dans le labyrinthe*, say, in order to pervert it). This raises an obvious question of structure. How Sollers resolves the problem of the organisation of his text is reflected in the novel's multi-purpose title.

The word 'drame' contains several distinct threads of meaning. It is an enactment, a drama in the sense of a crisis, as well as being a type of play falling outside traditional generic boundaries, somewhere between tragedy and comedy, with perhaps music added, too. Barthes, in his review of the novel, recalls its derivation from a word meaning 'doing'. It is also, anagrammatically, akin to a dream (or a 'Traum', as in Freud's *Traumdeutung*, his *Interpretation of Dreams*), and it is relevant that Freud himself uses the theatrical metaphor when, in the *Traumdeutung*, he refers to dreaming as taking place 'on the other stage' of the unconscious. 'Drame' also closely resembles, phonetically, the 'trame', the weft and the woof, of a fabric, or 'tissu' (which, Barthes often stresses, is the same word as 'texte'). Theatre, dream, fabric, enactment, the multiplicity of threads and the mixing of genres: these are the key elements that Sollers employs in organising his text. He does this first by giving his book a spatial structure. This space is that of books as such, and books, *Drame* suggests, take place in space rather than in time, or more precisely, in a world where time is converted into space, as though, perhaps, into a 'pays du temps où l'on ignorait le temps' (p. 23).

Modern and avant-garde texts have tended, of course, ever since Mallarmé's 'Un Coup de dés', to prefer space over time, and Sollers carries the process one step further. Mallarmé wrote of his poem that 'tout se passe, par raccourci, en hypothèse; on évite le récit' (Mallarmé, p. 455), and Sollers's main concern is much the same. The aim is to escape the linearity of time and the teleological narrative order which goes with the idea of a time-based plot (and it is worth noting that one of the distinctive features of the phenomenological approach to fiction, which is found, for example, in Sartre's novels, lies in the aligning of plot with human time; indeed it would be possible to write the history of modern fiction in France in terms of these two competing models of time and space). Unlike time, however, space is reversible and multi-directional. Therefore, to opt for space over time becomes, for Sollers, a way of emphasising the multivalent density of writing over the single-dimensionality of the spoken word. In *Drame* the temporality of story and plot becomes converted into space, and the book, as noted earlier, is built up according to sixty-four alternating segments which are said by the author to represent the sixty-four squares on the chessboard. This has a number of effects: firstly, the text demonstrates its own structure as a relational network and a verbal labyrinth having no single exit or entry point. Reading has to move backwards as well as forwards, and there is no sense of the end of the text representing a final point when reality or truth is revealed. In addition, writing is treated as a ludic adventure, as a challenge which has risks of its own, involving the transgression of fundamental norms. On more than one occasion the book is described as being a kind of 'échiquier mobile' (p. 21), as a game being played on a 'damier figurant le temps' (p. 23).

As the narrative structure of *Drame* suspends story, its place is taken by the theme of theatre. The metaphor of theatre and of theatrical space is prominent in a number of novels of the 1960s. Besides supplying the title of *Drame*, the stage is often the source for a number of images which refer to the dynamic creativity of language.

According to the stage metaphor language is bodily action, performative movement and process. In some ways, paradoxically perhaps, the theatre becomes a name for all that undermines representation: the use of language as gesture, the dissolution of subjectivity into a series of verbal roles or masks, the blurring of the boundaries between what is real and what is fictional, and the inclusion of the audience as an integral part of the performance. (A number of influences are behind this conception of the theatre, including, notably, the essays, letters and poems of Antonin Artaud, whom *Tel Quel* did much to re-establish, as well as Mallarmé's sketches for his all-encompassing 'Livre' which take the theatre to be the appropriate forum for his infinite, seamless Book. Here, as in a number of other areas, *Tel Quel* was heir to much that had first surfaced either in the context of Symbolism during the last quarter of the last century, or in the Surrealist movement of the 1920s and 1930s.)

In *Drame* the theatre serves as a device to stress the novel's performative quality. Notably, what the novel dramatises is the shifting and unstable nature of identity. Oscillating between 'je' and 'il' according to the chessboard pattern of black and white, the protagonist of *Drame* is dissolved into a rhythmically changing set of pronouns. It is never very clear to the reader in what ways, and to what extent, the two pronouns refer to the same or different personae, and the relationship between them needs constantly to be retrieved from the movement of writing. To this extent it is words which 'speak the protagonist' and words which are writing the endless story he himself is never able to summarise. He does not exist in the text as a controlling force but rather as a space in whom the pulsating segments of the text resound as though he were the stage on which they were being performed. Indeed, if one follows the critic Maurice Blanchot in the view that the third person is not really a person at all but more a species of non-person, then it becomes clear that words, far from securing the protagonist's sense of identity, undermine it quite radicaiiy. Many incidents in the book, starting with the very first which recounts a dream during which the main character finds himself in the library face to face with the spectre of his own death, evoke the mortality of the central character, and it is not surprising that *Tel Quel* became closely identified in the 1960s with the theme of the death of the author and of writing being somehow akin to the experience of death.

This idea of the dissolution of identity and personality into the relational play of words was linked by *Tel Quel* itself with Mallarmé's notion of the 'disparition élocutoire du poète' (Mallarmé, p. 366) and the experience of death and void explored in many Mallarmé poems. The idea is given forceful expression in Jean-Louis Baudry's novel, *Personnes* (1967). *Personnes* is reminiscent of *Drame*, the structure of which it both recalls and complicates. Like *Drame* it gives various clues in its title. 'Personne', the author reminds his readers, means a theatrical mask as well as a human person, and a character or persona as well as, in French, being a term for 'nobody'. The novel explores these different, seemingly contradictory meanings via the French system of pronouns. Using a spatial model again, the novel adopts a double-entry grid of eighty-one sequences, alternating between first and third person. Each of these short narrative segments is constructed on the basis of two related pronouns, the one as subject and the other as object of the narrative episode, and *Personnes* becomes a dramatic enactment of the tensions present in language between subject and object, human and non-human, masculine and feminine, dream and reality.

One of the more striking aspects of both *Drame* and *Personnes* is their refusal to conform to established rules of genre. Barthes, in his review of *Drame*, considered the term 'roman' on the cover of the book to be a provocation, and it is clear that Sollers's text, as well as a number of the other fictional works published by *Tel Quel*, aspires to the status of a total work of art, mingling novel, theatre, poem, essay and philosophical meditation in a fresh synthesis. The aim of this fusing together of different genres, however, is not to reduce all literature to an underlying sameness or monotony, but rather the reverse. For if all texts, because they are made up of language, are taken to be fundamentally continuous with one another, it becomes possible to undermine the artificial and historically contingent boundaries between genres. For *Tel Quel*, the rejection of divisions of genre was part of a broader revolt against all attempts to police the literary by the imposition of false boundaries.

This rejection of generic compartmentalisation is at the heart of Maurice Roche's first novel for *Tel Quel*, *Compact*, also published in 1966. It was followed throughout the '70s by a string of further works including *Circus*, *CodeX*, *Opéra Bouffe*, *Maladie Mélodie* and others. In all these books, most of which still, almost modestly, call themselves 'romans', Roche develops a mode of writing of startling originality. His novels exploit the spatial potential of the written form to the extent of incorporating within the fiction all manner of textual disturbance: puns, anagrams, spelling mistakes, quotations, portions of text in foreign languages, proof-reader's corrections to an already printed text, common textual symbols, different typefaces and printing styles, constant changes in layout, use of the page as a visual medium, underlinings, pictures, doodles, scribblings, graphisms, cartoons, extracts from musical scores, collages from other texts such as newspapers or historical documents.

Roche began as a musicologist and is the author of a monograph on Monteverdi. Reading his novels, it is easy to see the relevance of Roche's interest in polyphonic music, since the variety of materials he uses in his fiction transforms the usually predictable fictional space of literature into a massively intricate polyphony of voices. The fictional universe that Roche's novels inhabit is a carnivalesque one, full of gruesome jokes, uncanny collisions of meaning, comic parody and perversions of the commonplace. As a result his novels are radically unquotable and impossible to summarise. One recurrent preoccupation, however, is with the question of inscription. What characterises all the material Roche uses is its quality as written text.

This relationship to writing as a process of inscription is illustrated in *Compact* by an episodic story (printed in italic) about a Japanese tatoo artist acquiring (by fair means or foul) human bodies and skins (including that of the narrator) in order to cover them with decorative inscriptions. The surface on which writing is inscribed, Roche suggests here, is none other than the body, human skin and flesh. For Roche individual human subjects are ensnared, literally, within a network of writings, from the names which we are all given at birth to the legal statutes to which as citizens we fall subject. These texts form, as Roche's novel *CodeX* implies, a 'codex', a frame of written legal rules composed in some hermetic code. That code, however, can be challenged by a mode of writing which, like Roche's, is able to cross out (x) that code which steals our flesh, body and memory. The major part of Roche's work is concerned with reclaiming memory, with retrieving from history and from culture all manner of written texts for Roche's own – and his readers' – enjoyment. Time and again Roche dramatises his own death as though it could be a scene from one of his own novels, making it into a huge 'funferall', to use Joyce's term from *Finnegans Wake*. Roche's writing has links with modern performance art in that he is able, as a writer, to cover, or recover, his own body with, as it were, its own disruptive inscriptions and thus reject the oppressive imprint of a society and civilisation whose salient feature, for Roche, is its arrogant and exorbitant claim to speak in his place.

The year 1968 was important for *Tel Quel* as well as for the French intellectual world as a whole. It saw the events of May, which changed the entire political landscape in France, particularly for the Paris-based avant-garde. In the autumn of 1968 the Editions du Seuil published a collection of theoretical essays taken from *Tel Quel*, and entitled *Théorie d'ensemble*. This was intended as a summum of *Tel Quel*'s achievement in founding a comprehensive theory of the modern literary text. It was also part of the *Tel Quel* group's own response to May, which was to institute the meetings of its 'Groupe d'Etudes théoriques', at which, among numerous others, papers were presented by Sollers (later collected in *Sur le matérialisme*) and by Derrida (including his seminal Mallarmé essay, 'La Double Séance', later published in *La Dissémination* together with a long review of Sollers's *Nombres*). This gave some indication of *Tel Quel*'s desire to raise the literary and theoretical stakes in order to place writing at the centre of the cultural revolution which, as it seemed to some of its participants, May '68 had put on the immediate agenda.

Nombres, however, Sollers's second novel for *Tel Quel*, had been published shortly before May, and it began as a continuation of *Drame*. There was the same abstract, almost geometric organisation. One hundred page-long sequences were divided into four numbered groups of twenty-five sections each. One of each group is presented in turn, and numbered accordingly (1.5 or 2.34, for instance). These four thematic series, which can be read continuously through the novel (by skipping the intervening sections and returning to them later), or intermittently (by following the printed order of the book), are described as being like the four sides of an auditorium. Three are in the imperfect tense and the first person, while the fourth, occupying the position of the absent fourth wall, is addressed to the audience and is in the present tense.

In this way the novel exploits the same theatrical structure as *Drame* but with a clearer sense of subverting it by opening it out into a wider environment. *Nombres* (this is one of the meanings of the title) attacks closure and uses a number of devices to question its own limits. On occasion it quotes from *Drame* and incorporates sentences from the earlier text (p. 47). At one point Sollers even goes back to the opening sentence of his 1961 novel, *Le Parc* (not his first, but the first that he was prepared to acknowledge as his own in 1968): '"Le ciel, au-dessus des longues avenues luisantes, est bleu sombre": voilà en somme la phrase d'où j'étais parti –' (p. 30). The effect is to link all Sollers's writings as being extensions of one another, like a series of interlinked three-dimensional spaces. On another level it suggests that *Nombres* should be read as a remembering, as an anamnesis of the writer's birth into language. 'Le récit', Sollers writes, 'avait commencé brusquement quand j'avais décidé de changer de langue dans la même langue, quand le premier nœud de résistance s'était imposé, quand les répétitions avaient envahi leurs traits . . .' (*Nombres*, p. 27).

At issue here is a whole complex of relations and questions. The question of naming is a central preoccupation in most of Sollers's fiction (Sollers is a pseudonym, and his relation to his own family name – Joyaux – is explored in *H* and, later, in *Portrait du joueur*). In Sollers's work the name serves as a focus for the relationship between body and language, subjectivity and sexual division, words and eroticism. When *Nombres* re-enacts, in fiction, the writer's birth and rebirth into language and narrative it is these issues that are to the forefront. In 2.6, for instance, we read:

> Cependant j'arrivais du côté de ma propre histoire. Cela m'était signalé par la tentative de me situer à la périphérie d'un cercle qui serait passé par 'nous tous'. Je pensais que si j'arrivais au tissu qui nous composait, je saurais en même temps ce qui le maintient, le nourrit, l'anime – quelque chose devant malgré tout disparaître au moment de la réponse juste, se jeter dans ce qui autrefois avait été appelé 'mer' en criant . . . Cette réponse était liée à la prononciation d'un seul mot qui me désignerait à la fois de façon ramassée et multiple, une syllabe n'existant dans aucune autre langue connue, un nom pour toujours acide me brûlant la gorge, les dents? (p. 19)

One thread of the story in *Nombres* is a dramatisation of the sexual relations of the narrator and an unnamed woman. Sexuality and eroticism are another variation on the infinite text of memory, desire and difference which *Nombres* investigates. To this extent the relation to the other, and to the other sex, are crucial elements in the book. There is, however, a further dimension to the relation to the other. This is the question of other writings, in the sense of both writings written by other authors and writings from other cultures. Here *Nombres* innovates considerably in relation to *Drame*. Present in the text of *Nombres* are numerous quotations, signalled by quotation marks but not attributed to any source. These include fragments from Lucretius, the Chinese classics, Marx, Freud, Mao Zedong, modern mathematical textbooks, Artaud and many others. They take the form of gnomic sayings, axioms, famous quotations or theoretical pronouncements, all of which are woven into Sollers's own fictional text as part of its own argument, as well as serving to open the text out beyond itself into some infinite patchwork of writing composed by many hands (according to Isidore Ducasse-Lautréamont's recommendation that 'la poésie doit être faite par tous, non par un').

In addition the text of *Nombres* is interspersed with Chinese ideograms. These encapsulate one aspect of the whole argument about writing and spoken language which had been carried on in *Tel Quel* for some years. Chinese ideograms, the idea ran, retained their gestural density as written acts, as traces or inscriptions, in precisely the way western, alphabetical languages did not. The argument was that ideograms were not transparent ciphers of meaning (as alphabetical letters claimed to be according to a naïve view of language) but were visual, non-linear and dramatic. They required the whole body to write or perform them and were therefore not alienated. If (as Nietzsche once put it) the whole of western metaphysics derived from the Greek language, then, it was argued by *Tel Quel*, one could defeat that metaphysics by changing language, by drawing on the Chinese conception of the ideogram. What was claimed here about Chinese language (which had antecedents in the history of modernism, notably in the *Cantos* of Ezra Pound) was also claimed about the Chinese Cultural Revolution (which had been roughly contemporaneous with France's May '68), and *Nombres* is in this sense staged as a dialogue between East and West, between a radical society in transformation and an alienated world in decline, between the world of the numerous masses and that of the introspective individual. It was clear from its title where the sympathies of *Nombres* lay, and the book signalled the beginnings of *Tel Quel*'s support for what by 1971, when the editorial policy of the review took a sharp turn against the French Communist Party and towards the Maoist extreme left, the review began to call 'la pensée Mao Tsé-Toung'.

Lois, which appeared in 1972, is Sollers's most peremptory and assertive text. It marked a noticeable shift from the earlier, more ascetic fiction. The meticulously designed formal geometries of *Drame* and *Nombres* are abandoned for a much looser method of organisation. Sollers wittily expresses it on the cover of *Lois* by referring to the 'stucture du volume'. The novel registers in other ways much of the anarchic enthusiasm which followed the events of 1968, as well as responding to the significant theoretical doubts expressed by Barthes, Derrida and Kristeva about the implications of a narrowly formalist concept of writing. Instead, *Lois* occupies what Joyce in *Finnegans Wake* (p. 594) refers to as the 'trancitive spaces', and works on the basis of silent quotation and pastiche, by the reworking of mythical narratives and the invention of portmanteau words. The presence of Joyce in the text is acknowledged by Sollers by way of a homage-cum-translation of the opening to sections I and IV of *Finnegans Wake* (pp. 3 and 593); a later version of some of the same passages appeared the following year in *Tel Quel* 54, in a translation by Sollers and Stephen Heath:

en rune et rivière pour roulant courant, rivagé battant dans le rebaignant, passée la douadouane du vieux de la vieille, de mèrève-adam se repom-

> mifiant, recyclons d'abord, foutrement commode, circulés viciés ou gesti-
> culant, le château-comment sous périphérant, là où ça méthode, où ça
> joue croulant . . . Il y va-repique l'acteur au volant . . . Sandhyas! Sand-
> hyas! Sandhyas! dormourant le bas, appelant l'eau bas, résuractionné
> l'airveilleur du bas, o rallie-rallie, o relie-ravis, o reluis pleinphix tout
> brillant luilui, soit l'oiseau en vie, notre râle écrit, nos sémématières sur
> l'ossiéanie . . . (*Lois*, p. 41)

Like the *Wake*, *Lois* relies on a series of mythical narratives and
allusions to provide the framework for the novel. The formula was a
fruitful one for other members of the *Tel Quel* group, too, notably
Jean-Louis Baudry, whose 1970 novel *La 'Création'*, which had as its
subtitle, 'premier état: l'année', assembled the diverse creational
myths dealing with the yearly cycle in a lyrical epic which devoted a
different text to each day in the yearly process. Sollers's treatment
was more pugnacious than Baudry's and involved him in a lot of
frank sexual talking. In *Lois*, for instance, the Oedipus story is
recounted as the 'histoire du type aux chevilles enflées né à contre-
temps récité, condamné chassé et récupéré, meurtrier hasard et
nécessité, réponse en chemin par l'oralisé, puis baisant sa reine de
mère qui s'y attendait, puis jeté crevé dans son aveuglé appuyé fifille
aux creux des forêts' (p. 12). This use of narrative as the basis for
satire and for energetic (and at times cryptic) assertions about
sexuality, politics and the literary is characteristic of the novel,
which expends much of its energy in comic invective and pastiche.
Sollers's version of Lacan ('le docteur flacon') rewrites Lacan's
famous prosopopoeia in 'La Chose freudienne' ('Moi la vérité, je
parle', *Ecrits*, p. 409) as 'moi l'aspérité, je parle, je parle, mais ça
vient d'ailleurs, de tout autrefois, de futur en courbe et retourne-
moi' (*Lois*, p. 58) and continues in much the same vein. Other
pastiches have 'le professeur jacob strauss', the famous mythologist
(Claude Lévi-Strauss), welcoming his colleague 'le professeur levib-
sohn', 'la linguistique, comme vous le savez, en personne' (Roman
Jakobson) (p. 67) in a comic sequence of dubious humour but, no
doubt, well-planned satirical effect. 'Au commencement est la verve'
(p. 131), claims Sollers, and such seems to be the major concern in
the novel, which remains one of his less memorable books, though
one which represented an important shift in direction.

Less than a year later, Sollers published another novel, *H*. This is
how it begins:

> qui dit salut la machine avec ses pattes rentrées son côté tortue cata socle
> ses touches figées accents toniques hors de strophe elle a rêvé cette nuit
> que je lançais la balle très haut et très loin elle ne s'arrête plus elle allume
> en passant les cerceaux disposés méridiens plus ronds quand elle les

traverse et voilà la bombe qui retombe toute chaude enfumée grillée tiens on est en pleine montagne y d'la poudreuse regarde les cristaux blancs violets sens cet air et en effet on enfonce les chevilles dans la plaine mousse pour la première fois l'hallucination goutte à goutte est vue du dedans découpée foulée cata cata catalyse ça fait des jours et des jours qu'elle fait la tête dans son coin sinistre mais ce matin en route c'est l'ouvert le creux décidé y a-t-il une autre forme. (*H*, p. 9)

Without punctuation, without capitalisation, without paragraphs, the text continued in this way for 180 pages. Though there was an outcry among traditional critics, Sollers's method was simple. The idea was to inject into *H* the gestural rhythm of writing, its melodic effects, its non-linear movement across themes, allusions, scenes from the present and the past, and to this end all external punctuation was abandoned. The same step had been taken, though in more local ways, by Joyce (Molly Bloom's monologue at the end of *Ulysses*) and by Faulkner, both of whom began to be important presences in Sollers's work. By omitting from *H* all the external scaffolding of punctuation, Sollers was better able to exploit the internal punctuation of speech, which is conveyed by intonation, breathing, pauses, shifts in speed and rhythm. In this way writing became more musical, more percussive, and though this decision to explore the possibilities of spoken rather than written language was a new one for *Tel Quel* (and one that *Lois* had already instigated), the aim was to revalue speech and consider it as already a mode of writing.

H, as readers will have noted, differs from the earlier fiction by embracing a mode of verbal continuity built around the use of the first person. Yet the form *H* adopts, Sollers says in the novel, is not the 'monologue intérieur' of Edouard Dujardin, much used by early modernists, and which often tended to reflect a notion of subjectivity prior to language, but rather what Sollers calls the 'polylogue extérieur' (the term was taken up by Kristeva in her informative essay on *H* and used by her as the title of her 1977 collection of essays, *Polylogue*). The difference is that the 'polylogue' does not need to sustain any mimetic illusion and thus assume the existence of some final unity, a unity which is usually thought of as the diversity of a human personality. In the place of unity, *H*'s commitment is to dissonance and discontinuity (its musical analogue, Sollers suggests, is Schoenberg's 'Klangfarbenmelodie' of Opus 6 – p. 184). *H* develops in this way a highly mobile and differentiated idiom which touches upon a wide range of issues: literary, political, sexual and historical. As Barthes points out in his review (reprinted in his short book, *Sollers écrivain*), there is, physically, no single way of reading the novel. It is worth noting, too, as Barthes shows, that in addition to (or as part of) its intellectual sophistication *H* contains much that is seductive or evocative in traditional literary ways and offers many of the customary pleasures associated with novel-reading: wit, humour, insight, intelligence and energy.

In the later 1970s *Tel Quel*'s publication of fictional works fell away a little, partly as a result of the defection of former leading figures. But the reason had also to do with the political crisis that the avant-garde began to undergo. The fascination for the China of Mao Zedong did not survive his death in 1976, and by then *Tel Quel* had begun to turn to the United States as a possible spiritual home for its dissident style of marginal literary activity (*Tel Quel* 71/73, published in 1977, was subtitled 'Pourquoi les Etats-Unis?'). At the same time, the growing interest in Céline, an innovator in literary and stylistic terms but reactionary in his political or ideological convictions, was an indication that the link between avant-garde literary practice and avant-garde politics could no longer be taken for granted. Moreover, it seemed, from Céline's own texts and as a result of the extraordinary inflation of political discourse in the early 1970s, that any systematic approach to the political dimension was paranoid and totalising (if not potentially totalitarian) and was tantamount to a betrayal of the dissolving capacities of writing. How writing might intervene in politics (and what definition of politics that implied), rather than being taken as read, became intensely problematic, and the ever more prominent role taken by psychoanalysis in Sollers's writing in the 1970s reflected the desire to use Freudian analysis as a means of comprehending not only the literary and the sexual but also the political. Much of this history is researched in detail (if in indirect ways) in Kristeva's 1980 account of Céline, *Pouvoirs de l'horreur*, but it was central to Sollers's ongoing literary project of the 1970s, the novel *Paradis*.

Paradis was first published in instalments in *Tel Quel* in the spring of 1974, beginning with the special number on *Lois* and *H*. The model was clearly Joyce's serial publication of *Work in Progress* (later *Finnegans Wake*) in the pre-war Parisian magazine, *transition*. The first publication of *Paradis* in book form was not until 1981 (together with a tape-recorded version of the novel read by the author and lasting twelve hours), and a second volume followed in 1986. *Paradis* continues in the vein of *H*, as an unpunctuated 'polylogue extérieur', but concentrates more on the complex intertwining of sexuality, religion, language and writing. Though *Paradis* is perhaps Sollers's most imposing work, it is also perhaps one of his least accessible and the one which most needs a knowledge of Sollers's other preoccupations during the 1970s.

In 1983, however, the decision was taken to dissolve *Tel Quel* and move the review to another publishing house (Denoël, a subsidiary of Gallimard), under a different name, *L'Infini*. The move coincided with a fresh burst of novelistic activity on Sollers's part; he wrote for Gallimard, in swift succession, *Femmes* (1983), *Portrait du joueur* (1984) and *Le Cœur absolu* (1987). Voluminous, polemical, laced with eroticism and commenting in thinly disguised terms on contemporary events and personalities, these novels caught the best-seller market unawares and projected Sollers once more into the limelight. In novelistic terms they most closely resemble Céline's novels of the 1940s and 1950s (*Féerie pour une autre fois*, say, or the war trilogy). As such they also belong to a different history to that of *Tel Quel* and to a different avant-garde, if in the 1980s the word can be maintained with any conviction.

Bibliography

1. Main texts

Major novelistic or critical texts published by the leading members of the *Tel Quel* group and some of the main theoretical works which appeared in the Editions du Seuil *Tel Quel* series under the direction of Philippe Sollers

Barthes, Roland, *Le Degré zéro de l'écriture* (Editions du Seuil, 1953)
——, *Essais critiques* (Editions du Seuil, 1964)
——, *Critique et vérité* (Editions du Seuil, 1966)
——, *S/Z* (Editions du Seuil, 1970)
——, *Sade, Fourier, Loyola* (Editions du Seuil, 1971)
——, *Le Plaisir du texte* (Editions du Seuil, 1973)
——, *Fragments d'un discours amoureux* (Editions du Seuil, 1977)
——, *Sollers écrivain* (Editions du Seuil, 1979)
——, *L'Obvie et l'obtus* (Editions du Seuil, 1982)
Baudry, Jean-Louis, *Le Pressentiment* (Editions du Seuil, 1962)
——, *Les Images* (Editions du Seuil, 1963)
——, *Personnes* (Editions du Seuil, 1967)
——, *La 'Création'* (Editions du Seuil, 1970)
——, *L'Effet cinéma* (Editions Albatros, 1978)
——, *Proust, Freud et l'autre* (Editions de Minuit, 1984)

Derrida, Jacques, *De la grammatologie* (Editions de Minuit, 1967)

——, *L'Ecriture et la différence* (Editions du Seuil, 1967)

——, *La Dissémination* (Editions du Seuil, 1972)

Guyotat, Pierre, *Tombeau pour cinq cent mille soldats* (Gallimard, 1967)

——, *Eden, Eden, Eden* (Gallimard, 1970)

——, *Prostitution* (Gallimard, 1975)

Henric, Jacques, *Archées* (Editions du Seuil, 1969)

——, *Chasses* (Editions du Seuil, 1975)

——, *Carrousels* (Editions du Seuil, 1980)

Kristeva, Julia, *Séméiotiké* (Editions du Seuil, 1969)

——, *La Révolution du langage poétique* (Editions du Seuil, 1974)

——, *Polylogue* (Editions du Seuil, 1977)

——, *Pouvoirs de l'horreur* (Editions du Seuil, 1980)

——, 'Mémoire', *L'Infini*, 1 (1983), 31–54

Pleynet, Marcelin, *Prise d'otage* (Denoël, 1986)

Ricardou, Jean, *La Prise de Constantinople* (Editions de Minuit, 1965)

——, *Problèmes du nouveau roman* (Editions du Seuil, 1967)

——, *Pour une théorie du nouveau roman* (Editions du Seuil, 1971)

Roche, Denis, *Louve basse* (Editions du Seuil, 1976)

Roche, Maurice, *Compact* (Editions du Seuil, 1966)

——, *Circus* (Editions du Seuil, 1972)

——, *CodeX* (Editions du Seuil, 1974)

——, *Opéra Bouffe* (Editions du Seuil, 1975)

——, *Mémoire* (Pierre Belfond, 1976)

——, *Monteverdi* (Editions du Seuil, 1977)

——, *Macabré* (Editions du Seuil, 1979)

——, *Maladie mélodie* (Editions du Seuil, 1980)

——, *Camar(a)de* (Arthaud, 1981)

——, *Je ne vais pas bien, mais il faut que j'y aille* (Editions du Seuil, 1987)

Scarpetta, Guy, *Scène* (Editions du Seuil, 1972)

Sollers, Philippe, *Le Défi*, in: *Ecrire* no 3, pp. 1–35 (Editions du Seuil, 1957)

——, *Une Curieuse Solitude* (Editions du Seuil, 1958)

——, *Le Parc* (Editions du Seuil, 1961)

——, *L'Intermédiaire* (Editions du Seuil, 1963)

——, *Drame* (Editions du Seuil, 1964)

——, *Nombres* (Editions du Seuil, 1968)

——, *Logiques* (Editions du Seuil, 1968)

—— (ed.), *Théorie d'ensemble* (Editions du Seuil, 1968)

——, *Lois* (Editions du Seuil, 1972)

—— (ed.), *Artaud* (U.G.E., 1973)

—— (ed.), *Bataille* (U.G.E., 1973)

——, *H* (Editions du Seuil, 1973)

——, *Sur le matérialisme* (Editions du Seuil, 1974)

——, *Paradis* (Editions du Seuil, 1981)

——, *Vision à New York* (Grasset, 1981)

———, *Femmes* (Gallimard, 1983)

———, *Portrait du joueur* (Gallimard, 1984)

———, *Théorie des exceptions* (Gallimard, 1986)

———, *Paradis II* (Gallimard, 1986)

———, *Le Cœur absolu* (Gallimard, 1987)

[Numerous interviews and statements of opinion by Sollers are to be found in *Tel Quel* (1960–83) and, subsequently, *L'Infini* (1983–)]

Thibaudeau, Jean, *Ouverture* (Editions du Seuil, 1966)

———, *Imaginez la nuit* (Editions du Seuil, 1968)

Todorov, Tzvetan (ed.), *Théorie de la littérature, textes des formalistes russes* (Editions du Seuil, 1965)

2. Other texts referred to in this chapter include:

Joyce, James, *Finnegans Wake* (Faber and Faber, 1963)

Lacan, Jacques, *Ecrits* (Editions du Seuil, 1966)

Mallarmé, Stéphane, *Œuvres complètes*, Henri Mondor and G. Jean-Aubry, eds (Gallimard, 1945)

de Saussure, Ferdinand, *Cours de linguistique générale* (Editions Payot, 1972)

–5–

Marie-Claire Blais

ROSEMARY LLOYD

'une gageure, une vraie gageure, un
pari, comme toutes les œuvres d'art'
(Baudelaire)

One of Marie-Claire Blais's finest novels, *Le Sourd dans la ville*, opens
with the image of a youth staring through a window at 'l'environne-
ment de silhouettes dont le monde était fait pour lui' and resembling
in his attitude 'cette figure de la Douleur telle que l'a peinte Munch
dans "Le Cri"' (*SV*, p. 9).[1] Emblematic not only of the characters in
this novel but of all Blais's protagonists, 'ce personnage anonyme
poussant des cris silencieux' also offers a visual representation of her
conception of the novel as a reflection of humanity's suffering in a
hostile world. For Blais, who in a characteristic comment remarked that the *nouveau roman* left her 'presque indifférente',[2] is
uncompromisingly *engagée* in her writing, constantly using the
novel form to highlight what she sees as central human problems
in an implicit affirmation of the genre's power to reflect, through
language and form, a truth external to it. The window through
which Mike stares signals him as observer but also symbolises the
individual's estrangement from the world, simultaneously suggesting and throwing into question the power of narrative to represent
directly the reader's 'reality'.

Born in Québec in 1939, Blais published her first novel in 1959
and attained international fame when *Une Saison dans la vie d'Emmanuel* was awarded both the Prix Médicis and the Prix France-Québec

1. The following abbreviations are used: *BB=La Belle Bête* (Montréal, Pierre Tis-
seyre, 1968); *DS=David Sterne* (Montréal, Stanké, 1981); *I=L'Insoumise* (Montréal,
Stanké, 1979); *L=Le Loup* (Montréal, Stanké, 1980); *LP=Une Liaison parisienne*
(Paris, Robert Lafont, 1976); *NU=Les Nuits de l'Underground* (Montréal, Stanké,
1978); *PA=Manuscrits de Pauline Archange*, 3 vols (Montréal, Stanké, 1981); *S=Une
Saison dans la vie d'Emmanuel* (Montréal, Stanké, 1980); *SV=Le Sourd dans la ville*
(Paris, Gallimard, 1980); *VA=Visions d'Anna* (Paris, Gallimard, 1982).
2. Interview in *Le Soleil*, 18 July 1966.

in 1966. This novel, with its provocative blend of harsh realism and suggestive lyricism, has been translated into thirteen languages and adapted for the cinema, and for many readers it remains her finest achievement. Apparently oblivious, however, to demands that she simply keep writing further seasons in the life of Emmanuel, Blais has not only escaped the image of québécois literature to produce works transcending national frontiers, but has also refused to be pinned to any political stance or narrative style. Each of her works poses different problems for the reader, since each is clearly a response to a particular *gageure*, both thematic and technical. Such a conception of the novel is not without its pitfalls, and Blais has not always escaped the inherent traps. But it is this sense of danger and adventure, this mingling of contemporary themes with the Romantic conviction that it is the artist's duty to bear witness on behalf of the inarticulate and the suffering, that gives such a sense of vitality and immediacy to her writing.

Set in the context of her later work the three novels which preceded *Une Saison*, *La Belle Bête* (1959), *Tête blanche* (1960), and *Le Jour est noir* (1961), may seem, for all their originality, somewhat slight. All three are, to some extent, finger exercises, experiments in the adaptation of myth and poetic prose to convey the central themes of love and jealousy, despair and mortality. Yet it was on the evidence of these three works, together with the poetic short story 'Les voyageurs sacrés', that Edmund Wilson was able to proclaim her 'a true "phenomenon"; [. . .] possibly a genius' and to recognise that 'the idea that man is born to sorrow, the agony of expiation, is at the base of her tragic consciousness'.[3] Certainly *La Belle Bête* already contains in embryo many of Blais's central themes.

Written in a prose of quite remarkable intensity and purity, *La Belle Bête* places six characters in a harsh, rural landscape and, through a careful pattern of repeated images and suggested myths, explores the destructive nature of their relationships. The world Blais creates here is one of stark dichotomies in which beauty, which alone attracts love, is bracketed with stupidity and selfishness, while intelligence, which seems inseparable from ugliness, struggles in vain against universal hostility. Isabelle-Marie, perceptive but physically unattractive, is the first in a long line of protagonists rent in two by a rebellious refusal to submit to accepted values, but it is a rebellion which leads only to destruction. Jealousy is a prime mover in this bleak vision: Isabelle-Marie's jealousy of her beautiful but mentally defective brother Patrice leads her to disfigure him; Pat-

3. Wilson, *O Canada*, pp. 148, 153.

rice's jealousy of his mother's lover, the fatuous Lanz, drives him to ride his horse over Lanz in a murderous rage. Love, the potential redemptive force, is granted only to the beautiful: the disfigured Patrice is abandoned by his formerly adoring mother and Isabelle-Marie's briefly idyllic marriage to a blind boy who believes her to be beautiful comes to an abrupt end when his sight is restored. Isabelle-Marie is not even permitted the saving grace of loving her own daughter, whose ugliness repels her. The work ends with two suicides, that of Isabelle-Marie, who throws herself under a train, and that of Patrice, who drowns himself.

Structurally, the work's sense of inevitability derives partly from the repeated motif of the train, representing on a social level the crude mechanisation which threatens to destroy this rural world and more generally the inescapable tragic force which dominates the characters' lives. The train is a common image in Québec literature for the force that brings the evil of the cities, epitomised here by the dandified artificiality of Lanz, to destroy the tranquillity of rural settlements. The power of the novel, however, depends above all on its echoes of myth and fairy tale. Some of these echoes, taken out of context, are obvious to the point of appearing simplistic: Patrice, mirroring himself in the water in which he is later to drown, is Narcissus; on horseback, he becomes a centaur. Isabelle-Marie's mother Louise recalls the evil stepmother of fairy stories, while the title plays on 'La Belle et la Bête' to suggest the inseparability of the two epithets. More powerful resonances are created by passages such as the following:

> comme étranger à la tragédie qu'il venait de provoquer en jouant, Patrice suivait la canne d'or qui s'enfuyait comme un glaive en fusion, et aussi, ce qu'on n'avait jamais remarqué, la perruque de Lanz qui quittait son crâne. De plus, mêlée aux taches de sang, la barbe fausse de Lanz s'égrenait. Il se décomposait avant de mourir. (*BB*, p. 93)

Transformed into an image of mindless jealousy, Patrice not only kills his victim but decomposes him, strips him of the attributes – wig, beard, cane – which created his personality. In particular, that symbol of sexual and financial power, the gold cane, finds a brief metamorphosis into liquid form before disappearing completely. This image of decomposition is mirrored in the cancerous growth that destroys Louise's beauty, as though the evil and hatred Lanz has brought had assumed physical form. Lucien Goldmann, applying to *La Belle Bête* a rigorously sociological grid, presents it as a totally pessimistic portrayal of French-Canadian society in its death throes, while Philip Stratford sees in it 'a fascination with aberrant, fated evil in human form' and as such 'the baldest, most primitive expression of [her] haunted vision'.[4]

That haunted vision is shaped primarily by Blais's rejection of traditional social values, justified by a close study of family relationships and an exploration of sexual behaviour, and her bleak awareness of the horrors of existence, leading to a preoccupation with death and the temptation of suicide. Moreover, *La Belle Bête*, like Blais's later novels, centres on the *insoumis*, those who refuse to be cowed by the conditions imposed on them by society or by the absurdity of existence.

Perhaps one of the reasons for the popular success of *Une Saison dans la vie d'Emmanuel* is that it places these themes in the recognisable, contemporary world of French Canada and explores them through characters who retain an indomitable, earthy optimism. However one interprets the role of Grand-Mère Antoinette, for instance,[5] she is an undeniably human presence, humorously and compassionately depicted, the figure who both opens and closes the novel. The very first lines present her as massively present:

> Les pieds de Grand-Mère Antoinette dominaient la chambre. Ils étaient là, tranquilles et sournois comme deux bêtes couchées, frémissant à peine dans leurs bottines noires, toujours prêts à se lever: [. . .] des pieds vivants qui gravaient pour toujours dans la mémoire de ceux qui les voyaient une seule fois – l'image sombre de l'autorité et de la patience. (*S*, p. 7)

It is precisely because she combines traditional values (summed up as both authority and patience) with an unquestioning love for her grandchildren that the novel can be read both as a study of the narrow, bigoted and repressed world of the urban poor, especially the poor who have recently left the land and who are corrupted or destroyed by city life, and as a depiction of the power of the mind to overcome such limitations. Although it is possible to read this novel as an allegory of the French-Canadian predicament, to see it as presenting problems unique to Québec would be to deny its universal validity.

In the 'marée d'enfants' (p. 11) four children stand out as possessing an intense individualism, all the more remarkable in that so

---

4. Stratford, *Marie-Claire Blais*, p. 16.
5. 'Une société, un pan de notre histoire', according to M. Brûlé, 'Introduction à l'univers de Marie-Claire Blais', *Revue de l'institut de sociologie*, 42, 3 (1969), p. 510. She is more subtly analysed by M.J. Green as 'an allegorical mother-figure', but one whose reality 'extends beyond such characterization' in 'Redefining the maternal', *Traditionalism, Nationalism, and Feminism* (Westport, Connecticut, Greenwood Press, 1985), p. 128.

many of the others simply reproduce the submission of their elders. There are, for example, daughters referred to merely as 'les grandes A' and 'les petites A' who reflect the terrible fate of the submissive woman in Blais's world:

> les Roberta-Anna-Anita avancèrent comme un lent troupeau de vaches, chacune entourant de ses larges bras une espiègle petite fille aux cheveux tressés, qui, dans quelques années, leur ressemblerait, et qui, comme elles, soumise au labeur, rebelle à l'amour, aurait la beauté familière, la fierté obscure d'un bétail apprivoisé. (p. 45)

Only one of the daughters finds an escape: the aptly named Héloïse, rejected from the convent because of the very intensity of her need for love, finds happiness at last by working in a brothel, convinced throughout that she is a kitchen maid. The narrow, rule-bound, unloving life of the nuns is shown, in a typically Blaisian overturning of accepted values, to be corrupt, while the warmth and kindness that Héloïse craves are provided by the brothel: chastity and degradation are not allowed to retain their conventional, unquestioned associations. Le Septième, merely a number in this mass of children whose mother is too exhausted to love them and whose father is too bound to outmoded and blinkered values to be able to offer them any kind of guidance, seeks escape through alcohol and finds in the figure of a priest a would-be seducer: yet although the final pages of the novel show him convinced that he will end in prison and bearing the mark of his vampiric assailant on his neck, there is a sense of optimism in the sheer power of his individuality. The fate of Pomme, too, is ambiguous: he loses a hand to the mechanised god of the factory where he works, thus symbolising the mutilated victims of urban society, but the final page of the novel shows him leaving hospital under the spring sun in a paragraph which begins with Pomme's despair but ends affirming: 'Emmanuel sortait de la nuit' (p. 175). The disorienting shift from one character to another is a device developed and refined in the later novels.

But it is Jean le Maigre who most seizes the imagination in this novel. He may be dying of tuberculosis, but his sense of humour and his ability to express himself in his creative writing suggest that he symbolises the beginnings of a new québécois identity. The blend of acute observation with the creation of new myths that dominates his 'autobiographie' makes it a clear *mise en abyme* of Blais's own literary endeavour. Consider for instance the following arresting opening to the story of his life: 'Dès ma naissance j'ai eu le front couronné de poux! Un poète, s'écria mon père, dans un élan de joie. Grand-mère, un poète! Ils s'approchèrent de mon berceau et me contemplèrent en

silence. Mon regard brillait déjà d'un feu sombre et tourmenté'
(p. 65). This wry reference to the 'poète maudit' yields to a
perceptive realism, with its ability not only to create the value
system of a child's world but also to find the pithy and evocative
descriptive phrase: 'grâce à un échange de bâtons de réglisse et de
choix de places pour la nuit – *sur le lit, sous le lit ou à travers le lit,*
Pomme était toujours assis près du poêle, son ventre rond respir-
ant au degré de la flamme' (p. 76).

Equally important in terms of Blais's subsequent novels are two
narrative techniques: the attempt to capture the rhythms of colloquial speech and the use of shifting narrative perspectives. The
third-person narrative voice moves almost seamlessly into the first-
person narrative of Jean le Maigre through his autobiography or
through his other writings, notably his portrait of Héloïse, where the
carefully balanced periods contrast sharply with the more abrupt
rhythms of the third-person narrative. In two parallel descriptions of
Héloïse's childhood, three narrative styles, those of the unnamed
narrator, of Jean le Maigre and the spoken words of Grand-Mère
Antoinette, are displayed almost as virtuoso responses to an initial
challenge:

> Dès l'enfance [writes Jean le Maigre], Héloïse a manifesté cet amour de la
> torture. Quand tout le monde trayait les vaches autour d'elle, Héloïse, à
> genoux dans le foin, méditait, les bras en croix, ou bien regardait jaillir
> des gouttes de sang de ses doigts transpercés d'aiguilles. Combien de fois
> ma grand-mère ne lui a-t-elle pas arraché des mains le glaive et la
> couronne d'épines dont elle s'accablait pieusement le vendredi.
> (p. 37)

The spoken intervention of Grand-Mère Antoinette breaks in as
though there were no difference between Jean le Maigre's text and
that of the narrator:

> – C'est assez, disait Grand-Mère Antoinette, qui ne perdait jamais la
> mesure (ou si elle la perdait, croyait-elle, ce n'était que par orgueil).
> Calme-toi un peu.
> Etrangère au travail, dédaigneuse de ses sœurs, qui, vers leur treizième
> année, se transformaient en lourdes filles, et qui, aux champs, travail-
> laient comme des garçons robustes, méprisant ces visages bouffis, Héloïse
> [. . .] choisissait le couvent. (p. 37)

In many ways a work of dark despair at the human predicament, an
evocation of a world dominated by physical and spiritual suffering,
where parental love is stifled by either incomprehension or exhaustion, where those meant to guide and solace the sufferers are more
likely to pervert them, and where the individual is crushed by the

materialism and mechanisation of the age, *Une Saison dans la vie d'Emmanuel* is also an affirmation of the power of love and of art to triumph, however briefly, over the forces of darkness.

The incomprehension of one generation for another, together with the individual's rebellion against the conditions of existence, are also central motifs in *L'Insoumise* (1966) and *David Sterne* (1967). In both works, too, Blais continues to experiment with shifting narrative positions. Each novel charts her attempt to find a narrative style fluid and elastic enough to convey the essential enigma of the individual. *L'Insoumise*, according to Philip Stratford's succinct formulation, labours after its first sixty pages under 'the dead weight of the loss of its most interesting character'[6] and even the generally enthusiastic Françoise Laurent describes it as 'une exploration qui n'est pas arrivée à terme où des personnages sortis du drame bourgeois du dix-neuvième siècle portent leur symbole comme un vêtement enfilé à la hâte pour cacher une médiocre nudité'.[7] Yet the novel is considerably more interesting and inventive than either judgement suggests.

Four voices speak in this work. Madeleine is the *insoumise* of the title, who discovers her son Paul's diary and who finds herself as a result of reading it 'seule et démunie, étrangère à tous ceux qui hier étaient de proches bien-aimés que je chérissais sans le savoir' (*I*, p. 129). Her husband, Rodolphe, appears to be the typically cold, authoritarian father, opening his section of the narrative with a sentence that makes a passing salute to Camus: 'Lorsque Madeleine me téléphona, à mon bureau à l'hôpital, pour m'apprendre la mort de Paul, c'était un beau matin d'automne' (p. 185).

Nevertheless, as his account progresses it becomes clear that he is considerably more complex than Madeleine perceives him to be. Indeed, the central thrust of the novel concerns the characters' inability to interpret each other's deeds and actions. A variation on the manuscript discovered after a suicide, the journal ultimately reveals less about the writer than about its readers, so that the text enables Blais to explore the ways in which readers interpret the written and spoken word. Madeleine sees Paul's account of his affair with a married woman as reproducing an adulterous affair of her own. This awakens emotions of jealousy and guilt which in turn drive her to attempt to come to terms with herself in writing.

6. Stratford, *Marie-Claire Blais*, p. 47.
7. Laurent, *L'Œuvre romanesque de Marie-Claire Blais*, p. 59.

Rodolphe, however, interprets the journal and other written evidence differently, coming to the conclusion that his son was a homosexual. His response to this conviction is firstly jealousy, then a determined endeavour to replace his son with Frédérik, the boy he suspects of being his son's lover. It is Frédérik's own narrative which closes the text on a form of suicide consisting in a willing sacrifice of his own identity and his youth: 'il y a peut-être un certain courage à livrer sa jeunesse à la mort, puisqu'il faut se livrer, de toute façon. Soit à l'amour, à Dieu ou à quelque humaine ambition, pourquoi ne pas se livrer simplement, aujourd'hui, à l'inconnu . . .' (p. 238).

L'Insoumise, then, is a work which, through its narrative structure and through the embedded passages from the journal, stresses the loneliness of the individual, the impossibility of knowing others, the despair of adolescence and the power of the written word to transform its readers, for evil as well as for good.

Similar themes, and a similar shifting narrative viewpoint, are to be found in *David Sterne*. In this novel, Blais depicts adolescents on the fringes of the criminal underworld, experimenting in evil out of a sense of despair at the disintegrating, meaningless world in which they find themselves. Stylistically, the novel ranges from such dry aphorisms as 'Rameau enfantait son suicide, moi, ma déchéance' (*DS*, p. 23) to a form of lyrical free verse:

> Mon Dieu Mon Dieu
> Contre le mur je pleure de dégoût
> Je vomis mon sang mes larmes
> Qu'est-ce que cela peut vous faire à vous
> Les passants s'éloignent
> Et soudain, c'est le silence, on commence à m'oublier,
> Le jeune policier au sourire vainqueur range sa bicyclette
> Tu as assez volé assez couru David Sterne rentre chez toi
> La balade est finie.
>
> (pp. 56–7)

Both thematically and stylistically it points forward to the later novels, but whereas here the bleakness of the vision remains that of nightmare, elsewhere it is transformed into art by a series of deeper resonances.

Childhood and adolescence are again at the heart of a series of three novels published in 1968, 1969 and 1970, *Les Manuscrits de Pauline Archange*.

Here, however, she regains some of the bitter humour and stubborn optimism of *Une Saison dans la vie d'Emmanuel*. Episodic in form, the novels' twin nuclei are the friendships forming Pauline's character and her discovery of herself as a writer. Charting her development from early childhood to the verge of adulthood, the novels set her in an uncompromising and unrelievedly bleak world of poverty and suffering. Illness is a dominant feature of this existence, whether it is accepted with resignation by the sufferers or with rage by the young doctor Germaine Léonard. While most of those Pauline meets regard life, with all its grimness, as something unchangeable, and social and sexual conventions as being beyond question, Germaine offers the young schoolgirl an image of intelligence, emancipation, free thought and intense, barely controlled, passion. There is little doubt that her role in the novel is not merely that of awakening Pauline to other possibilities but most importantly to represent Pauline as adult, a character of singular intensity and complexity, fired by pity and revolt.

In a world of grey depression, grinding poverty, and narrow-minded bigotry, only three forces offer a means of protection: love, the imagination, and *insoumission*. As in some of the earlier novels, *Pauline Archange* offers love as a saving grace, with the very young Pauline desperately longing to love her friend Séraphine forever, since this alone can offer protection against the world's hostility. Yet, as elsewhere in her writing, Blais emphasises that love itself can degenerate into hatred through a fear of vulnerability: if Germaine wants to sever her relationship with Pierre Olivier, it is less for the moral reasons she adduces than through a 'crainte plus cachée et plus orgueilleuse, celle qu'elle avait de le perdre et [. . .] pour cette raison elle préférait rompre dès maintenant des liens qui, dans leur continuité, risquaient [. . .] de se terminer dans l'humiliation ou l'aridité' (*PA*, vol. III, p. 201). It is, however, *insoumission* which most defines Pauline and lends so crisp an edge to her autobiography. Few writers have captured the rebellion of childhood with quite the intensity and simplicity that Blais reveals in passages such as the following:

> même lorsque vous étiez tout petit, livré à ces inquisiteurs, lavé, soigné par eux, survivant aux maladies de l'enfance grâce à leurs soins vigilants, petite chose rebelle agitant ses pieds et ses mains dans son lit à barreaux, hurlant, gémissant sur son absence de liberté, même en ce temps-là, personne ne semblait remarquer votre peine ingrate, votre volonté de vivre seul, sans être touché par des mains incestueuses. (*PA*, vol. I, p. 25)

It is partly this sense of revolt which compels Pauline to write, as an act of rebellion against the conditions of existence: 'ce qui me désolait le plus, c'était de penser qu'il était si long, si dur pour moi de vivre, et que dans un livre, cela ne prendrait que quelques pages, et que sans ces quelques pages, je risquais de n'avoir existé pour personne' (*PA*, vol. I, p. 207).

The conviction that the writer's task is to recapture lost time recurs with similar intensity in the opening pages of the trilogy's final volume: 'Je rêvais tant d'écrire la vie que je croyais parfois la posséder; mais quand je voulais écrire ces choses du passé, elles semblaient disparaître dans la brume' (*PA*, vol. III, p. 13). But the desire to write is also a response to an intense awareness of the beauty of existence, the arrival of spring after the rigours of a Canadian winter or Pauline's growing awareness of the joy of music and painting, a theme Blais develops in her later writing. It is this openness to beauty and joy that allows the series of novels to close on a note of optimism which, far from glossing over the despair at suffering, is revealed as the only possible positive response to that suffering. In the final moments of her autobiography, Pauline catches sight, significantly through a window, of a friend not seen for a long time: 'Il s'approcha de la fenêtre givrée et me sourit. Il y avait dans ce sourire une telle amitié, une si tendre vaillance que je sentis soudain renaître mon courage et, emportant cette vision dans la tempête, je courais en pensant avec joie: C'est lui . . . l'ange de Dürer, je l'ai vu, enfin!' (*PA*, vol. III, p. 205). Structurally, Pauline's narrative has come full circle, from her birth in a tempest to this moment of insight in a storm. Both the cyclical structure and the reference to a work of art which assumes emblematic significance are typical of Blais's later novels.

It is characteristic of Blais's narrative flexibility that, even in a work purporting to be written by the central character in the first person, she introduces passages of internal monologue based on other characters, especially Germaine, together with narrative commentary of a psychological sophistication inaccessible to the young Pauline. There is here less a sense of experimentation with conventions than a refusal to be bound by logic, but it does lay the foundations for what must be seen as more conscious experimentation later on.

In two studies of love published in the 1970s, the elements of experimentation and *gageure* seem to operate less at the level of form than at that of subject. With *Le Loup* (1972) Blais gives us a first-person narrative written, in accordance with the long tradition of the psychological novel, with the aim of reaching deeper understanding: 'j'ai maintenant derrière moi, à l'âge de vingt-quatre ans, un lourd passé sensuel dont je voudrais pénétrer davantage le mystère et la complexité' (*L*, p. 12). The major difference here is that the love which lies at the heart of this novel is that of 'des garçons pour les hommes, des hommes pour les garçons' (p. 11). As elsewhere in her work Blais focuses on those in whom the longing for love is crushed by a fear of accepting love. The narrator, Sébastien, prepares us for such figures from the outset in a passage which, typically, identifies love with suffering:

> j'ai longtemps rencontré, pendant cette recherche de la tendresse masculine, des êtres tourmentés qui ne pouvaient répondre à aucun amour même lorsque dans l'approche de la vieillesse, la lassitude de leur corps, ils venaient humblement se réchauffer en vous, leur cœur demeurait sourd à toute supplication: ces êtres souffraient trop pour se pencher vers la souffrance d'autrui. (p. 11)

In Blais's universe this vast band of those who fear love joins, and is often identical with, the *insoumis*.

To analyse this love Sébastien places a language almost classical in its sobriety at the service of what at first seems an uncompromisingly clear gaze. His lover Eric, for instance, is described in the following way: 'il est comme une ascèse, un chant de douleur qui entre de force dans la chair, et même dans l'intimité ses exigences sont si rigoureuses que pour peindre le plaisir qu'il prend ou qu'il donne, je l'appellerais non pas plaisir mais volupté sévère' (p. 13). Love is presented as a 'dur combat' (p. 90), sensuality becomes a form of nobility (p. 91), the individual appears eternally and irrevocably isolated, an 'être autonome, définitivement seul jusqu'à la mort' (p. 93). Indeed, this awareness of solitude, piercing the young Sébastien with such intensity that he all but faints, provides the key not only to his various lovers but also to Sébastien himself.

As in all confessional novels we are, of course, being manipulated by the privileged status granted the first-person narrative. Sébastien subtly portrays himself as saint, constantly offering love to all in need, providing redemption, charity, nourishment. Yet, apparently incapable of fidelity, he transforms this nourishment into 'ce poison de la jalousie' (p. 223) making his lovers confront his dreams of perfect harmony with the cry: 'quel malheur de vous avoir connu!' (p. 242). Even the concluding passage, with its admission that his life may merely have been 'une approche de plusieurs âmes qui n'étaient que blessées et que je laisse mourantes' (p. 243), is imbued with the kind of irony that defies complete deconstruction: 'il est possible aussi qu'un amour donné sans mesure, même très mal donné, ne soit pas complètement perdu; si cette goutte de sang avait un jour le pouvoir d'abreuver celui qui m'a lié à lui par sa soif et par sa souffrance, alors, oui, j'aimerais y destiner encore ma vie' (p. 243). A study of love and jealousy which gains much of its resonance from the use of Christian vocabulary and imagery, *Le Loup* remains – no doubt deliberately – cerebral and polemical, a coolly intellectual survey. *Les Nuits de l'Underground*, published in 1978, is a very different matter.

Here, Blais chooses to depict relationships between women for whom '[la] patrie est un lieu où il n'y a que des femmes' (p. 69). Written in the third person and making frequent allusions to works of pictorial art, *Les Nuits de l'Underground*, for all its occasional *temps faibles* and for all its indebtedness to Proust, has a richness and a warmth, as well as a sense of the complexity and variety of human relationships, which place it with the best of lesbian novels. Moreover, its constantly shifting linguistic registers, from the colloquial to the highly formalised, from metropolitan French, through québécois dialect, to a cosmopolitan blend of German and American-English, make it, in Françoise Laurent's phrase, an image of the 'spectre linguistique du Québec'.[8]

The opening passages are particularly arresting, raising the central question of Lali's identity and nature, establishing and justifying the tissue of artistic references, and creating a series of powerful and seductive rhythms:

l'amour de Geneviève Aurès pour Lali Dorman naquit comme une passion pour une œuvre d'art. Sculpteur, Geneviève éprouvait déjà, pour le visage humain, une curiosité profonde; cet amour de l'art lui avait fait parcourir de nombreux pays, et elle préparait une exposition au Canada, et une autre à Paris, lorsqu'elle vit pour la première fois, dans les chaudes ténèbres d'un bar, par une nuit d'hiver, ce visage dont elle s'éprit peu à peu, croyant découvrir dans ces traits aveugles les plus pures expressions, austères jusqu'à la morosité parfois, de la peinture flamande. Longtemps, elle ne sut le nom de l'être qui portait un tel visage. (p. 9)

While Geneviève struggles to accept her lesbian nature, Lali affirms hers unflinchingly: 'elle était de ceux qui depuis longtemps assument le choix d'une sensualité prisonnière des lois du monde, [. . .] les radieux libérateurs de la race fière qu'ils représentent aujourd'hui' (p. 15). Geneviève's other major love affair, with the Parisian Françoise, is likewise explored in terms of an individual's acceptance of her sexual personality. Françoise, who in the past suppressed her love of women and accepted traditional marriage instead, is shown

8. Ibid., p. 158.

as being just as powerful and free as Lali. Despite her 'apparence d'une grande enfant docile prête à toutes les soumissions' she has 'le pouvoir de mettre toute son imagination dans sa vie, de transformer même un mariage malheureux en un festin plus compatible à ses désirs' (p. 209).

If these three central characters allow Blais to suggest some of the complexity of lesbian love, the women who gather in the bar, the *Underground* of the title, offer a microcosm of interrelationships, 'tout un monde complexe et délicat' (p. 262), as Blais puts it. This world is set firmly into a social context by a question at the opening of the novel and a statement at its close: the initial question – 'mais une femme pouvait-elle toujours vivre seule, lorsque tout, en elle, l'isolait des lois sociales?' (p. 10) – finds its counterpart in the affirmation of 'un amour dont l'existence menaçait le monde masculin et ses lois' (p. 262). Lesbianism is presented here as an image of both social and metaphysical revolt, at once part of a particular historical moment (the anti-feminism of québécois society until the last few decades is notorious) and symbolic of forms of *insoumission* which have nothing to do with time or gender.

Nevertheless, rather than being centred uniquely on lesbian relations, the novel explores in general terms the nature of desire and the mechanisms of seduction. Participating in a long tradition of studies of love, it recalls, perhaps inescapably, certain aspects of *A la recherche du temps perdu*, particularly in some of its formulations and in the tendency of its central character to adapt the world to conform to works of art. Proust's insistence that in the act of possession one possesses nothing, for instance, finds its echo in Geneviève's awareness that 'au fond de toute conscience, même enfiévrée par le plaisir d'aimer, une certitude est là qui dit: "Non, on ne possède personne, et personne ne peut te posséder"' (p. 232), an awareness rendered particularly poignant for her by the fact that Françoise is gravely ill. As one could well expect, in her evocation of jealousy, Blais specifically mentions Proust, demanding that we read her study with its intertext clearly in mind: 'elle imaginait ce passé de Françoise, et la fluidité de ce déluge d'images qu'elle ne pouvait pas atteindre ni capturer lui causait une méchante douleur, telle cette jalousie de Proust imaginant les infidélités d'Albertine, auprès de sa constellation d'amies' (p. 208).

And like Swann or Marcel, Geneviève attempts to instil some meaning into her suffering by seeing it 'à travers l'allégorie tragique d'une œuvre d'art' (p. 264). However important the dialogue thus established with Proust and the resonances set off by it, Blais draws also on others in the tradition of studies of love. Embedded in her long, flexible sentences can be found formulations recalling the pithiness of Stendhal in *De l'amour*. If, for example, Geneviève is disturbed by the photo of Françoise's husband, it is, we are told, because 'ceux qui nous précèdent nous semblent toujours les plus forts' (p. 208). And, as so often in her writing, Blais also incorporates echoes of her own novels, intensifying a vision of the world which remains largely constant within the variety of narrative techniques employed. Once again, for instance, the reader is made aware of the intimate relationship Blais perceives between love and violence, desire and destruction: 'car la vie des couples est faite de la même violence que la vie elle-même et tout ce qui sommeille ou s'agite entre deux êtres n'est souvent connu que d'eux seuls qui le subissent' (p. 72). In this 'comédie sacrée de la passion' (p. 126) the strongest passion is without doubt that of the narrative voice for words: long sinuous sentences in finely wrought prose, epigrammatic formulations, polyglottal dialogues, colloquial discourse are all infused with a delighted and infectious fascination with language.[9]

Chronologically between these two explorations of homosexual love there appeared in 1976 the novel *Une Liaison parisienne*, which deals mainly with heterosexual relationships. It seems in narratological terms a response to the *gageure* of writing a novel which is completely traditional both in treatment and in the central plot, a triangular relationship experienced by a naïve hero. To some extent, too, it is a *roman-à-clef*,[10] a thinly-veiled artistic version of a relationship Blais herself experienced. The work is marred by various weaknesses, not least in the presentation of the two central characters, the aptly named Mathieu Lelièvre and the obviously caricatural Mme d'Argenti. Since their relationship never appears based on more than sensual gratification, it is difficult to see Mathieu's distress at its conclusion as anything more profound than a fit of pique at finding another preferred to him. Nevertheless, it does offer clues to a deeper reading of other of her novels.

First, although the title suggests both sexual and geographical

---

9. This delight in language is also very much present in *Un Joualonais, sa joualonie* (1973), a work written entirely in the form of a highly colloquial internal monologue. The most comic of all Blais's works, it is a light-hearted romp through typical Blaisian themes and is of interest mainly for the sheer imaginative power of its dialogue. To discuss it in adequate detail would require more space than is available here.

10. See Mary Meigs, *Lily Briscoe, a self-portrait* (Vancouver, 1981).

links between the Canadian protagonist and 'le pays tant vénéré depuis son plus jeune âge' (*LP*, p. 9), the work articulates a major theme Blais shares with many of her compatriots, that of alienation. Lelièvre's veneration of France arouses the scorn of his Canadian comrades, and his lack of knowledge of French social customs as well as his accent and dialect make him appear crude and un-civilised to the French. This specific form of alienation is metonymic here for metaphysical estrangement and particularly for modern mankind's isolation in the city, but whereas in other of her novels this alienation is seen as essentially tragic, here it appears primarily as comic.

Since her central character is a writer, Blais is also able to explore various literary ideas within the context of the novel itself, opening up the kind of self-reflexivity that Huysmans, Proust and Gide, to mention only three, have accustomed us to expect. Her narrative structures, moreover, enable her to undercut, through subtly suggested irony, many of Lelièvre's pronouncements. This is, for instance, the effect of the alternation of narrative voice and direct discourse in the following passage:

> comme il avait dit à Pierre-Henri Lajeunesse, il était 'avant tout écrivain, donc un observateur' et ce rôle, si théorique qu'il fût, exigeait de lui une attention de chaque instant, 'la rigueur de l'analyse et l'abandon de celui qui aime l'expérience'. 'N'est-ce pas dangereux de choisir les deux à la fois?' dit Pierre-Henri Lajeunesse, mais Mathieu répliqua que malgré son ignorance il avait l'impression 'd'être un sage au milieu des fous' et que sa vigilance rationnelle le sauverait toujours de tout péril. Pierre-Henri Lajeunesse sourit à son ami avec hauteur: – C'est ce qui arrive, dit-il, quand on n'a aucune imagination, comme toi, on choisit la raison et on se fracasse les côtes plus qu'un autre! (p. 12)

Yet, as in Gide's *Les Faux-Monnayeurs*, one cannot help suspecting that the combination of verbal and dramatic irony ranged against the author-persona may well be a form of protection of the author. Certainly the blend of emotion and analysis, of lucidity and sensual response, posited here by Lelièvre closely resembles Blais's own.

A more complex game of mirrors is provided by Lelièvre's reading of one of Mme d'Argenti's novels, in which the fictional novelist herself appears, but in disguise, to proclaim in highly clichéd terms: '"Ma voix vient d'un autre monde, d'un lieu sans conscience, d'une terre sourde à tout appel de pitié"' (p. 24). As a result reader and writer become as one, both 'surgissant ensemble, en une seule voix' (p. 24), as Lelièvre suggests, in an expression which accords closely to Blais's own methods in bringing the reader into the text. Yet, again, this union of reader and writer is abruptly undercut by an ironic comment on the expression 'terre sourde à tout appel de pitié': 'même si, pour Mathieu Lelièvre, le sens de cette phrase demeurait obscur' (p. 24). Because of the ironic treatment of the central character, the concluding paragraph of the novel leaves us uncertain as to whether we should condemn him for considering literature as Emma Bovary does or let him, for all his naïvety, represent Marie-Claire Blais refusing to countenance an unbridgeable gulf between literature and reality:

> Mathieu s'envola cette nuit-là vers son pays en songeant qu'il avait vécu 'une histoire comme dans un livre', il avait maintenant refermé le livre troublant: Madame d'Argenti, en ce sens, était morte, il ne pourrait la faire survivre que par la littérature, et encore on lui dirait 'que les romans ne sont pas comme la vie . . .' (p. 175)

Lelièvre's naïvety is evident again in one further aspect of the way in which we respond to novels, for he finds himself forced to ask the hoary old question: 'Confondait-il l'écrivain et son œuvre, jumeaux spirituels qui sont bien souvent [. . .] des antithèses physiques?' (*LP*, p. 60). This kind of confusion, moreover, extends more directly into his day-to-day existence, leading to the following assertion: 'N'était-ce pas qu'à Paris que l'on rencontrait, pour son malheur, un caractère de Balzac dans son lit, et pour son bonheur, un fragment du Temps Perdu dans un Café moderne réchauffant encore dans son antre quelque atmosphère ancienne?' (p. 163).

Françoise Laurent claims that what saves *Une Liaison parisienne* from being 'une vaine errance dans les sentiers vengeurs de l'autobiographie'[11] is the compassion Lelièvre reveals for the poor and oppressed of Paris. We may well feel, however, that this sympathy, however important it may be for Blais, is too loosely associated with the central themes of the novel to appear as anything other than a side issue, marginalised by the novelist's personal involvement with this particular text, and that it is the manipulation of irony and the flashes of humour which are Blais's greatest achievements in an otherwise rather undistinguished work.

With two further novels, written in tandem but published three years apart, *Le Sourd dans la ville* (1979) and *Visions d'Anna* (1982), Marie-Claire Blais finds an ideal medium for the thematic and psychoanalytic explorations that dominate all her work. Her supple, extremely long sentences move seamlessly from one mind to

11. Laurent, *L'Œuvre romanesque de Marie-Claire Blais*, p. 151.

another, creating an admirable vehicle for conveying her image of the fragmented human psyche in a destructive modern world. Her constantly shifting perspectives not only enact the fragility of human relationships but also create a constant dialogue, or perhaps more accurately, a polyphonic discourse in which the isolation of the individual is still poignantly emphasised but where the anger and revolt of her *insoumis[es]* are transformed from egotism by an overriding sense of compassion. This kind of dialogue, and the way in which Blais's narrative voice acts both to reveal the character's thoughts and to prevent a complete identification of narrator and character, can be illustrated by the opening lines of *Visions d'Anna*:

> Il faisait ni beau, ni froid, dans le cœur d'Anna, ni frais ou brûlant, c'était le vide, pensait-elle, pur et tranquille, une profondeur intacle qu'ils ne pouvaient même imaginer, ils étaient ces autres qui la laissaient errer ainsi, sans but, sans raison, parfois, ils lui souriaient avec humour, l'effleuraient de leur dérisoire affection, puis ils revenaient à eux-mêmes, à leurs préoccupations d'adultes, ne lui demandant plus ce qu'elle ressentait et pensait, il y avait longtemps déjà qu'ils n'osaient plus rien lui demander, car dans leur découragement, ils avaient peut-être décidé eux aussi qu'elle était entièrement libre. (p. 9)

Equally important in establishing the relationships between narrative voice, reader and fictional entities is the consistent use of the third person, creating a narrative focus which denies autonomy to the characters and constantly reminds us of their alterity. The central question of many *nouveaux romans* remains pertinent here: who speaks? Narratologically, this passage slips from narrator's discourse ('Il faisait ni beau, ni froid, dans le cœur d'Anna') to *style indirect libre* or what Dorrit Cohn would call narrated discourse[12] ('il y avait longtemps déjà qu'ils n'osaient plus rien lui demander') to grey areas that cannot easily be attributed to any particular voice. One of the results of this slippage is a sense of aimlessness, of loss of reason in a world overpopulated and threatened by ecological disasters and nuclear war, a world in which adolescents can see no purpose. The danger that this aimlessness might make the novel itself seem to lack direction is overcome through a series of structural devices, especially an intricate patterning of repeated phrases and metaphors.

Le Sourd dans la ville presents the reader with a fugal structure in which voices and lives weave in and out of each other, each exploring in a different way a question which may be that put by Gloria – 'le rôle du sexe dans la vie, qu'est-ce que c'est hein?' (*SV*, p. 14) – or

---

12. See D. Cohn, *Transparent Minds* (Princeton, N.J., Princeton University Press, 1978).

that of Florence – 'quel homme est donc libre en ce monde?' (p. 41) – or which may be a more general question, intimated through intertextual reference rather than directly expressed, a question concerning the purpose of existence. The conceptual link between the wide array of characters is that of suffering physical, psychological or moral; each, as Florence puts it, appears as 'une sublime figure de la douleur de vivre' (pp. 32–3). A further link is provided by the constant presence of a connecting narrational focus created by the uncharacterised narrator. Mike, the *sourd* of the title, suffers from a cancer which is slowly eating away his skull, but in a traditionally Romantic overturning of physical and spiritual, he is the one who is most sensitive to the suffering of others, most able to hear their unspoken cries of despair and loneliness. Moreover, through him Blais explores, as she did in *La Belle Bête* with the character Louise, the symbolism of cancer where individuals are destroyed by internal forces which are a part of them but over which they have no control.

Mike's mother, Gloria, is wholly at the mercy of sexual appetites which lead her to link her life with brutish criminals for whom she is merely an object. Here, too, Blais uses Mike to subvert conventional images, for just as in *Une Saison dans la vie d'Emmanuel* the prostitute and the saint become indistinguishable one from the other: 'Gloria se transformait la nuit pour son fils en une image de crucifixion sévère, la Mère de la Douleur, c'était elle' (p. 22).

Gloria's counterpart, and the person to whom she first asks the question concerning the 'rôle du sexe dans la vie', is Judith Langenais, known as Judith Lange. Judith, too, sees Gloria as a victim, 'une victime de tous ces paradis impulsifs que nous créons à notre image' (p. 65). A philosophy teacher enraged at the problems of the human race, Judith is faced with the fact that philosophy can provide so few answers to the predicaments of modern life, and what answers it does provide she is unable to convey to her pupils: 'Judith reprit son livre, Descartes, Descartes, et eux ne l'écoutaient pas, ils fixaient leurs yeux sur cette branche de lilas, à la fenêtre' (p. 28). Seduced by the beauty of the world, Judith's pupils teach her that 'il n'y avait de philosophie sainte que dans la vie' (p. 29; see also p. 33). Indeed, as we shall see, images of the natural world have an unusually important place in this novel compared with other Blais texts. Judith is above all a force for redemption, as her nickname (L'Ange) rather obviously suggests, another reworking of Dürer's angel of melancholy, but a force which remains powerless against despair and prejudice.

This prejudice is seen particularly in the character of Judith's mother, a bourgeois housewife sharply contrasted with Gloria, starved for love but incapable of accepting it when Judith offers it, for Judith not only runs counter to Mme Langenais's image of womanhood, but also offers her an individuality she has submerged in her role of wife, since Judith alone refers to her by her given name, Joséphine. Yet, as the novel progresses, Mme Langenais gradually moves towards a heightened awareness of herself as an individual, and begins to break down the carapace of conventions she has unhesitatingly accepted. Through Judith, therefore, in a reassessment of the traditional relationships between mother and daughter, Joséphine Langenais perceives a truth based on love and individual values, to which the a priori judgements of society had previously blinded her.

Whereas Judith seeks truth and her mother comes to question conventions, Mike's older sisters each represent a form of escape. Berthe, terrified by her mother's mindless promiscuity, tries to deny her own physical personality and devotes all her energies to intellectual pursuits in an existence of extreme loneliness bereft of ambition and purpose: 'rien', she tells us, 'n'était plus pénible que d'être jeune et accablé d'une vie dont on ne savait que faire, sinon de l'éteindre dans un idéal mesquin, étroit' (p. 101). Her terror of her own sexuality makes it impossible for her to envisage any kind of relationship with others: 'la moindre libation d'elle-même lui semblait un cauchemar, même sourire, tendre la main, rien, elle ne pouvait pas' (p. 102). Even her studies offer no real substitute: 'ces livres [. . .] ne signifiaient rien pour elle, sinon la morne explosion sonore de son silence intérieur' (p. 106). The *métaphore filée* of deafness and silence is thus woven into Berthe's drab existence, just as the word *explosion* points to the gun shot that brings the novel to a close. The sterility of Berthe's choice is paralleled by her sister Lucia's flight from reality through drugs and sex, a flight Blais explores at more length in *Visions d'Anna*.

Much of *Le Sourd dans la ville* centres on Florence Gray, who epitomises the problem of women who allow their identity to become incorporated in that of their husband. Florence, who at one point identifies herself as 'la femme du doctor Gray', is the *être secondaire* who suddenly discovers not only that 'les autres [. . .] c'est un autre livre [. . .] dont les mots sont absents' (p. 59) but also that those 'autres' deny her the possibility of expressing herself as a woman: if at Chartres life is depicted as the gift of a man rather than a woman it is because 'les bâtisseurs qui étaient des hommes, bâtissaient la vie selon une architecture, un prolongement masculins' (p. 67). It is this failure to create an identity of her own that leads Florence inexorably, inescapably to the suicide that brings the novel to its abrupt end.

The resonance of the novel is a product partly of the contrapuntal dialogue set up by these separate voices as they weave their variations on the basic themes of loneliness and suffering, and partly of the numerous references to other works of art. These references culminate in Florence's realisation that Mike and Gloria are 'à l'image de ces œuvres d'art qu'elle avait admirées autrefois dans les musées, sans reconnaître alors, entre l'œuvre d'art et la vie, cette tragédie de l'existence qui liait l'une à l'autre, les rendait inséparables' (p. 196). Throughout the novel's long meditation on death and love, works of art – paintings, music, novels – act as crystallisations, embedding in the text mirrors which not only reflect Blais's primary themes but also set up chains of refracted images. One of the central figures is Edvard Munch,[13] whose dark, tormented depictions of individuals equally threatened by death and their own sexual drives provide a perfect counterfoil for Blais's own vision. Mike enters the novel mirrored by Munch's 'The Scream', while Gloria participates in the ambiguity of Munch's vision of the Madonna: 'on ne savait si le modèle du peintre, avec sa forme fortement agrandie contre le mur sombre de la nuit, si elle était une figure du plaisir ou la vaillante représentation d'une madone sans mystère' (p. 82).

Attitudes and responses also evoke parallels with Munch's art: 'cet avenir, ou ce présent, on préférait le voir venir de dos, comme les trois jeunes filles sur le pont, de Munch, entourées d'une rivière de feu' (p. 141). These references, which articulate Munch's work according to Blais's own code, lend particular force to her claim that the individual always extracts from art what is most central to his own needs and personality: 'l'art dépassait sans doute nos plus lugubres tragédies, pensait Florence, car si on se souvenait peu ou vaguement du visage de Munch, on ne pouvait oublier cette courbe mélancolique qu'il avait révélée d'un profil d'enfant, lequel jamais plus ne se tournerait vers nous' (p. 71). Indeed, the image of the artist, and particularly the artist's task of giving expression, however transient, to pain as a powerful protest against the suffering of humanity, is central to this study of the interrelationship of art and death. The dialogue set up here, not only among the characters of the novel, but also between them and a variety of artists, of whom Munch is the supreme example, has as one of its purposes the desire to set up resonances through time. This is particularly obvious in the

---

13. For a detailed treatment of this theme, see Stephens, 'Polarisation and stereotype'.

following quotation, where Florence realises that the prime concern of artists such as Lautrec and Degas is to show the unchanging nature of the human lot:

> quand l'art faisait ainsi violence à la vie, quand il allait la chercher dans les entrailles de la terre, c'est le créateur, l'artiste qui devait payer et souffrir pour cette transparence, car les prostituées de Lautrec, comme les buveurs d'absinthe de Degas, c'était l'évocation transparente d'une race de femmes et d'hommes qui allaient subir nos épreuves, celles de notre temps, des victimes, comme nous, d'une apocalypse sociale et indivi-duelle. (p. 101)

This dialogue extends to other writers and to musicians as well as to painters. Kafka's bleak depiction of a threatening, nightmarish existence, for instance, is inscribed in filigree behind Blais's own by the following statement, 'Kafka avait révélé au monde les couches souterraines de ce sol sur lequel nous croyions danser à l'aise' (p. 141), as is Dostoevsky's vision of man as both sentimental and evil. But what Blais is eager to emphasise about both writing and painting – and this bears on our understanding of how she perceives her novels affecting her readers – is that they are not immutable, with a meaning entirely graspable once they are completed, but rather they attain their force only through time and only when contemplated by a receptive mind, represented here by that of Florence on the point of suicide. Indeed, Florence as reader is an image Blais gives us near the beginning of the novel when she describes her carrying a case filled with old letters, and the link between reading and death is clarified by a statement attributable either to Judith or to the narrative voice: 'on eût dit que ce poids de mots écrits et livrés, pendant toute une vie, l'aiderait à partir' (p. 29). Where the traditional image is of the suicide leaving behind a document to be read as a kind of *voix d'outre-tombe*, Florence prepares for death by contemplating the art of others. The dialogue set up in *Le Sourd dans la ville*, therefore, constantly invites the participation of an implied reader.

This realisation, to which Florence's long meditation on art has gradually led, also means that the dialogue takes place through time: writing, she insists, is prophetic, only slowly gathering the momentum it needs to 'frapper l'inconsistant bavardage de son épée muette' (p. 141). Memory, therefore, is a central theme, as well as being of structural importance, for the movement through past and present in the novel is largely a result of the pulse of Florence's memory. Both creative and destructive, prisoner and warder, 'la mémoire était un instrument de possession, un être emmuré mais qui avait pour son jeu de tortures tous les pouvoirs, et de nous posséder, et de posséder encore les autres, par le souvenir' (p. 156). It is of course supremely ironic that this dialogue, between characters, through time, with artists and above all with death, should take place under the title *Le Sourd dans la ville*, for all these debates are internalised, serving merely to deepen the individual's utter isolation. That isolation is further intensified, moreover, by the fact that Blais emphasises the alterity of these voices by means of inserting into the French discourse phrases of American English.

Blais employs a further device, in addition to the artistic resonances, to prevent this internalised debate from appearing too abstract and to strengthen the novel's structure by a delicate architecture of repetition: the creation of symbolic landscapes. Foremost among these are the hot desert lands to which Gloria promises to take Mike and where he believes he will be cured. The elements of this landscape – 'le cactus, l'indigo bush qui guérit, la lavande et le miel' (p. 163: see also p. 81) – are repeated to create a 'mélodie' in Mike's mind, yet both he and the reader are aware that this landscape is in fact the 'paysage absolu de la mort' (p. 164). Florence, too, is associated with various landscape images. There is, for instance, an unattainable 'espace inoccupé, fait pour être peuplé, malgré tout, par l'intégrité de ses plus simples désirs' (p. 44), but more typical of Florence's despair is the 'immensité désertique [. . .] sans horizon, la sensation d'avancer ou de reculer vers ces montagnes de givre est une sensation neutre, indifférente' (p. 53). In this desert, created by absence, separation and death (p. 76), Judith Lange appears as 'le soleil d'été' (p. 56), revealing to us, as do the 'montagnes de givre', that this is a Munchian desert of frozen wastes, not the hot desert of Mike's dreams. Moreover, the two repeated motifs, that of Munch's art and that of Florence's spiritual landscapes, unite in the final passages when Florence realises that 'elle était aujourd'hui dans cette Agonie de Münch sur laquelle descendait le brouillard incandescent et froid' (p. 197).

The existential anguish of *Le Sourd dans la ville*, therefore, is expressed in terms both of contemporary social issues and of timeless human predicaments and given particular intensity by the references to works of art, by the evocation of spiritual landscapes and by the circular patterning of the structure, where, between the opening images of Mike observing life and the final ones of Florence closing her eyes in death, repeated phrases and images combine to create an impression of tragic inevitability.

With *Visions d'Anna* Blais is dealing with much younger central characters facing the difficulties of adolescence, 'ce long jour sans sommeil qu'on appelait une vie' (*VA*, p. 10), using the focus of what one of her characters, a writer, calls 'le seul sujet d'un romancier aujourd'hui [. . .], la survie de l'espèce' (p. 15). We are presented with what seems to be a single day in Anna's existence, filled with the kaleidoscopic visions produced by drugs and memory, and leading to Anna's final choice between 'drifting' and being 'de retour', two terms which recur as leitmotifs throughout the novel. Woven into Anna's visions are those of her younger friend Michelle, whose description of the fugue she wants to write offers a synesthetic *mise en abyme* of the novel's structure:

> Michelle écrirait une fugue wagnérienne dans laquelle elle raconterait la confusion de sa vie, sa fièvre, son inquiétude, ses larmes sèches seraient sonores comme des cloches, on ne dirait pas 'c'est une fugue comme toutes les fugues' mais quel chaos rutilant et dur, aux sons des cloches se mêlent l'écho des bombes et les cris de ceux dont les larmes ont e.p´té brûlées. (p. 158)

As in *Le Sourd dans la ville*, voices and themes surface, disappear, reappear, but here the linking theme is the need for love.

Variations on Anna's own need for love are provided by a range of further voices. Her mother, Raymonde, is a social worker who not only finds that the problems she encounters in her work with delinquent and disturbed children are repeated in her own daughter, but also feels that Anna's predicament may well be a response to her meetings with those children. Her resultant sense of guilt is exacerbated by a conviction that the social structures against which these delinquent girls fight are the creation of adult males and thus produce a world from which they are estranged so that they choose instead to 'drift': 'la liberté de *drifter*, pensait Anna, c'était aussi l'émotion de l'errance, loin du pays étranger, de la maison étrangère, à l'aube, au soleil couchant' (p. 80). The theme of being an outsider in one's own land is central to Blais, as it is to many French-Canadian writers, and intimately connected with the feminism of her vision. As so often in her writing, Blais sets up here a dialogue with others of her own novels: like Lucia in *Le Sourd dans la ville* Anna seeks emotional fulfilment in the escapism of drugs – 'c'était cela, *drifting away*, se livrer à l'extase de l'instant' (p. 44) – but comes to realise that this is 'le chemin secret vers l'épouvante' (*SV*, p. 137). Equally, through the voice of Raymonde, Blais continues the exploration of the relationship between philosophy and existence that she embarks on with Judith Lange. In a discussion with her daughter, Raymonde is forced to acknowledge the dichotomy between theory and practice: 'les mots qui sortaient de la bouche d'Anna étaient lucides, ils évoquaient cette philosophie de l'existence que Raymonde avait autrefois embrassée d'un seul élan dans les œuvres de Sartre, Camus, ces œuvres avaient exalté l'imagination de Raymonde quand les réflexions de sa fille la désolaient' (*VA*, p. 22). And despite Raymonde's lucid acceptance of her daughter's alterity, she faces the despair of realising that 'Anna vivait ailleurs, loin d'elle, du moins, dans la transparence d'un univers qui lui était étranger' (p. 23).

Despite the novel's title, its focus oscillates between Anna and her friend Michelle, together with the network of relationships surrounding them. Michelle, believing herself unloved, allows her musical gifts to lie fallow and turns instead partly to drugs and partly to lavishing her love on society's outcasts, tramps whom she tries to bring into the house or whose dereliction she attempts to share by sleeping outside. More than anything else, Michelle's voice explores 'cette action béante qui était la préparation de la vie, plus que la vie elle-même, elle comprenait soudain que la vie elle-même n'avait jamais eu lieu, que tous tentaient de la modeler, de la refaire à leur image, quand il n'était pas sûr, pensait-elle, qu'elle fût vraiment sortie du néant' (p. 75). If she does finally manage to escape from the void, it is not through the help of her parents, who see her as 'un cas pour le psychiatre' (p. 75), but through the unquestioning love of her sister Liliane. Presented in one of those sharply-focused vignettes at which Blais excels (p. 112), Liliane, like Raymonde, calmly and unflinchingly places humanity above society, the individual above convention. Her lesbianism affronts 'les sexologues qui n'admettaient qu'une seule forme de la sexualité, condamnant toute différence comme l'eût fait la société' (p. 131), while her participation in an ecological group – 'si elles ne pensaient pas à sauver le planète, qui le ferait à leur place?' (p. 104) – is a quiet condemnation of 'une négligence universelle qui venait de s'abattre sur chacun' (p. 110). In Blais's sharply polarised world this concern is also a sign of feminine protection of an environment plundered by men: the ecological meeting is described as 'encore une réunion où il n'y aura que des femmes' (p. 114).

The novel charts a passage from pessimism and, drifting to a form of clear-sighted optimism which leads to Raymonde's final realisation that Anna is at last truly 'de retour', provides an overall structure for these varied responses. What makes this passage possible is the gradual awareness that a sense of optimism can be united with an awareness of despair and suffering. Blais indicates through this novel that imagination can provide a momentary key to the problem, for Anna realises that 'l'anarchie de l'imagination triomphait pour un instant des valeurs vides de la société' (p. 70), but more weight is placed on the need for warmth and compassion in human relationships, exemplified by Liliane's love for Michelle and Raymonde's for Anna. Moreover, Blais explores these relationships in the novel partly through a close study of the minor causes of ephemeral emotions and sentiments – consider, for example, the following evocation of affection on Liliane's part and jealousy and fear on her mother's: 'Liliane regardait sa mère tout en effleurant la joue de Michelle, ce petit creux de ses joues, disait-elle, qu'il faudrait gonfler, arrondir, du bout de ses doigts forts et carrés, et Guislaine avait fermé les yeux comme si cet effleurement machinal l'eût blessée' (p. 112) – and partly through psychological studies of the characters. These studies tend to come late in the novel, after our interest in the relevant character is aroused, as though Blais is attempting a mimetic representation of the way in which relationships develop in life. Thus, it is only after seeing Guislaine overwhelmed by doubts and incapable of expressing and accepting love in her relationships with her daughters that we are told that she had been a 'boursière pauvre' and finds herself 'hantée par tous les doutes qui perturbaient sa fille, mais il ne fallait pas se trahir auprès d'eux' (p. 117). The masculine pronoun provides a further clue here: Guislaine, like Florence, is shaped by and for the vision of the male other, whereas Liliane accepts responsibility for her own individuality.

Perhaps one of the most rewarding ways of reading *Visions d'Anna* is to see it as part of the tradition of novels of education, particularly those which deal with the rites of passage from adolescence to adulthood. Seen in this focus the novel opens up a series of productive dialogues and reveals itself as an attempt – at least in part – to find a structural and thematic solution to the problem of adapting this tradition to the realities of modern existence.

Those realities lie at the heart of Blais's most recent, and arguably least successful novel, *Pierre: La Guerre du printemps 81*, first published in 1984. Her decision to republish it in a revised form in 1986 points, perhaps, to her own uneasiness about the work, although most of her revisions are stylistic. In this novel, written in the first person, the eponymous hero joins a gang of motorcyclists and participates in a wave of violence and eroticism. This attempt to explore the fascist mentality and to project a male vision of the world, where woman – here represented by the enigmatic Stone – is a communal possession for physical pleasure, is, to my mind, vitiated by a range of weaknesses. The desire to depict and the longing to polemicise are never successfully united, the descriptions of violence and sexual intercourse remain so clinical as to be more than faintly embarrassing, and perhaps most serious of all, we are at no point convinced that such a character would choose to communicate with the outsider the reader is forced to remain, since the structure of the novel constantly alienates us. Here the *gageure* of entering a violent male mind and presenting his discourse in the first person proves too great a problem for Blais to handle successfully. Although any study of her novels cannot pass over it in complete silence, I would argue that what interest it has lies more in the extent to which it shows the dangers of her kind of experimentation with a wide range of subject matter than in any intrinsic value, and that it adds little to her achievement.

Despite the considerable variety of subject matter and narrative technique encountered in Blais's writing, certain constants are clearly detectable: to the horrors of existence she opposes the refusal of individuals to be crushed; images of suicide are confronted with examples of determined but clear-sighted hope; metaphors of drifting and cruising find a counterpart in those of stability and being 'de retour'. Her fascination with language, with its possibilities and its misfires, together with an apparently unquenchable desire to attempt different styles and an undeniable ability to handle both lyricism and classical concision, makes her a writer of great eloquence but equally leads her into the temptation to state rather than suggest, to tell rather than persuade. The *nouveaux romanciers* have taught us to expect novelists to reveal considerable critical sophistication, a fascination with technicalities, a tendency to see the genre as an infinitely adjustable arena for meticulously created puzzles. Blais demands and deserves a different response. Her experimentation is far more instinctive than intellectual, born less of a desire to explore the novel's potential than of a need to express the world's despair. One can prefer the controlled, delimited, cerebral world of the *nouveau roman*; one can lament Blais's occasional failure to recognise her own limitations and to play to her strengths; but one cannot deny the intensity and integrity of her work.

Bibliography

Novels by Marie-Claire Blais

La Belle Bête (Montréal, Institut littéraire du Québec, 1959)
Tête blanche (Montréal, Institut littéraire du Québec, 1960)
Le Jour est noir (Montréal, Editions du Jour, 1961)
Une Saison dans la vie d'Emmanuel (Montréal, Editions du Jour, 1965)
L'Insoumise (Montréal, Editions du Jour, 1966)
David Sterne (Montréal, Editions du Jour, 1967)
Les Manuscrits de Pauline Archange (Montréal, Editions du Jour, 1968)
Vivre! Vivre!: Les Manuscrits de Pauline Archange vol. II (Montréal, Editions du Jour, 1969)
Les Apparences: Les Manuscrits de Pauline Archange vol. III (Montréal, Editions du Jour, 1970)
Le Loup (Montréal, Editions du Jour, 1972)
Un Joualonais, sa joualonie (Montréal, Editions du Jour, 1973)
Une Liaison parisienne (Montréal, Stanké/Quinze Editeurs, 1976)
Les Nuits de l'Underground (Montréal, Stanké, 1978)
Le Sourd dans la ville (Montréal, Stanké, 1979)
Visions d'Anna (Montréal, Stanké, 1982)
Pierre: La Guerre du printemps 81 (Montréal, Primeur, 1984; revised edition Paris, L'Acropole, 1986)

Interviews

'Libre conversation avec Marie-Claire Blais', *Québec français* (October 1981)
'Je veux aller le plus loin possible', *Voix et Images*, 8, 2 (Winter 1983), 191–210

Selected Critical Studies

(For a detailed bibliography see *Voix et Images*, 8, 2 (Winter 1983), 249–95)
Atwood, M., 'Un petit rat heureux', *Le Maclean*, 15, 9 (September 1975), 19–21, 43
Brûlé, M., 'Introduction à l'univers de Marie-Claire Blais', *Revue de l'institut de sociologie*, 42, 3 (1969), 503–13
Cliche, E., 'Un rituel de l'avidité', *Voix et Images*, 8, 2 (Winter 1983), 229–48
Fabi, T., *Le Monde perturbé des jeunes dans l'œuvre de Marie-Claire Blais* (Montréal, Editions agence d'Arc Inc., 1973)
Goldmann, L., 'Note sur deux romans de Marie-Claire Blais', in his *Structures mentales et création culturelle* (Paris, Editions Anthropos, 1970), 410–14
Laurent, F., *L'Œuvre romanesque de Marie-Claire Blais* (Montréal, Fides, 1986)
Marcotte, G., *Le Roman à l'imparfait* (Montréal, La Presse, 1976), 93–137

Nadeau, V., *Marie-Claire Blais: le noir et le tendre* (Montréal, Les Presses de l'université de Montréal, 1974)

Smith, D., 'Les vingt années d'écriture de Marie-Claire Blais', *Lettres québécoises*, 16 (Winter 1979–80), 51, 53–8

Stephens, S., 'Polarisation and stereotype: the representation of woman in Marie-Claire Blais's visual novel *Le Sourd dans la ville*', *British Journal of Canadian Studies*, 1 (1986), 230–7

Stratford, P., *Marie-Claire Blais* (Toronto, Forum, 1971)

Tremblay, V., 'L'art de la fugue dans *Le Loup* de Marie-Claire Blais', *French Review* (May 1986), 911–20

Viswanathan, J., 'Echanger sa vie pour une autre: focalisation multiple dans *Mrs Dalloway* et *Le Sourd dans la ville*', *Arcadia*, 2 (1985), 179–94

Wilson, E., 'Marie-Claire Blais', in his *O Canada. An American's Notes on Canadian Culture* (New York, Farrar, Strauss and Giroux, 1964), 147–57

–6–

Agustin Gomez-Arcos

ANN DUNCAN

Agustin Gomez-Arcos's novels, so far numbering nine, are refreshingly different from most contemporary European fiction. They display a vigour and a passionate sense of commitment particularly rare in recent French narrative. This polemical vein expresses itself, moreover, through a curious blend of lyricism on the one hand and down-to-earth realism on the other. The compelling mixture in Gomez-Arcos's novels of fantasy and realism, of *disponibilité* and commitment, without there being any distinction between them, is an intrinsic part of Surrealist poetry but is not often found in the French novel. It springs from a heightened perception of a reality that is in itself bizarre, but which is no fantasy. It is composed of the dreams, beliefs and fears which are an intrinsic part of the world the narrative reflects. It is in many ways reminiscent of the so-called 'magical realism' of the contemporary Latin-American novel.

Gomez-Arcos has the time-honoured gift of being a good story teller, enhanced by caricatural verve, moral indignation and human warmth. The text is not self-sufficient. It alludes to an outside reality which we are intended to re-examine critically. This fundamental realism isolates Gomez-Arcos from the purely self-reflexive tendencies of the *nouveau roman*, as does the precise social reality portrayed. Franco's Spain is the background to all but two of Gomez-Arcos's novels. (He was born in Andalusia in 1939 and began his literary career writing for the theatre; his work included translations and adaptations of the work of Jean Giraudoux. In 1966, after certain of his plays were banned, he left Spain to take up permanent residence in France. All his novels have been written in French, and it is as a French writer that he must now be considered.) Yet if his narratives are concerned fundamentally with revealing the truth about a repressive régime, they are, like most contemporary fiction of an experimental sort, manifestly poetic in structure. They develop through echoes and allusions, through patterns of imagery and suggestion, rather than through action or argument.

His first novel, *L'Agneau carnivore* (1975), has, like all its successors, a very succinct plot: one person is waiting for another. Gradually the person waiting is revealed to be masculine, the person awaited his lover. Slowly, the gender of the adjectives reveals that the lover is also masculine. As the narrative progresses through flashbacks, we deduce that they shared the same childhood, possibly the same mother, are indeed brothers. The text recounts the growth of their love in adolescence, their separation in adulthood and the elder brother's return. Interspersed with this evocation of passion is a struggle for identity and for the freedom not to repeat the mistakes of a previous generation – the ones which lost the war, which lost love. This struggle is therefore both personal and collective, psychological and political. The political dimension is treated explicitly, the psychological is suggested through echoing images and casual statements. The novel operates, then, on three levels. Firstly, there is the love story of the two brothers, a bizarre drama of family life. On the political level the subject is the failure of the Republic and the asphyxiating tyranny of Franco's régime, perpetuated by the lies and self-interest of the church and the bourgeoisie. On the metaphysical level it is a drama of the search for autonomy and self-knowledge, of the urge to return to one's origins and to recapture a lost paradise. It also shows the destructive power of possessive love. (The title refers to a pet lamb that the mother adored, then slaughtered because she preferred it as a rug.)

The second novel, *Maria Republica* (1976), is a far more virulent political satire. It is much funnier, too, with greater stress on the grotesque but a concomitantly greater sense of outrage. The eponymous protagonist, orphaned in the Civil War, has been driven to starvation by her wealthy and pious aunt so that she will relinquish her younger brother, who is then made a priest (culmination of outrage to Maria). The girl then becomes a prostitute. The narrative covers the aunt's attempt to 'recuperate' Maria by shutting her up in a convent, interspersed with flashbacks to childhood. The sexual perversion, cruelty and debasement of religion in the community act as an allegory for the ruthless tyranny of the Phalangist government, as seen by Gomez-Arcos, and underline the unholy alliance between church and state, which is one of his major themes.

On the anecdotal level the book narrates a girl's mourning for her parents, shot in the Civil War, and for the brother taken from her by poverty. It constitutes her cry of revolt and grief. The scabrous account of the nunnery serves as ornamentation to this level of the narrative, although it is also an essential part of the political diatribe. This constitutes a biting satire of corruption in a police state.

The Republic takes its revenge at the end, in the fire with which Maria symbolically destroys the whole society, including the assembled bourgeoisie, the jailer-nuns and their victim-novices. From this destruction, the phoenix of liberty will arise. The political message adumbrates the metaphysical drama. The moral 'regeneration' of Maria, which the nuns and her aunt profess to desire to further their aims of political oppression, is paradoxically turned against her oppressors and becomes the rebirth of liberty through revolt.

The third novel, *Ana non* (1977), is indubitably Gomez-Arcos's masterpiece. The narrative framework is remarkable for its simplicity. An old woman leaves her home in the south of Spain to visit her one surviving son, a prisoner in some unspecified town in the north. The narrative follows her journey on foot across the entire length of Spain, guided by the tracks of the railway that she cannot afford to use. This geographical and chronological progression is enlivened and fragmented by her memories which recount, in random order, another journey – that of her life.

Ana's peregrinations through Spain closely resemble the peripeteia of the picaresque novel. She, like the *pícaro*, is destitute, persecuted and perpetually hungry.[1] As in the picaresque novel, the protagonist's wanderings and chance encounters give rise to social satire. They provide many anecdotes which keep the narrative moving and create the impression of time passing for Ana. They also build up suspense as we share her yearning to reach her symbolic goal: the north – her son and the death she knows awaits her at the end of the journey. (In both French and Spanish, the north can also mean one's sense of direction.) Ana's physical journey, and her travelling back and forth in memory, obviously signify all journeys through life. We follow Ana through her youth, her fulfilment through marriage to the fisherman, Pedro Paücha, and her happiness with their three sons. Her husband and two of her sons are killed in the Civil War; the youngest is imprisoned for life (which means 'for death', says the blind man who accompanies her for a while). Ana's sudden and multiple bereavement signifies all loss and injustice; while her struggle with exhaustion and hunger on her journey is an extension of her previous life, symbolising the hardship of all who are poor: 'Elle n'a pu la raconter à personne, son histoire.

---

1. The parallel is obviously intentional, underlined by the episode when she guides a blind man and they pass by the city of Tormes, the birthplace of the famous *pícaro*, Lazarillo.

Elle n'était pas un cas isolé, mais le miroir où se reflétait la détresse des autres' (p. 28).

The universality of the themes is underlined by the way in which the narrative is alternately third-person and first, though it is always Ana's consciousness through which events are filtered. Moreover, it is always the protest implicit in the name 'Ana non' to which the narrative returns. For there is, as usual, a political dimension to the novel. There is firstly a passionate denunciation of war, coming from the voice of the bereaved; secondly, there is a series of acerbic comments on the establishment – the police, the church, the rich – coming from the voice of the poor and the oppressed. There is, then, much of the same bite and vehemence of the other novels, tempered here with far more poignancy. It is the only novel in which Gomez-Arcos portrays a happy and natural relationship, and the only one where tenderness and joy figure as prominently as suffering and injustice. The stark simplicity of the narrative structure, centring on the ancient theme of the quest, enhances the important metaphysical dimension of the novel, which is closely incorporated throughout with the anecdotal level.

The moving mixture of realism and lyricism in *Ana non* was followed in 1978 by an entirely different kind of book, *Scène de chasse (furtive)*. The themes are the same as in the previous novels, but the violence, hatred and perversion central to *Maria Republica* are here exacerbated. The central event is the funeral of a Chief of Police in a mining town in the north of Spain. The narrative begins with an unnamed female figure making up her face in front of a mirror. Her present gestures alternate with memories and her story is gradually built up through a series of fragmented recollections, revealing how she came first to marry the police chief, then to hate him. The reconstruction of her past is interspersed with the equally dislocated stories of his mistress and a doctor, with their respective reasons for colluding with him, thereby enabling him to develop his inclinations for sexual perversion and torture, which constitute another series of flashbacks. A face glimpsed in the crowd at the funeral introduces a new narrative thread: the story of one of his victims, whose husband was tortured to death before her eyes and whose son was born the same night with pre-natal memories of torture imprinted on his unconscious mind. The woman rears her son with the aim that he should be the torturer's assassin. This brings a kind of detective story element into the novel. The deed has obviously been accomplished before the book begins, although we do not know the identity of the murderer until the beginning of the fifth and last chapter. It is not a question of discovering the murderer, however, but of tracking down the stages of his (furtive) hunt for the right opportunity. The investigative process also examines the unvoiced hatred of his mother, the police chief's wife and the doctor who was forced to sign the death certificates of the victims.

The subject is more overtly political than in *Ana non* or *L'Agneau carnivore* and less metaphysical. It constitutes a scathing denunciation of the methods and aims of a police state and of the alliance between church and state. The prejudices and egoism of the rising middle classes and impoverished aristocracy, and of all who support the establishment, are exposed. Society is variously equated with a brothel and a torture chamber. The perversions practised in both are not made humorous, as in *Maria Republica*, but emphasised, to elicit the maximum of disgust. Through all this there gradually emerges the voice of the anonymous and silent masses. The novel vocalises their search for an identity; it is their strangled cry of protest, their struggle to free themselves from oppression. Through the murder the boy frees himself from his mother's horrific experiences, and he is reborn, to hear the word *bonjour*, which she has never been able to say to him before.

Gomez-Arcos's fifth novel, *Pré Papa ou Roman de fées* (1979), is completely different in outer form from all the others, although the narrative technique and the themes are very similar. It is a parody of science fiction, as well as being a satire of contemporary moral values and social customs and the abuse of high technology. The scene is some unspecified European town which has emerged from the rubble after a nuclear holocaust. Paris no longer exists, and everything is dictated by The Centre and its computers. The ideal couple, John and Mary, resplendent in their super-perfect habitat designed by Monsieur Gadget, decide that they will have a child. But Mary fails to become pregnant. Overwhelmed by this disaster, John falls ill. His initial refusal to accept the idea that it is he who is having the baby turns to acceptance, and the book ends with his mock-heroic departure in a spaceship, to found a new world suitable for his child.

Although this novel might seem to lack Gomez-Arcos's usual realism, and to be inspired by fantasy, it too contains a passionate commitment to an ideal. The danger here is presented as the loss of real values through the worship of technology, and the possible destruction of everything by a nuclear catastrophe. It calls for a return to sanity, while fantasising a regeneration of society in which everything, even primary biological functions, would be revised.

With *L'Enfant miraculée* (1981) we return to rural Spain and a certain degree of realism. The narrative framework is again taut: a twelve-year-old girl, Juliana, narrowly avoids being raped by her foster brother. Hailed by the villagers as a saint, she is set apart from the rest of her family and forced into a role of piety. Finally, like Maria Republica, she expresses herself in an orgy of destruction in the church, then escapes to the town. On the way, she yields to a stranger, whom she castrates and kills as dawn rises over the horizon. The main subject of the book is the suppression of Juliana's identity by the narrow superstition of those around her. Gomez-Arcos attacks his usual targets of social and religious hypocrisy. There is a vividly impressionistic picture of a rural community in Andalusia. The voice of the chorus, whether family or society, is an important feature of the narrative.

L'Enfant pain (1983) also gives a lively picture of village life, with its customs and types. It is so far the only novel by Gomez-Arcos to present a united and loving family, whose tribulations are caused entirely by poverty and political victimisation. The narrative is seen through the eyes of a six-year-old boy whose world is dominated by hunger. The time is the aftermath of Franco's victory; the child's father had been the Republican mayor. The rest of the village, the conquerors, prolong the combat after the war itself is over by their harassment of this family. The child has to watch his mother make bread for others which he is not allowed to eat. There are no real events, merely a succession of scenes all reflecting daily life and simple, symbolic actions. The past intertwines with the present, as is usual with Gomez-Arcos, and the narrative interest passes from one member of the family to another, creating the effect of a collective voice. The combination of realism and lyricism, so characteristic of Gomez-Arcos's work, is particularly salient in this novel, which has the simplicity and compassion of *Ana non*.

The second most recent novel by Gomez-Arcos, *Un Oiseau brûlé vif* (1984), re-creates something of the unsavoury, claustrophobic atmosphere of *Scène de chasse*, as well as the political hypocrisy portrayed in *Maria Republica*. The atmosphere invariably leads in these novels to violent hatred and a desire for vengeance. For the first time, however, with the exception of certain sections of *Scène de chasse*, Gomez-Arcos portrays a protagonist, Paula, who is an ardent supporter of Franco's régime. We are told things through her words but not from her viewpoint. Denunciation of her views is effected through the style and structure and through ironic contrasts between her words and deeds. Moreover, the personage and story of her servant, Feli La Rouge, further serve to situate Paula's conduct in a critical perspective. On the anecdotal level, the novel explores Paula's veneration for her frigid, hypochondriacal mother and her hatred for her father, as well as her victimisation of La Rouge. On the political level, the narrative depicts the crumbling of Franco's régime, accompanied by the fear and fury of his supporters as their illusions are lost and their stranglehold on society threatened. There is the momentary hope of the opposition when he dies, followed by the symbolic self-burial of La Rouge when the monarchy is restored, dashing Republican dreams. The analysis of the political situation is more explicit than in most of the previous novels, and the events are more topical; so our involvement in the issues is greater. The self-righteous, narrow-minded middle classes, with their cult of appearances and their oppression of the poor under the guise of religion, are satirised as virulently as in the previous novels, with the characteristic note of caustic humour erupting into anger. At a deeper level, the book examines the search for autonomy and the stagnation which comes from false idealisation of the past.

Bestiaire, Gomez-Arcos's most recent novel, is his first to be set in present-day France, even a recognisable Paris, and to deal with specifically French issues. The ostensible subject is the rise in xenophobia among the French, and the excesses of the extreme right, although in an equally satirical vein the first part of the narrative presents the excesses of the post-1968 left, looking for a new cause. The female protagonist, fresh from the barricades, sets out to complete the revolution by corrupting the purity of the French blood-stream through her sexual mores. Her plan backfires when she produces blond, blue-eyed triplets who take over the narrative and the genetic regeneration of France – but as they understand it, which is as Le Pen might. The sibling rivalry of the triplets (one male, one female and one dubious) animates the narrative, as does their precocious sexuality, its excesses matching those of the political views in this *bestiaire*, which culminates in the hominoid which is born of the triplets' vengeance on the left.

The style and narrative technique of this vivacious and salacious novel show how Gomez-Arcos constantly renews himself, experimenting with new approaches to the novel, sharpening his satirical verve, renovating his linguistic games, while fundamentally dramatising the same concerns. It is a ferocious novel, directed against extremes but also against the mediocrity of excess, as well as against the mediocrity of the sheep without strong views, who let themselves be brainwashed by the media, by slogans, by their peer group. The savagery of Céline and Tournier and the inventive, joyously sadistic fantasies of Vian characterise Gomez-Arcos's first incursion into the contemporary French scene.

As with most contemporary fiction, character and narrative are fragmented in these novels. They develop piecemeal, in a non-linear and non-chronological manner. The text usually begins with a gesture: Ana closing the door on her past, the heavy convent door closing in *Maria Republica* ('porte à jamais'), a woman making up her face in *Scène de chasse*. As the narrative gradually unfolds, the characters are pieced together like a jigsaw. The identity of the protagonist, the context of the action and the motives behind it are only gradually revealed, thereby maintaining suspense and keeping our critical faculties alive.

We never learn more than what is necessary for the coherent development of the themes. This results in a certain poetic condensation: 'Elle avance, fatigue têtue, se rapproche du Nord, de son fils, de sa mort. Elle n'a d'autre paysage que celui, obstiné, de sa mémoire' (*Ana non*, p. 90). Yet the characters are not sketchy outlines without antecedents, mere voices for the text, as in the *nouveau roman*. Nor are they rounded characters in the traditional sense; they are clearly symbolic, to a degree that is unusual in the modern French novel, though frequent in Spanish-American fiction. The final picture is convincing, however, because we see the characters from inside, through their feelings, as well as through the action taking place in a credible context.

Action is, however, reduced to a minimum. As with many contemporary novels, the emphasis is shifted from structural nodes to satellites. The tenuous plot is a pretext: apparent digressions, lyrical refrains, intertextual references convey the real meaning of the novel, enshrined in the memories and feelings provoked by the experiences alluded to. The reverberation of these feelings in the characters creates the lyrical force of the novels. It also creates the dramatic force, since it both precipitates the dénouement and clarifies it: 'Tu m'as faite veuve, mon fils t'a fait cadavre' (*Scène de chasse*, p. 263).

The end of the book is often foreshadowed at the beginning, yet the texts are not circular; there is a definite progression. Even when the narrative begins at a time which we only reach on the last page, the text has served to complete our understanding of the enigmatic situation of the first pages. *Scène de chasse* begins with an allusion to a corpse and a funeral and ends with the murderer's rebirth as he finally eradicates the victim from his memory. Through the text, the meaningless ceremonies of the funeral and of the woman masking her face for it become full of significance. *L'Agneau carnivore* begins with the expectation of the elder brother's return and ends when the disappointment of the return itself has been allayed by the subsequent renewal of their bonds – episodes which derive their significance from the drama re-enacted by the younger brother's memory as he waits.

Chronology is not rendered meaningless, as in Robbe-Grillet's work, where it is often impossible to place events in a sequence, since they may not have happened at all, and where the narrative consists of continual replays of a nucleus of images which vary but never progress. In Robbe-Grillet's novels this absence of chronological order is concomitant with the absence of cause and effect in motivation or circumstances. Gomez-Arcos, on the contrary, is pointing firmly to the causes behind various politico-social or psychological situations. It is always possible to reassemble the memories and flashbacks in Gomez-Arcos's novels in a significant order, even though they are presented to us in a random sequence. The technique is more like that of Butor's *La Modification* or *L'Emploi du temps*, where the protagonist's mind ranges freely over various moments in the past, both personal and collective, which, none the less, progress within a definable framework. But Gomez-Arcos's characters have none of the panic which afflicts Butor's, who try to understand things logically and are overwhelmed by the swiftness and multiplicity of experience. Gomez-Arcos's protagonists have a quiet assurance that they will attain their end.

So Gomez-Arcos, though he is fascinated with the craft of fiction, is not primarily a ludic writer, producing self-reflexive narratives. There is a purpose behind his novels, both for him and for his characters. Although his plots are minimal, there is a continual air of animation and an element of suspense that hold the reader's attention. The various peripeteia which delay the final resolution, or *coup de théâtre*, are entertaining in their own right and also illuminate the main theme. The structure, which is fragmented on the narrative level, is therefore closely unified on the thematic level. Moreover the absurdity of many of the episodes and dialogues in these books exposes not a fundamental lack of meaning in the universe itself but a distortion of real values by a particular society. This affirmation of meaning sets Gomez-Arcos apart from many other contemporary French novelists. The meaning he discerns is, however, a strictly humanistic one. It is the meaning of the word *bonjour*, which cannot be said by the victim of torture. A nucleus of passionately held beliefs forms the mainspring of his fiction. It is this idealism which gives his work its affirmative quality in spite of its vituperative nature. These beliefs are not, however, expressed as intellectual abstractions or developed through rational exposition. For Gomez-Arcos is a resolutely non-intellectual writer, although a highly intelligent one. His convictions are conveyed poetically through suggestive patterns of structure and style; they are presented dramatically, in terms of the actions, interactions and perceptions of the characters. The response provoked in the reader is therefore emotional.

We participate in events both through the characters' own feelings and through their words. As most of the characters symbolise some aspect of Franco's Spain, this device is often used for satirical purpose, and the characters are made to denounce themselves. The Reverend Mother in *Scène de chasse*, for instance, talks of 'Cadres supérieurs, ministres et banquiers [. . .] belle race [. . .] respectueux de l'Eglise et de l'Ordre établi [. . .].' 'Enfin, des gens qui se comportent de façon naturelle' replies the police chief (p. 213). A satirical perspective can also be introduced by conveying the suggested reactions of the listener to reported speech: 'On lui demande d'éviter les accrochages de rue (d'accord), le sang (ne répond pas); on lui conseille l'isolement des éléments gênants (est pour; isolement éternel)' (ibid., p. 201).

Alternatively, the irony may come from an interjected comment by the protagonist/narrator: 'Sa faute! J'ai déjà renoncé à savoir à qui incombait la faute. (Ajoutons à cela un brin de sarcasme pour rendre un son juste. Seulement, le sarcasme de maman, c'est de l'épicerie fine)' (*L'Agneau carnivore*, p. 89).

L'Agneau carnivore is almost exclusively told in the first person, and indeed Gomez-Arcos usually presents the narrative through the viewpoint of the protagonist. But in several novels the narrative shifts frequently from first person to third. Liberal use of *style indirect libre* and dialogue further diversify third-person narrative. In *Un Oiseau brûlé vif* Gomez-Arcos accomplishes the difficult feat of presenting the narrative through a protagonist whom he intends us to find repulsive. The ironic viewpoint is conveyed through *style indirect libre* reinforced by structural parallels. In *L'Enfant pain* the narrative interest passes from one member of the family to another, though the viewpoint is always that of the small boy. Considerable prominence is given in *L'Enfant miraculée* and *L'Enfant pain* to the role of the collective voice or chorus. This sometimes suggests perspective, as in 'une sorte d'aisance que les gens de par ici appellent *richesse*. Mais c'est trop dire' (*L'Enfant miraculée*, p. 11); above all it denotes the communal nature of the experience.

It is usual in Gomez-Arcos's novels for the focus of narrative interest to shift occasionally within each text so that more than one subjectivity is portrayed. Thus in *Bestiaire* a kind of collective voice representing the political spectrum is provided by passing the narrative from the unmarried mother to each of the triplets in turn (followed by their voice in unanimity) and then to their neighbour

Thérèse d'Avila (no saint), a midwife, thesis-writer and 'new psychologist' with whose despair about the labelling of apartments as 'left' or 'right' the book ends. This multiplicity of perspectives reaches its greatest complexity in *Scène de chasse (furtive)*. The murdered police chief is mainly significant through the effect he had on others. The novel is both a detective story and a documentary, but the events are highly personalised. There are numerous narrators, who are in turn the focus of interest, and the narrative voice oscillates between first, second and third person. This is particularly evident throughout chapter 3, relating the story of Teresa, the tortured woman, mother of the murderer. The past, conveyed in a third-person narrative made vivid by use of the present tense, alternates with first-person recollections, designated by the tense as past: 'Sait que son nom Teresa quittera ses pensées, car il a des choses plus importantes à résoudre que leurs relations d'homme et femme, leurs personnes ou leurs rêves. Rêves, quel mot! me disais-je en soupirant' (p. 276).

As her thoughts are penetrated, she addresses other characters in the second person, so that inner monologue becomes dialogue, critical observation by the author merges with the character's subjective impressions. Words from the religious ceremony also echo her private hymn of praise: 'Tu es sous terre. Pour ceux qui sont comme moi, c'est déjà ça de gagné. Alléluia. La femme grise quitte le cimetière, lentement, sous la pluie, elle regagne la ville' (p. 313).

Elsewhere in the novel dialogue fuses with parodic authorial comment:

> 'Tu as volé les objets sacrés et tu les as vendus, n'est-ce pas, crapule?'
> La crapule dit oui.
> 'Et [. . .] tu t'es payé une nuit de putes, n'est-ce pas, dégénéré?'
> Le dégénéré dit oui.
> 'Le reste, tu l'as donné aux anarchistes, n'est-ce pas, espèce de subversif?'
> L'espèce de subversif dit oui. [. . .]
> Tout le monde est ravi. La Mère Directrice félicite l'officier de police pour son langage. (p. 144)

And yet another innocent is tortured to death.

In *Maria Republica*, although the viewpoint is almost always that of the eponymous heroine, Gomez-Arcos varies the presentation through the insertion of parodic documents, tape recordings and other voices. Maria keeps a notebook in which she comments on events, and the author uses this literary exercise to mock his own imagery: '(Notes de Maria qui se complaît dans des images apocalyptiques)' (p. 224). Life at the convent is ruled by the computer (referred to as 'L'Ange de l'Informatique'), whose oracular pronouncements function almost as a Greek chorus, warning of impending disaster.

For the computer has become God in our society. This is part of the central theme in *Pré Papa*, as well as providing an additional source of narrative voice, through the computer's comments: 'Notre Seigneur l'Ordinateur, rond et sacramentel [. . .] allume incontinent son écran-hostie et délivre son message: "[. . .] ne savais-tu donc pas que Dieu n'existe plus? Ton salut, tu dois le demander au Centre"' (p. 296). Throughout this novel runs a network of communications through which the characters are exposed to voices from other spaces, whether scientific or para-psychological: 'Sous la forme d'appels téléphoniques et de messages télévisés, les avertissements du Centre se multiplient. Le réseau de voix persuasives prie John de rentrer au bercail [. . .] ces voix le préviennent des innombrables dangers du monde extérieur [. . .] Ce sont les mots de sa mère, ou presque' (p. 286). Literature is seen as a vital part of the preservation of truth: 'Il n'existe pas une seule cassette, bande vidéo ou document quelconque où cet événement ait été enregistré pour les générations postérieures. Ça se dit, passe de bouche à oreille, comme une rumeur lointaine venant du fond des âges [. . .] une tradition orale [. . .] Mais Mary [. . .] garde le Livre. Elle en parlera à John' (p. 72).

All these allusions to documents, to official media pronouncements and to the diverse methods of communication, technical, oral and literary, diversify the narrative technique. They create an effect of animation and at the same time involve the whole of society in the personal drama. In several novels the oral and social function of the experience is complemented by the role of newspapers. In *Scène de chasse* newspaper cuttings play a direct role in the drama, as a source of information. They also exemplify twisted propaganda and official platitudes. '(Légitime, cette douleur, d'après le journal de la ville, dernière édition, première page)' (p. 8).

In this way the whole question of communication, which is central to Gomez-Arcos's work, is brought to the fore. We are invited to examine the manner in which information is transmitted and to consider the ways by which our views are formed by the press, textbooks or public opinion. Gomez-Arcos emphasises the problem of censorship (whether that of the state or the individual super-ego), the problem of the freedom of thought, as well as freedom of speech, and the tyranny of the *lieu commun*.

Showing the cunning distortion of the words used by the oppressors, Gomez-Arcos reveals the pathetic inadequacy of the words available to the humble folk who are his main protagonists: 'bien sûr tu ne dis pas "horreur de l'inutilité" parce que le nom des choses t'échappe' (*Maria Republica*, p. 45). The contemporary focus on the difficulty of self-expression acquires a social dimension in these novels. His narratives attempt to remedy the inarticulacy forced on the masses. The text constitutes in many cases the effort to make audible the mute protest of symbolic characters who cannot themselves find the words or may be prevented from doing so. We are told of the tortured Teresa: 'Et ce qui n'était jusqu'à présent qu'un effort de mémoire, un monologue intérieur vicié par le silence de toute une vie, éclôt soudain en mots, explose comme une bombe de paroles [. . .] elle parle' (*Scène de chasse*, p. 311).

We are, then, made aware in all the novels that the text represents the characters' attempts to find words with which to communicate their experience. The first part of *Ana non* is narrated (in the third person) with an eloquence she herself would not have possessed. Half way through she learns to write: 'Elle prend une décision soudaine: elle va raconter l'histoire de sa vie. Puisqu'elle sait enfin lire et écrire, elle peut parler d'elle-même. Elle n'a pas besoin des autres, de leurs voix, de leurs mots. Elle n'a pas besoin qu'on dessine son personnage [. . .] elle revendique le droit à la parole. Elle parle' (p. 161). The narrative henceforth switches to Ana's own first-person narration of her memories, so that she seems to be offering her story of poverty, bereavement and love to others, as well as speaking to herself in order to occupy her mind during the journey. Now that Ana is literate, she can re-create 'le mot *amour*. Un mot d'où jaillit un ruisselet miraculeux d'eau de pluie. Amour liquide où le soleil reparu se mire' (p. 114).

In this book perhaps even more than in the others, the naming of things creates them, as in contemporary poetry. Through their names they acquire for the reader the symbolic values they have for the speaker. At the beginning of the novel Ana non carefully bakes a loaf of almond bread to take to her son in prison: 'Un pain aux amandes, huilé, anisé et fortement sucré, Un gâteau dirait-elle' (p. 8). This phrase acts as a lyrical refrain throughout the narrative, bearing witness to Ana's fidelity and abnegation. She clutches onto the loaf through all her adventures, fighting a ravenous dog for it, retracing her steps if she drops it, refusing to eat it even when starving. The refrain serves, too, as a structural device, since the bread's loss of weight as it dries up charts Ana's path through life and her gradual shrivelling through age and debility. It becomes an object 'qu'elle n'a plus la force d'appeler un *gâteau*. [. . .] Poids sec. Définitivement désséché. Poids mort' (p. 252). Without a name, it loses substance: 'Pas un vrai gâteau, se dit-elle. Tout bêtement un rêve' (p. 268). It is referred to several times as 'son éternel paquet illusion', or her 'paquet mythique'. As such, it represents the dreams we all carry through life, which motivate us to carry on.

Ana's name, too, symbolises her identity. It is not just an arbitrary code of reference attached to her by the author. She lost her husband's name of Paücha when she was widowed, to become the 'Ana non' of total protest: 'ma solitude c'est le *non* qui me colle à la peau comme à d'autres une identité' (p. 48) – (and the *non* obviously recalls its homonym *nom*). As she becomes literate, able to tell her own story and to designate those responsible for her deprivation, she refuses to be called Ana non and reaffirms her identity as Ana Paücha. The author also calls her Ana fantasque, Ana jeune, Ana secrète, Ana seule, Ana non de solitude – just as Clara in *L'Agneau carnivore* has many roles, such as Clara servante, Clara simple, Clara paysanne, Clara finie, Clara écœurée, Clara personne. When Ana is preparing to face death, the text declares: 'Plus d'Ana non. Ce personnage honteux, anonyme, est resté à jamais sur la voie ferrée, enseveli sous la neige comme un tas de guenilles [as she soon will be]. Vive Ana oui' (p. 296). She and the blind man have searched in vain for the name of her menfolk on the monument to the dead at the Valle de los Caidos. The book ends with a list of their names and a revindication of their rights to an identity. The text fills the void on the state monument and in life, where 'nulle mémoire n'en garde trace'. Heroes of protest, they are 'des anti-noms. Des non' (p. 311).

Since people exist through what they are called, they cease to exist if no one names them. The victims in *Scène de chasse* are 'sans nom et sans visage. Sans voix. Une douleur, un cri muet, une agonie parfaitement anonyme' (p. 261). The torturer himself is nullified by the hatred he inspires: 'Carlota ne dit jamais *votre père* mais *le Chef de Famille*, le réduisant ainsi à sa seule nature de Chef de Police' (p. 223).

The mother's repudiation of the narrator in *L'Agneau carnivore* is made manifest by her use of the words 'mon fils' solely to designate his brother, and by the fact that, until the last page, he is the only character in the narrative to be nameless. The absence of a name or of words is the destructive silence which these novels are attempting to remedy, on the psychological level within the fiction and also on a deeper political level. In *L'Agneau carnivore* the brothers are stifled by their parents' 'loi aberrante du silence'. Almost the last sentence in *L'Agneau carnivore*, spoken by the hitherto taciturn servant, Clara, is: 'Je viens de me prouver à moi-même que près de quarante ans de silence ne m'ont pas tuée, comme vous deux' (p. 306). She is addressing the boys' parents, who symbolise the defeated Republic. Silence for these characters, as for an author or, even more, a dramatist, is deadly: 'C'est quoi la torture? Je le sais maintenant. C'est le silence. Supporter jusqu'à la mort le poids insupportable du silence. Gémir comme des bêtes [. . .] Mais ne pas parler. *Ne pas parler*' (*Scène de chasse*, p. 296).

The bullets that kill the torturer at the end of this novel are newly made 'mais âgées de dix-neuf ans de silence' (p. 372). In *Pré Papa* silence destroys the couple (pp. 239–64), and Mary kills herself because she feels that she no longer exists, faced with her husband's silence and her own inability to communicate with him.

Closely linked with silence is the Cry.[2] Each book formulates a passionate cry to be heard, from an individual symbolising a group whose problem comes alive for us through the novel. The cry of poverty is vocalised by Maria Republica as a child, frightened that her baby brother will die of hunger: 'Ce cri que tu sens déjà germer au plus profond de toi, dans un coin de ton âme, ce cri que tu n'arrives pas à étouffer par ton silence' (*Maria Republica*, p. 44). The anguish of her childhood is reflected in the impotent fury she feels when confronted with a tortured companion in the convent. It is this anger that fuels her final revenge:

> Maria n'y peut rien [. . .] noyer ce cri qui s'échappe du vide, incapable de s'enfuir, incapable de se taire, cri continu. [. . .] Il lui faut entendre ce cri [. . .] car il est des tourments qui doivent être communs à tous pour prendre conscience d'où ils sortent [. . .] Le cri hurlant dans ses tympans, épousant sa chair même, Maria [. . .] ouvre la bouche pour donner à ce cri [. . .] une autre échappatoire possible. Une autre issue. Mais rien ne sort. (p. 181)

Each narrative is the violent cry of the oppressed. It is the author's response to the presence of suffering in the world. For Ana non, there was marriage and the news of her husband's death: 'Entre ces deux cris, ma vie: Pedro Paücha' (p. 183). As she faces death Ana utters her last cry of protest: 'Tu croyais que j'allais mourir en silence, soumise, Ana non pour toujours [. . .] Terre de la patrie, je t'accuse de meurtre' (p. 310). The cry is often stifled throughout the characters' lives. If they support a repressive régime they themselves stifle it: 'Et Madame retient un cri d'angoisse [. . .]

---

2. This cry, in Gomez-Arcos's novels, fulfils the same function as the *grito* in the *cante hondo* of the poetry and dances of Andalusia. It is a deep cry of passion that expresses inarticulate rage, hatred, fear, love or the moment of vengeance. Lorca uses it in this sense in his plays and poetry.

Un cri lourd, nourri de la lourde misère du passé, et qui pousse, grandit et monte en elle d'un violent coup de force [. . .] ce cri [. . .] sans horaires, sans repos, cri fou, cri besoin [. . .] mais elle ne va pas crier, ne libérera jamais ce cri étouffant' (*Scène de chasse*, p. 56). If they rebel against the régime, others silence them. It is Juliana's *cry* which prevents her from being raped: 'Un hurlement s'échappe de sa gorge d'enfant, déchire le silence nocturne qui se met aussitôt à se remplir de cris' (*L'Enfant miraculée*, p. 93). But these echoing cries stifle her identity, force her to become a ghost of herself. Four years later she erupts from her imprisonment in a false self and explodes in a final cry of liberation (p. 3).

It is evident that a deep social and moral commitment informs Gomez-Arcos's novels. This is not expressed dogmatically; the irony is pervasive. In *Maria Republica* and *Scène de chasse* particularly, the grotesque humour makes repulsive passages readable, as they have to be if the message is to reach us. In *Scène de chasse*, for instance, the alimentary and sexual obsession of the Chief of Police with viscera is presented with baroque exaggeration; we find it incredible and almost funny. But all his behaviour is equally compulsive, and his profession gives this terrifying scope. Indefatigable industry, normally thought of as a virtue, is revealed by the style to be a vice if misapplied: 'On assistait à la naissance d'une vocation sacrée: celle de flic [. . .] il s'adonna à cœur joie au commerce des polices totalitaires, extorquant, dénonçant, torturant et tuant dix-neuf heures par jour' (p. 174).

This picture of a world heading for disaster because its values have been overturned recurs in all Gomez-Arcos's novels. Confusion of values is often shown by mockery of the illogicality of *idées reçues*: 'Elle est vieille sa chienne. Pauvre. Laide. [. . .] Vagabonde. Elle est donc républicaine. Rouge. Communiste. Tout ça veut dire la même chose. A mettre dans le même panier. Compris dans le prix' (*Ana non*, p. 68). Much of the humour in the novels comes from the fact that the characters and their views are commonplace. In *Scène de chasse* Carlota marries the police chief largely because she has been 'properly' brought up to respect money and social prestige. ⎯ne dame ne rit pas. Une dame sourit. Dixit maman [. . .] Mère consciente d'avoir sur ses épaules la lourde charge d'une fille à marier *comme il faut*, (mère lieu commun)' (pp. 14–15).

There are also longer passages of sustained humour, such as the scene in which some rich townspeople have a 'Day of the Poor', and Ana is adopted for the duration of two meals. The unctuous words with which the bishop and assembled company welcome Ana – 'nous te voulons pauvre et sale. C'est comme cela que nous t'aimons'

(p. 103) – reveal the bishop's true feelings; the rich do indeed wish to keep the poor as they are, deprived and unpleasant to look at. They can only be fed and cherished as part of a theatrical performance (significantly, the banquet is being televised), isolated from the context of real life.

This desire for the revision of social values goes hand in hand with a renovation of the language that expresses them. Language, like society, is treated as a set of conventions to be reformulated. Words define roles, and for Gomez-Arcos, the way in which things are said reveals their underlying nature. The police, referred to as 'la Gristapo', for their grey uniforms as well as their methods, become 'une infection galopante de flicaille' (*Scène de chasse*, p. 258) as they rush in to suppress a demonstration.

Not all the satire is political or malicious. Some is good-humoured, inspired by delight in language playing on observed reality. Like Queneau, Ionesco, Vian and many contemporary writers, Gomez-Arcos raises language to the status of protagonist; it is as important a part of the drama as the ideas which it expresses. For example, a guest arrives to dine with Super-Couple John and Mary: 'Si brillante qu'on la dirait aluminisée de fond en comble et prête à partir en voyage spatial. Elle a sans doute garé sa fusée dans la cour, se dit John' (*Pré Papa*, p. 173).

The exuberance of Gomez-Arcos's novels does not only arise from linguistic virtuosity; the text is further animated by his essentially theatrical vision. (He was a dramatist before he became a novelist, and left Spain after his plays were banned.) His characters often organise performances, and audience reaction is part of the narrative. Paula in *Un Oiseau brûlé vif* conducts rituals with a collection of dressmaker's models, attired to represent her family and acquaintances: 'les divers rôles de l'actualité sociale et politique, du Généralissime au maire de la ville, seront distribués au reste de la troupe' (p. 123). This acting-out of her fantasies has replaced reality for her, in the domestic arena as in the political.

This theatrical manner of presentation is not just a narrative device. By drawing our attention to the use of masks and role-playing in daily life, Gomez-Arcos is exposing the hypocrisy of society. 'Mais Paula ne se laisse pas émouvoir par son attitude théâtrale; elle sait qu'il s'agit d'un geste hypocrite, un de plus' (*Un Oiseau brûlé vif*, p. 91). Paula plays a part herself: '[elle] adopte des poses. Elle a des gestes hardis de femme adulte' (p. 98). In this way Gomez-Arcos points to the overriding importance of appearances, pomp and ritual, which are all designed to impress but have no moral substance.

Many actions in Gomez-Arcos's novels reveal outward show devoid of meaning. For example, each visit to the Mother Superior in *Maria Republica* is a ceremony with preordained roles and rituals: 'Madame la Duchesse Sa Révérence [. . .] tordue comme un mauvais acteur de théâtre, soulève les rideaux et fait son entrée dans l'oratoire' (pp. 222–3). This builds up to the climax of the public ceremony staged by the convent and up-staged by Maria on the day when she is intended to take her vows. The elaborate performances organised in the brothel in *Scène de chasse* are compared to 'un impressionnant show sado-maso-dingue [. . .] un concert de cris de damnés' (p. 120). The opening scene of this novel is highly theatrical, focused on a series of gestures accomplished by an as yet unidentified character: 'Figée dans un geste à demi finissant, à demi commencé [. . .] Madame regarde dans le miroir son visage de deuil. Il lui sied, le deuil. Peut-être mieux qu'à Electre. [. . .] pour mieux réussir ce chef-d'œuvre que son miroir reflète [. . .] Madame a quitté pour de bon sa propre personne [. . .] Artiste accomplie' (pp. 7–8).

The narrator's mother in *L'Agneau carnivore* is likewise less moved by events than attentive to the figure she can represent. When she thinks that her younger son has been born blind, she orders an entirely black wardrobe 'pour promener dignement mon désespoir dans tout le pays' (p. 17). All her entrances and exits in the novel are theatrical: 'Maîtresse de son personnage, maman compose avec soin sa voix et ses gestes' (p. 48). Descriptions are often presented as stage directions: 'Attitude: elle, maman, raide à côté de son piano, entourée des vieilles photos de famille comme d'anges gardiens' (*L'Agneau carnivore*, p. 27). The other characters are also presented as actors, and this, moreover, is how they see themselves.

> C'était vraiment la grande scène sur le champ d'honneur. Il avait dû la préméditer pendant la nuit et lui donner sa forme définitive ce matin [. . .] dans la famille, on avait un penchant jamais négligé aux situations mélodramatiques [. . .] Après quoi, j'ai fini de monter l'escalier comme une vedette suivie par les projecteurs. Je ne voulais pas me priver, moi non plus, de ma sortie. (pp. 109–10)

The effects here have been carefully engineered to achieve the maximum effect, so that both readers and participants regard the scene as memorable.

Gomez-Arcos's role as social satirist, and as creative artist, requires a public. Likewise, his characters, or actors, need an audience. Gomez-Arcos stresses how the character's monologue is always aimed at a listener. The function of spectators/readers is therefore important, because they turn a text or monologue into a dialogue. We are told of the servant Clara, witness to the mother's mono-logues: 'Dans cette comédie sournoise, elle n'est qu'une figurante. Jamais elle ne dira un mot. Elle est là parce que, au théâtre, on ne peut pas parler dans le vide' (*L'Agneau carnivore*, p. 56). Later in the novel the mother ('devenue démocrate') permits Clara a small role, but there is still no real conversation: 'Elles se donnaient du Matilde et du *ma chère*. C'était Versailles, côté fourneaux' (p. 260). Much of the early part of the narrative is based on the information acquired by the child narrator from his mother's endless telephone conver-sations, treated as monologues because only one side of them is presented to the audience.

In *L'Agneau carnivore* the narrator is often present as a bemused spectator, whose participation is not expected. He does not exist for his mother as a person; he is never once named throughout the narrative until the ironic coda. In his words (pp. 89–90):

> La scène est tellement absurde que je n'en crois pas mes yeux ni mes oreilles. On dirait que cette scène a été répétée des milliers de fois avant d'être jouée devant moi. [Ils] sont là [. . .] ils parlent de moi. Mais ni eux ni moi ne sommes concernés. On s'est trompé de scène, d'acteurs, de personnages [. . .] ça ne ferait pas non plus partie du spectacle [. . .] je ne suis pas dans la peau de mon personnage, moi non plus.
> (Fin du premier acte et rideau.)

The dramatic highlights of the characters' lives occur against a background of daily rituals (awakening, bath and meal times), which all contain their element of drama and ceremony and are invested with solemnity by the style (as in Proust). The servant makes her entrance 'cassée en deux comme une servante de mélodrame' as she goes about her household duties (*Un Oiseau brûlé vif*, p. 9). Even in *L'Enfant pain*, the most simple and realistic of Gomez-Arcos's novels, where the generic and unexceptional nature of people and setting is emphasised by the chapter headings ('Père', 'La rue', 'Le pain', 'Le chien', 'Les lentilles', 'La maison', 'Le village', etc.), the presentation is consistently scenic and dramatic. The cat stalking a sparrow is presented by 'l'enfant, qui avait suivi le drame inachevé' (p. 213). This underlines the magical value of such spectacles for the child.

The first eight pages of *Ana non* recount a succession of simple gestures – lighting the oven, closing the door, putting the key in its place – that have suddenly become significant because 'il est des gestes qu'elle ne fera plus. Jamais' (p. 13). The text then moves back from the present, celebrating 'd'autres choses qu'elle ne fera plus', sketching in her past for the reader from the plausible viewpoint of Ana's present reflections. Gestures thus appear as archetypal, symbolic not only of Ana's daily routine but also of the sort of life led by women in fishing villages, and of the gesture of a woman leaving her past to go towards death. This metaphysical function can also be conveyed by the presence of spectating characters, forming a kind of fatidical Greek chorus: 'attentives, elles sont trois à épier cette inéluctable descente dans la sénilité' (*L'Enfant miraculée*, p. 129).

There is little distinction between melodrama and the everyday. Just as the humdrum can be raised to the magical, so can horror become accepted as normal. Daily life in Gomez-Arcos's *comédie humaine* often resembles the *Grand Guignol*. The characters, like the observer-writer, just have to look about them: 'la rue, théâtre de massacres. C'est dans la rue que le chasseur a décidé d'observer attentivement la nature de la bête' (*Scène de chasse*, p. 357). In *Maria Republica*, too, the subject is not the moving drama of everyday life but the appalling drama of daily horror. The ostentation of the gestures and setting, enhanced by lighting effects, stresses the falsity of the whole social system, built on appearances. Everything is done for effect, nothing for simple or genuine motives.

> Maria s'approche, soulève les rideaux, et passe la tête [. . .] Sa Révérence prie [. . .] elle donne l'impression de veiller le cadavre syphilitique et invisible de Madame la Duchesse [her former title]. Comme dédoublée: la vie et la mort [. . .] l'impression d'avoir tout laissé en plan avant d'avoir terminé, comme un spectacle interrompu par une panne d'électricité avant l'adieu des amoureux. (pp. 164–5)

The politico-social struggle in *Maria Republica*, as in other novels by Gomez-Arcos and as in Genet's plays, is developed through the sexual mores of the contestants. Dramas of exploitation and submission, repression and liberation are enacted in the sexual sphere, arousing strong, instinctive reactions in the reader. As a prostitute Maria reaches the conclusion that each man is 'un être politique'. Accordingly, she deliberately sets out to infect the entire bourgeoisie of the town with the syphilis she has contracted. She starts with her most assiduous client, a prison governor, described ironically as a 'héros national, solide pilier du Régime' (p. 155): 'un homme honnête s'il en est, courageux, irréprochable. Les doigts de ses mains additionnés aux orteils de ses pieds n'auraient pas été suffisants pour chiffrer le nombre d'exécutions dont il a été responsable pour la gloire de la Patrie' (p. 150). His child is born deformed through hereditary syphilis, and Maria feels personally avenged since this man made her fornicate on the Republican flag as a deliberate act of humiliation. She feels, moreover, that she has avenged her parents, shot as communists during the Civil War, and that she has carried out an effective campaign against the future of the ruling class through the only means at her disposal, sex. She is at the same time denouncing the hypocrisy of this clique, which professes to condemn prostitutes and adultery and to uphold the tenets of the Catholic church.

Much of the humour in this novel is derived from the parallel between the ex-prostitute Republican novice and the ex-duchess Reverend Mother, who suffers from a more advanced stage of syphilis. Through this analogy, sentimental idealism is eschewed, since the oppressed are no more free from imperfections than their overlords. Yet at the same time, the Reverend Mother, and through her the religious community and the political régime that it actively supports, are satirised as unhealthy, worldly and corrupt. It is doubtless significant that Maria's syphilis was imposed on her by an exploiter, and that she was forced into prostitution by poverty, whereas the ex-duchess acquired her infection through marriage. The cancer rotting society was chosen by those who supported the Franquist cause; it was imposed on those who had fought for the Republic.

The predominance of the grotesque and the fantastic in Gomez-Arcos's novels is a feature inherent in the satirical novel. But the bizarre rituals are all the more sinister because they take place against a background of sober realism which makes them only too credible. This is particularly evident in *Scène de chasse*, where the perverse and sadistic sexual tastes of the Police Chief are central. His pathological behaviour inspires disgust in the other characters, as well as the reader. It establishes a thematic analogy with his role as torturer. It underlines how repulsive and abnormal this is, and it does so by instigating a (literal and figurative) gut reaction in the reader, which reinforces our intellectual condemnation. The total violation of the individual, represented by this man's private and professional vices, is therefore a drama which involves us, and not a debate revolving round abstract issues.

Significantly, the main torture episode in this novel is presented not in the third person by a narrator who was not even a witness, as are the brothel scenes, but in the first person (interspersed with second-person invocations to the torturer) by one of the victims, who watched her husband die under torture. Our involvement is therefore physical and emotional; the reasons for Teresa's murderous hatred are all too comprehensible. In this way the novel drives home its passionate protest against torture in any shape or form, against any attempt to degrade other human beings, against all those who condone totalitarian régimes which rely on such methods, whether by active support or merely the failure to protest.

Sexuality is rarely free from political connotations in Gomez-Arcos's novels, since his attitude to politics is essentially a moral one. It is bound up with his desire for the freedom of the individual, for equality and sincerity, all values which are reflected in sexual behaviour. It is, however, not always perverse. The most moving and unequivocally loving of all the relationships in Gomez-Arcos's novels is that of Ana Paúcha's devotion to her fisherman husband, extended to 'le petit', the son in prison. Her memories of their courtship are contradictory, and their love was mute – 'Pedro Paúcha et moi ne nous sommes jamais parlé d'amour [. . .] On laissait ça aux autres' (p. 190) – but it was real, of a reality that transcends fiction: 'Ana, la petite Ana anonyme, épousait *son* homme. Il n'y a pas eu d'histoire d'amour, vous savez' (p. 182).

Even in *L'Agneau carnivore*, where the brothers' incestuous and homosexual love is unorthodox, it is portrayed as deeply affectionate and authentic. It is an integral part of their search for autonomy in the face of the hypocrisy and repression which surround them. It is a statement of the equality, liberty and *fraternity* on which the Republic was founded. It is also an attempt to rekindle the political and personal ardour of the previous generation.

In *L'Enfant miraculée* the way in which Juliana's character is warped by other people's attitudes after the attempted rape is psychologically moving. But, as usual with Gomez-Arcos, it adumbrates the political discussion (kept to the minimum in this novel) by illustrating the individual's struggle for freedom and for truth. The end clearly signifies the revolt of the silent masses and emasculation of the oppressors.

It is from this refusal to be limited by an unsatisfying reality, the refusal to have the cry of liberty or sense of self stifled, that the vitality of Gomez-Arcos's novels springs. The question of freedom is metaphysical as well as personal, social and political. Gomez-Arcos does not extol freedom only because certain régimes have repressed it. He claims it as a basic human right: 'le goût de la liberté, seul vrai héritage transmis par sa race' (*Maria Republica*, p. 18). But the experience of freedom is almost unknown to his characters, resident in a police state. Significantly, there are few images of freedom in these novels but many of suffocation. The images of being stifled, however, are integrated with the call to revolt, on the part of both the reader and the protagonist, which these novels incite; they serve to build up the tension and make the final release inevitable.

For Gomez-Arcos's characters are not only choked with fury, they are also ablaze with hope. The society that he describes is corrupt, vicious and repressive; it leaves no scope for individual or collective freedom, for justice or truth. But he does not present despair. The fury which devours his characters may be impotent, but they are avenged in words. The political defeat of the Republic is turned into a vigorous affirmation of ideals through his novels. The disaster of the present becomes a message of optimism for the future.

Each of the novels, however violent the narrative, has a more or less optimistic ending. Gomez-Arcos does not see this as an absurd world in which everything is meaningless. It is merely the accepted meaning which is a travesty to be mocked; this leads to the adventure of redefinition, and the rediscovery of the real meaning.

The last words of *L'Agneau carnivore*, spoken by Clara, are 'Ça fait vivre, vraiment' (p. 306). There follows a sort of litany, or parodic cast list, of all the characters. All the minor personages are dead, as well as the actor whose presence underpins the whole action: 'Mon pays s'appelle l'Espagne. Morte. (Détail curieux: on attend toujours sa résurrection.).' The family survives through the sons. The narrator names himself for the first time: 'Moi je m'appelle Ignacio. Présent. Triomphant. Vivant' (p. 307).

Maria Republica ends with the symbolic burning of all that Maria hates – the bourgeoisie, the church, the flag. She frees the canary, casts off 'sa fausse identité' and dies with the words 'je m'appelle toujours Maria Republica' (p. 327). The idea will be perpetuated through the abolition of the individual personality (an idea central also to *Pré Papa*). A sort of poem which follows calls on all who are lethargic to wake up and react, to become aware that

> nous pleurions un cadavre
> qui n'a jamais existé,
> un cadavre qui n'a jamais cessé d'être vivant
> Alors, [. . .]
> tous les hommes enfin réveillés
> commencent [. . .]
> à penser à demain.
> Car demain
> est un mot vivant lui aussi.
> Vivant.
> Laissons-les parler de la vie.
> C'est le plus beau sujet de conversation
> que peuvent avoir les hommes.
> (*Maria Republica*, p. 329)

Another violent and disillusioned book, though animated by the same satirical verve of these two early novels, is the more recent *Un*

Oiseau brûlé vif. It ends, apparently pessimistically, with the bird called Liberty thrown into the fire by a furious Paula, who has lost everything 'foi, fortune, illusion'. But Paula is not a likeable character; politically she symbolises the blindness of Phalangism (her last action is to replace her 'lunettes d'aveugle' with hands trembling with fear). Moreover, La Rouge, her Republican servant, who buried herself alive when she thought that the hopes of democracy were over, has been rescued, physically and politically, by the latest developments. So the conclusion is not entirely pessimistic.

Ana non ends on a plural negative ('des nons'). But the text has been a gradual move from the negative 'non' of rejection and abandonment, to the positive 'non' of antagonistic affirmation. It is here juxtaposed with its homonym of creation: 'des noms'; it personalises anonymity.

The last words of *Scène de chasse*, the most violent and vituperative of all these novels, are: 'Ils éclatent de rire, mère et fils. Mangent à leur faim. Se comportent comme s'ils venaient d'entrer dans ce monde. De plein droit. Comme si dès maintenant, ce monde était habitable' (p. 374).

The last seventy pages of *Pré Papa* are written in a mock-heroic vein, expressing an idealism which is the mystical counterpart of the protagonist's previous naïve and total acceptance of technology. Beneath the irony, however, is an invitation to us to give a sharp, critical look at the direction in which modern society and its values are taking us, to refuse to substitute the god of Science for the God of Christianity, and to create instead a new way of life, based on our real needs. At the end, after reflecting on the inevitable recurrence of war, John prepares to leave for another planet, so that he can be 'Libre! Libre de dire mon fils, viens quand tu voudras [. . .] Libre de lui donner la vie sans penser à la mort. – Oui. Une expérience unique, le commencement d'une immense aventure' (p. 320).

The end of *L'Enfant miraculée* is violent, but the final paragraph is full of positive words (plaisir, aube, joie, nouvelle, douce, grâce, soleil), and the final sentence leaves us in no doubt that Juliana, like the equally iconoclastic Maria Republica, has abolished slavery and lies through her act of destruction: 'L'enfant miraculée devient phare, bûcher, cri de liberté dans ce matin nouveau-né' (p. 288). *L'Enfant pain* is permeated with fear, hunger and sadness. Yet the last actions are the exchange of mourning for bright clothes, the family finally sitting down to a meal, and the child narrator going happily to bed.

Despite the bitterly destructive satire, then, these novels are vibrant with the instinct for life. The omnipresence of death and suffering in the world undermines the quality of life. But the response is the angry protest which impels both characters and text onwards: 'Dire non à la mort. Et aller de l'avant' (*Ana non*, p. 11). Gomez-Arcos may set out to denounce imposture and injustice, but he does this with the constructive aim of initiating renewal and progress. He writes with the confidence that, with wit and courage, human beings can survive any situation, however extreme. This optimism is in itself rare in an age of doubt and widespread cynicism.

If it is political fervour that gives these novels their satirical edge, it is the vivacity of their language and warmth of characterisation that gives them their appeal. Gomez-Arcos's savage wit and iconoclasm recall writers such as Céline, Pinget and Tournier. Yet there is a tenderness, a gaiety and an idealism in his work that is absent from theirs. It is present in the work of Vian and Queneau but seems otherwise to have become submerged in the modern French novel under an increasing complexity of techniques, which effectively delete human beings and their stories from literature.

Gomez-Arcos delights in telling stories and has no time for intellectual abstractions. Both these things are unusual among contemporary French novelists. This distaste for abstraction obviously does not signify a lack of ideas. There are in fact many ideas and even arguments developed in his novels. But they are communicated through action and interaction; they are made concrete through gestures and situations, as on stage. This gives a tremendous impression of vitality to his novels. The ideas, like the characters, come alive. As Teresa says of the books Luis used to pass around among the factory workers, the words had sometimes been effaced because so many hands had thumbed them: 'mais ils sont une bombe de contenu. [. . .] le texte vit' (*Scène de chasse*, p. 275). Gomez-Arcos's novels also have the explosive force of a bomb. They are socially subversive, and they make an aesthetic impact through their striking metaphors and innovative style.

Gomez-Arcos therefore builds on techniques in the *nouveau roman*, while seeming to return to the tradition of Realism. A story is told, convincing characters are created, and a message is conveyed. Yet what happens is less important than the feelings behind it. Above all, these narratives – by turns sad, entertaining and horrifying – move us because they are not just fictions, however invented or even fantastical the individual anecdotes may be. The events particularise real life issues: 'Je ne parle pas de ma vie, ni de ma vie toute seule. Je parle de la vie de mes pareils, de leur vie totale', says Teresa (*Scène de chasse*, p. 267). There is an undeniably documentary role to his narratives, yet their main force lies in their portrayal of human values. The fact that only *Un Oiseau brûlé vif* and *Bestiaire* are situated in recent years (the other novels being more immediately post-Civil War) suggests that the aim of political actuality is less crucial than that of highlighting the moral issues beneath it which transcend a specific place and time.

For this is committed literature in the truest sense. The author is committed to his beliefs, and the reader is committed to the act of reading. We are not passively spellbound; our critical faculties are left intact – sharpened even. But we are involved in the novel; we experience the situations and feelings, as in the theatre, and we cannot remain unaffected. The text gains validity through reference to a reality we know to exist, but it is compelling because it exteriorises unconscious drives which do not belong to the logical world of argument. They can only be brought to the surface, into the familiar and accepted world, through an explosion of repressed material. This explosion, so often the subject and dénouement of Agustin Gomez-Arcos's novels, is also their substance. It is this which gives them their significance.

Bibliography

Novels by Agustin Gomez-Arcos

L'Agneau carnivore (Stock, 1975) – Prix Hermès, 1975
Maria Republica (Stock, 1976)
Ana non (Stock, 1977)
Scène de chasse (furtive) (Stock, 1978)
Pré Papa ou Roman de fées (Stock, 1979)
L'Enfant miraculée (Fayard, 1981)
L'Enfant pain (Editions du Seuil, 1983)
Un Oiseau brûlé vif (Editions du Seuil, 1984)
Bestiaire (Le Pré aux clercs, 1986)

Review article

Christian Andejean, '*Ana non*', *Esprit*, 5 (1977), 124–30

-7-

Patrick Modiano

ALAN MORRIS*

Uniquely among the major authors of his generation, Patrick Modiano was thrust into novel writing by emotional necessity. Born in Boulogne-Billancourt of a half-Hungarian, half-Belgian actress and a mysterious, Mediterranean, Jewish *apatride*, he quickly came to see himself as an individual of dubious pedigree, an exotic mass of Franco-Semitic contradictions. A childhood plagued by upheaval and solitude – he was first abandoned by his father, then his brother, and his close friend Rudy died – served to nourish the feeling of insecurity which this confused heritage brought him, and so the older he grew, the more he found himself looking backwards with a sense of loss and disappointment. Being unable to appease this inner turmoil elsewhere, he duly turned to creative writing as the answer to his problems, revelling in the freedom this gave him to re-invent the past and hence establish a more satisfactory life history for himself. As he declared in 1976, following his interview with Emmanuel Berl: 'En face de Berl, je retourne à mes préoccupations: le temps, le passé, la mémoire. Il les ravive, ces préoccupations. Il m'encourage dans mon dessein: me créer un passé et une mémoire avec le passé et la mémoire des autres.'[1] It is in the light of this revelation, then, and, of course, in the light of the identity crisis which subtends it, that the *œuvre* of Patrick Modiano can most usefully be approached.

Modiano burst onto the literary scene in 1968 with a startling novel which won two worthy prizes and a great deal of critical acclaim. Its title, *La Place de l'Etoile*, was a reference both to the famous Paris landmark and to the place where the Jews wore the star of David during the Occupation – over the heart. This is significant, for the book is basically a French Jew's *cri de cœur*, a

*I gratefully record my indebtedness to David Gascoigne and Ian Higgins, whose encouragement and suggestions have been invaluable.
1. Emmanuel Berl, *'Interrogatoire par Patrick Modiano' suivi de 'Il fait beau, allons au cimetière'*, p. 9.

passionate examination of Jewish identity. Modiano was not the first to tackle the thorny subject of the *question juive*, but he deals with an old topic in an excitingly new way, namely by creating Raphaël Schlemilovitch. A composite of many different, stereotyped personalities, Schlemilovitch is the unlikely embodiment of all things Semitic, an archetypal token of his people as a whole, as one critic immediately noticed: 'Qu'ils s'aiment ou non, qu'ils s'acceptent ou non, tous les juifs de ce monde sont un seul juif, qui s'appelle toujours Raphaël Schlemilovitch – et un seul juif, hélas! porte le poids de tous les autres, présents, passés et à venir.'[2] In other words, to make a comparison based on the novel itself, he is just like the kaleidoscope his father makes: 'un visage humain composé de mille facettes lumineuses et qui change sans arrêt de forme . . .' (pp. 109–10).

Because of this splintering of its narrative voice, *La Place de l'Etoile* cannot be judged as though it were a classical novel. It must be recognised for what it is: an incongruous, comical voyage in space and time, where the primary logic to which Raphaël adheres is the logic of Jewish precedent. For example, he imitates Sachs and Joanovici by becoming a 'juif collabo'; he works hard to get into the *Ecole normale supérieure* like Fleg, Blum and Henri Franck, and he even falls victim to tuberculosis simply because Franz Kafka had had the disease before him. In fact, surprising as it may seem, his 'retour à la terre' phase can also be interpreted in this manner, for Pétain's seminal dictum which he adapts and appropriates – 'Je hais les mensonges qui m'ont fait tant de mal. La terre, elle, ne ment pas' (p. 83) – was, in reality, conceived by Emmanuel Berl, a Jew.[3]

Thus, singular or plural, Raphaël sticks closely to the path laid down for him by history. But it is not merely historical figures and events which give him his *raison d'être*; he is equally dependent on present-day (anti-Semitic) assumptions about what makes a Jew a Jew. This is apparent from the opening paragraph, for his reference to his 'héritage vénézuélien' plays on 'well-known' Jewish internationalism (a point taken up later when he mentions his cousins in Cairo, London, Paris, Caracas, Istanbul, Trieste and Budapest), and his very name would satisfy most people as being 'typical' of his race. Indeed, all through the novel Raphaël openly acknowledges his debt to popular prejudice, readily accepting the roles he is allotted – 'Je jouerai à ma façon le rôle du jeune milliardaire' (p.

---

2. Josane Duranteau, 'Un début exceptionnel: *La Place de l'Etoile*, de Patrick Modiano', p. I.
3. See Emmanuel Berl, *'Interrogatoire par Patrick Modiano'* suivi de *'Il fait beau, allons au cimetière'*, p. 88.

34); 'Je jouerai à la perfection mon rôle de persécuté' (p. 62) – and brazenly admitting to all imputed crimes:

> oui, je dirige le complot juif mondial à coups de partouzes et de millions. Oui, la guerre de 1939 a été déclarée par ma faute. Oui, je suis une sorte de Barbe-Bleue, un anthropophage qui dévore les petites Aryennes après les avoir violées. Oui, je rêve de ruiner toute la paysannerie française et d'enjuiver le Cantal. (p. 35)

Obviously, then, character-acting is something Raphaël excels at.

This penchant for theatricality is again displayed when Raphaël meets Charles Lévy-Vendôme, who is the-Jew-as-seen-by-the-anti-Semite *par excellence*. As his name suggests, Lévy-Vendôme personifies the Semitic 'threat' to France, for not only does he send young French women to work abroad in brothels, he transforms literary classics into erotica: 'Non content de débaucher les femmes de ce pays, j'ai voulu aussi prostituer toute la littérature française' (p. 68). Needless to say, Raphaël is easily persuaded to emulate this behaviour, and quickly becomes involved in the white slave trade himself. He then crowns his subversive activities by having an affair with a marquise – because she dresses up as a different celebrity each time they make love, the symbolic result is that 'il souilla la France à loisir' (p. 95).

As if this anti-Gallic stance were not provocative enough, Raphaël extends his repertoire to take in the role of anti-Semite. He joins the team of *Je suis partout*; he mingles with Maurras and his companions on the extreme right; he acts like a *camelot du Roi* in assisting Debigorre; and finally, to cap it all, he goes so far as to become a Nazi. Such conduct appears entirely irrational at first glance, but it is not. By putting himself in the place of his avowed enemies, Raphaël is able to get a different perspective on things and hence achieve a better understanding of his position and status as a Jew. Furthermore, while he is doing this he can indulge the other half of his schizophrenic character – he can show himself to be well and truly *French* and accept the anti-Semitic heritage which, historically, this implies.

Hand in hand with this quest for self-awareness goes a deep-seated desire to lay down roots, for throughout the novel Raphaël is extremely conscious of the fact that he is an alien in France. 'Je ne suis pas un enfant de ce pays', he observes (p. 12), and his feelings of isolation are rendered the more intense by the near-total absence of his parents. He occasionally refers to his mother, and he does meet with his father at one stage, but these two characters soon disappear completely from his life, as he makes perfectly clear later: 'Notre mère était morte ou folle. Nous ne connaissions pas l'adresse de notre père à New York' (p. 103). (Note how the use of *nous* here underlines his lack of a stable identity.) Though Raphaël finds a measure of consolation for this rootlessness in the work of Henri Bordeaux – 'Juif apatride, j'aspirais goulûment le parfum terrien qui se dégage de ces chefs-d'œuvre' (p. 73) – the remedy to which he turns most frequently is the creation of additional family ties. First, by planning to marry: he has fiancées in every province when working *la traite des blanches,* and he seems quite eager to wed any woman he encounters, whether it be Rebecca, the Israeli soldier, or Hilda, whose father is a strict SS disciplinarian. Second, by linking himself to surrogate relatives: he thinks nothing of claiming to be 'le frère jumeau du juif Süss' (p. 113), nor does he hesitate to speak of 'mon père, le vicomte Lévy-Vendôme' (p. 85), 'Des Essarts, mon frère' (p. 105), 'mon cousin, le peintre juif Modigliani' (p. 113), 'mon grand-père, le colonel Aravis' (p. 75) or 'mon grand-oncle Adrien Debigorre' (p. 75). His view of Maurras and his helpers at *L'Action Française* further reflects this state of affairs: 'Depuis mon enfance je rêvais à des grands-pères de ce genre. Le mien, juif obscur d'Odessa, ne savait pas parler français' (p. 25).

This search for some sort of anchorage reaches its peak when Raphaël sets off for Israel, 'la terre ancestrale' (p. 122), but on arrival in Tel Aviv he quickly discovers that he is no more welcome there than he was in France. The Israelis are obsessed by strength and have nothing but disdain for their European counterparts: 'Nous ne voulons plus entendre parler de l'esprit critique juif, de l'intelligence juive, du scepticisme juif, des contorsions juives, de l'humiliation, du malheur juif et patati et patata' (p. 133). Such a depiction of the Jewish homeland no doubt derives from the popular belief that Israel is composed of militarists, all determined to assert their power and ensure that they are never victimised again. Nevertheless, there is also a nightclub in the capital where German uniforms must be worn, so the stereotyped 'couple éternel du SS et de la juive' (p. 22) has by no means been forgotten.

On an entirely different level there is one final way in which Raphaël tries to establish roots – by writing, which allows him to attach himself to a whole cultural tradition. His portrayal of the marquise de Fougeire-Jusquiames has distinct (and avowed) overtones of Proust, while his liking for literary regionalism can clearly be attributed to François Mauriac, among others. These are not the only writers on whom he draws, though. As long as he plays the role of Franco-Jewish-author-in-search-of-an-identity, he is, of course, in exactly the same position as Modiano himself. This being the case, it is no surprise that he can be found to share a common background with the man who invented him. For example, in one of his incarnations, he too, like his creator, was born in Boulogne-Billancourt, lived on the quai Conti in Paris, had family origins in Thessalonika and was just under two metres tall. There is another area of contact as well. 'Comment se fait-il que vous vous rappeliez tout cela', Freud asks him in the closing pages of the book, 'vous n'étiez pas né' (p. 150); it is a remark which could just as easily be addressed to Modiano himself, for he was not born until after V-E Day either (not until 30 July 1945, to be exact). Because of this, then, *La Place de l'Etoile* can perhaps best be interpreted as an apocryphal autobiography, a therapeutic exercise in which the memories recounted are almost wholly fictitious. In short, it appears to be a work designed to assuage the anguish of narrator and author alike.

Modiano's second novel, *La Ronde de nuit* (1969), takes up virtually where his first leaves off – in the dark, dank world of the wartime French Gestapo. The same gang of *gestapistes* is discernible in both texts, and the sense of continuity is further heightened by the new narrator's resemblance to his predecessor, as the focus of his reading illustrates: 'Quelques livres: *Anthologie des traîtres, d'Alcibiade au capitaine Dreyfus, Joanovici tel qu'il fut, Les Mystères du Chevalier d'Eon, Frégoli, l'homme de nulle part*, m'éclairèrent sur mon compte' (p. 122). What is more, the theme of identity which pervaded *La Place de l'Etoile* is still very much in evidence, for as Modiano explains: 'Dans les deux livres, c'est toujours la recherche d'une identité: l'identité juive, pour le premier et dans le second plutôt une fuite instinctive devant toute identification.'[4]

This authorial summary of *La Ronde de nuit* is particularly helpful, for the central character is indeed extremely hard to pin down. At first (if the chronology of events is reconstructed), things are simple enough – he is Swing Troubadour, a *gestapiste* working at 3bis square Cimarosa for le Khédive and M. Philibert. The picture becomes more obscure, however, after he has been asked by his employers to join the Resistance as an undercover agent. He successfully completes the mission, receiving the *nom de guerre* Princesse de Lamballe, but is then delegated to infiltrate the Gestapo. It is at this point that confusion really occurs, for his attachment to both sides means, in effect, that he belongs to neither. Whenever he is a *résistant*, his persona of Swing Troubadour is annulled and vice versa: 'Agent double? ou triple? Je ne savais plus qui j'étais. Mon lieutenant, JE N'EXISTE PAS' (p. 132). Similarly, when he denounces Lamballe

4. Jean Montalbetti, 'Patrick Modiano ou l'esprit de fuite,' p. 42.

as the head of the network, he is on the one hand asserting his own identity (giving himself the status of the leader) and on the other immediately destroying it (earmarking himself for liquidation). It is consequently quite natural for him to conclude: 'A ce jeu-là, on finit par se perdre soi-même. De toute façon, je n'ai jamais su qui j'étais' (p. 175). This would in turn partly explain why he often dresses up as a woman, and why he can claim to be Marcel Petiot, Landru, Philippe Pétain, Maxime de Bel-Respiro and King Lear.

The same personality crisis colours Swing Troubadour/ Lamballe's treatment of Coco Lacour and Esmeralda, his two imaginary friends. Being to all intents and purposes an orphan – his mother is far away in Lausanne and his father (the infamous swindler Alexandre Stavisky) is dead – he finds in these peculiar comrades a kind of compensatory presence, a means of escape from his deficient family background: 'Nous menions, square Cimarosa, une vie de famille' (p. 163), he confesses. Moreover, by using his ill-gotten gains to protect this vulnerable couple, he can, to a certain degree, both justify his criminality and convince himself of his personal importance:

> Coco Lacour et Esmeralda. Misérables. Infirmes. Toujours silencieux. Un souffle, un geste aurait suffi pour les briser. Que seraient-ils devenus sans moi? Je trouvais enfin une excellente raison de vivre. Je les aimais, mes pauvres monstres. Je veillerais sur eux . . . Personne ne pourrait leur faire de mal. Grâce à l'argent que je gagnais square Cimarosa, en qualité d'indic et de pillard, je leur assurerais tout le confort possible. (p. 160)

Yet despite this statement of good intentions, he sometimes feels like abandoning his helpless companions, or far worse, pushing them under a train in the metro. As the couple gives him his reason for living, their symbolic murder again shows his propensity for self-destruction.

This uncertain, schizophrenic approach to life permeates every aspect of Swing Troubadour/Lamballe's behaviour, for not even his treachery is as clear-cut as is generally the case. First of all, his recruitment by the Gestapo in no way represents a commitment on his part; like the eponymous (anti-)hero of Louis Malle's film *Lacombe Lucien* (1974), the screenplay of which Modiano helped write, he joins up not by conscious choice, but rather by accident (pp. 101–2). Secondly, he relentlessly denies that he is malicious, no matter how much evil he actually generates. 'Je n'étais pas plus méchant qu'un autre', he protests; 'J'ai suivi le mouvement, voilà tout. Je n'éprouve pour le mal aucune attirance particulière' (p. 141). Thus, to use the author's own phrase, 'l'action se situe dans un contexte moral, mais elle est vécue par un être dépourvu de tout sens moral'.[5] Swing Troubadour/Lamballe is, in other words, doubly ambiguous. Not only does he have no permanent physical identity; he has no moral identity either.

The result of this dilemma is that Swing Troubadour/Lamballe finds himself trapped in an ever more distressing *ronde* of mental torment. Initially, it is because of the pressure placed on him to be decisive for once that his head goes into a spin, the *gestapistes* seeming to rotate rapidly as they encourage him to betray the Resistance: 'Une ronde autour de moi, de plus en plus rapide, de plus en plus bruyante, et je finirai par céder pour qu'ils me laissent tranquille' (p. 90). Yet, when the act of treachery has been committed, there is no appeasement for him; he becomes subject to pangs of remorse, so his state of mind remains unchanged, as he himself admits: 'Le RE-MORDS. Ces visages n'en finiront pas de tourner et, désormais, vous dormirez mal' (pp. 54–5).

What makes *La Ronde de nuit* such a polished work is the fact that the narrator's *vertige* is not merely *described* in this explicit manner, it is, above all, *evoked*. The entire text is punctuated with echoes and reflections of what has gone before, to such an extent that the novel, as its title suggests, follows a circular and not a linear course. The very first section of the book turns back in on itself, starting and ending with laughter in the darkness, and many sentences and phrases are repeated at regular intervals, with only slight variations, if any: 'un beau coup de filet en perspective' (pp. 15, 49, 68, 118, 123) and 'Aucune importance' (pp. 133, 155, 156, 163, 168), for instance. Furthermore, there is frequent reference to the constantly turning caterpillar at Luna-Park and, more importantly, to the Princesse de Lamballe's downfall, whether it be the execution of the historical figure (p. 61), the tipping of someone from a bed at a fairground stall (p. 92) or Goya's painting of her demise (p. 140). Princesse de Lamballe is, of course, the name the narrator uses in his guise of *résistant*, so his death is allusively forecast once more.

It is in the closing pages, however, that the impression of impending doom is at its most intense. Having failed in an attempt to kill le Khédive, Swing Troubadour/Lamballe is trying desperately to drive away from his former colleagues, but without success. They are hot on his heels, tracking him and toying with him, ready to take their revenge at any minute, and because of this, his days appear to be well and truly numbered.

Or do they? Elsewhere in the text there are strong indications that Swing Troubadour/Lamballe's nightmare is, in reality, over and

5. Ibid.

that he is now simply *remembering* the events he relates. Probably the clearest demonstration of this is the incident which occurs, significantly, roughly halfway through the book (pp. 83–4). On a day when, again significantly, the sun is shining brightly, he looks at the house at 3bis and claims that, although strange things went on when he used to live there, the shutters have been closed for a long time. Such an unequivocal revelation firmly establishes the time-scale in the work. Swing Troubadour/Lamballe's treachery and remorse, at first assumed to be experienced in the present, are in actual fact part of the past, which a stroll round Paris forces him to re-enact. He even reflects at one point: 'Vous voudriez oublier le passé mais votre promenade vous ramène sans cesse aux carrefours douloureux' (p. 118). It is therefore fitting that during his walk he should come across '*La Ronde de nuit*, une opérette bien oubliée' (p. 105); the operetta is no doubt a symbol for his own *ronde de nuit, forgotten* in the sense that it belongs to a bygone era, yet still playing, still haunting him at the current moment.

While the intrusive quality of memory is plainly the root cause of the narrator's anxiety, it would be wrong to infer that the power of recollection is cast solely in an unfavourable light in the novel. Far from it. On a more positive note, the ability to remember things is seen as an effective counter to the ravages of time. Throughout the book the central character is fully aware of the ease with which people and objects disappear, leaving no trace at all of their brief existence on the planet. 'De tant de frénésie, tumulte, violences, que reste-t-il?', he wonders, thinking back to the Fair at Luna-Park; 'Une esplanade vide en bordure du boulevard Gouvion-Saint-Cyr' (p. 92) is his sad reply. But he also knows that, by preserving his unique memories in print, irrespective of whether they are real or invented, he can at least save something from the obscurity which beckons: 'Le temps a passé. Si je n'écrivais pas leur nom: Coco Lacour, Esmeralda, il n'y aurait aucune trace de leur séjour en ce monde' (p. 91). In other words, like *La Place de l'Etoile* before it, Modiano's second text can be viewed as a (frequently imaginary) form of memoir.

It is in this context that a comparison between *La Ronde de nuit* and Rembrandt's famous canvas of the same name (*The Night Watch* in English) bears fruit. Like its fictional counterpart, the old master's painting depicts a gathering of military men and has an atmosphere of dreamy unreality. But more notably, to the left in the picture, doused in bright light, stands a young girl. Many critics see in this figure a personal intrusion by the artist, the reflection of somebody close to him, and this suggests that in the book, too, the illuminated character is linked to his creator. This being the case, it seems fair to conclude that, behind the walker of the sunlit streets of Paris, it is Modiano himself who is composing the fictitious autobiography.

The next landmark in Modiano's career is *Les Boulevards de ceinture* (1972), winner of the prestigious *Grand Prix du roman de l'Académie française*. This *récit* (to give it its proper generic classification) brings a marked refinement to the atmosphere of hallucinatory anguish found in the first two novels, but in most other respects continuity is maintained. The focus of the narrative – the world of collaborationist journalism – palpably builds on Raphaël Schlemilovitch's spell at *Je suis partout*; incidents mentioned earlier are elaborated upon; and established characters and well-worn phrases and images reappear. Moreover, the major concern of the work is still the question of identity, although the topic is now approached in a slightly different way – via the search for an absent parent.

It is the narrator, Serge Alexandre, who feels the need to embark on this quest, but his venture is by no means easy to undertake, for it requires a tremendous input on his part:

> On s'intéresse à un homme, disparu depuis longtemps. On voudrait interroger les personnes qui l'ont connu mais leurs traces se sont effacées avec les siennes. Sur ce qu'a été sa vie, on ne possède que de très vagues indications souvent contradictoires, deux ou trois points de repère. Pièces à conviction? un timbre-poste et une fausse Légion d'honneur. Alors il ne reste plus qu'à imaginer. (p. 148)

By using his imagination in this manner Serge is able to travel back in time to the Occupation and successfully make contact with his father, who is passing himself off as Baron Chalva Deyckecaire. But this success is understandably short-lived. At the end of the book the baron ages by thirty years as the temporal perspective is reestablished, and Serge readily concedes that he is no further forward than he was at the start: 'Qui êtes-vous? J'ai beau vous avoir suivi pendant des jours et des jours, je ne sais rien de vous. Une silhouette devinée sous la veilleuse' (p. 198). Like the ring roads of the title and, indeed, like the structure of the *récit* itself, he has gone round and round in a circle, because the only vital information he has obtained has been of his own making. He has, in fact, unwittingly followed the same path as Marcheret: 'Orphelin, Marcheret l'avait toujours été. Et s'il s'engagea à la Légion, ce fut peut-être pour retrouver la trace de son père. Mais il n'y avait au rendez-vous que la solitude, le sable et les mirages du désert' (p. 75).

Serge's failure is not total, however, because one essential goal *has* been achieved. If he has not been able to discover what his father was *actually* like, he has at least managed to choose a certain *kind* of father for himself, one who satisfies his emotional requirements: 'Par quel prodige vous avais-je connu quand vous n'étiez pas encore mon père? [. . .] Pourquoi avais-je voulu, si tôt, être votre fils?' (pp. 142–3). It does not matter that the details he dreams up cannot be corroborated, for he feels that they are true, and that is the important thing: 'je n'invente rien. Non, ça n'est pas cela, inventer . . . Il existe certainement des preuves, une personne qui vous a connu, jadis, et qui pourrait témoigner de toutes ces choses. Peu importe. Je suis avec vous et je le resterai jusqu'à la fin du livre' (pp. 161–2). Clearly, then, the very undertaking of the quest has brought a measure of psychological relief, and it is not hard to see why – by 'adopting' the parent of his choice, he has momentarily acquired the identity he lacks. For as he reveals: 'C'était *moi* que je traquais sans relâche' (p. 166).

Yet it is not simply the question of who he is that obsesses him, because this particular problem is linked to a far more general one, namely the destructive power of time. If nearly all trace of his father had not vanished with the passing of the years, he would not now be in the predicament he is in. Consequently, his quest is also an attempt to rescue the past for posterity, as his fascination with curricula vitae demonstrates:

> Je sais bien que le curriculum vitae de ces ombres ne présente pas un grand intérêt, mais si je ne le dressais pas aujourd'hui, personne d'autre ne s'y emploierait. C'est mon devoir, à moi qui les ai connus, de les sortir – ne fût-ce qu'un instant – de la nuit. C'est mon devoir et c'est aussi, pour moi, un véritable besoin. (pp. 68–9)

Such dedication to the task in hand is exemplary, but as already noted, there remains something extremely peculiar about the way Serge executes his project. Despite such reassuring statements as 'Bien des années ont passé, mais les visages, les gestes, les inflexions de voix restent gravés dans ma mémoire' (p. 172), the 'knowledge' on which he draws is largely fictitious and eminently questionable. For this reason, *Les Boulevards de ceinture* must be approached with caution. The work is not the straightforward autobiography it often appears to be; it is, on the contrary, a complete fabrication. The memories portrayed are *not* those of the narrator. And more notably perhaps, they are not those of the author either.

La Place de l'Étoile, *La Ronde de nuit*, and *Les Boulevards de ceinture* thus show a considerable amount of overlap when analysed together, and so strong are the obvious similarities between them that a fruitful new line of attack becomes possible. While these texts

can be read and appreciated individually, as self-contained arte-
facts, there is, nevertheless, a lot to be gained from tackling them as
a sort of informal trilogy, for by Modiano's own admission:

> On pourrait dire qu'il s'agit d'un seul livre. On retrouve à travers les trois
> romans les mêmes thèmes, tantôt esquissés, tantôt amplifiés (ainsi le
> thème du père est esquissé dans le premier roman puis développé dans le
> troisième). Ces trois romans ne constituent pas une suite chronologique
> mais un enchevêtrement, une sorte de miroir dont les trois faces se
> renvoient les mêmes images.[6]

Some of these reflected images are patently the themes of identity,
time, memory and the past, as may now be apparent, but there is
another major leitmotif which is no less worthy of mention here –
the focus on the dark years of the German occupation.

Each book in the 'trilogy' (and *Lacombe Lucien*, too, for that
matter) derives a great deal of its impact from a unique, carefully
studied re-creation of the *années noires*; so much so that Modiano has
often been hailed as the trailblazer of *la mode rétro*.[7] Justified though
this epithet may be, however, it is in many respects misleading, for
the novelist denies that he is interested in the war years in themselves. His interest, he asserts, is to a large extent literary: 'Il y a eu
un quiproquo à propos de mes trois premiers livres. L'époque ne
m'intéresse pas pour elle-même. J'y ai greffé mes angoisses. Mais
mon Occupation est une Occupation rêvée. C'est en quoi elle relève
de la littérature, et pas de l'histoire ou de la médecine mentale.'[8]
What is more, he has consistently pointed to links between the 1940s
and more recent times, and hence argued that, under the guise of
portraying the past, he is really discussing subjects relevant to the
present. The validity of this claim can hardly be queried, for
although the principal concerns of his first two novels – the *question
juive* and treachery – were highlighted most poignantly under
Pétain, few would contest that they remain issues of moment today.
And the same can be said of *Les Boulevards de ceinture*, because

> Ce père minable et fantomatique que recherche le narrateur peut être le
> symbole de beaucoup de choses. Symbole de l'effritement des Valeurs
> (avec un grand V), de la disparition de tout principe d'autorité et de toute

6. Victor Malka, 'Patrick Modiano: un homme sur du sable mouvant', p. 2.
7. *La mode rétro* embodied a nationwide renewal of interest in the Occupation and was
   one of the most dominant trends in the post-Gaullist France of the 1970s. For
   fuller details of the movement and Modiano's part in it, see my article, 'Attacks on
   the Gaullist "myth" in French literature since 1969'. See also Colin Nettelbeck,
   'Getting the story right: narratives of World War II in post-1968 France', and
   Pascal Ory, 'Comme de l'an quarante. Dix années de "rétro satanas".'
8. Dominique Jamet, 'Patrick Modiano s'explique', p. 36.

assise morale, etc. . . . toutes choses qui étaient liées à l'image traditionnelle du Père. Le père des *Boulevards de ceinture* est une sorte de dérision
désespérée du Père dans l'absolu.[9]

One reason for Modiano's obsession with the Occupation, then, is
a purely professional one – the period provides him with an evocative, symbolic setting in which the timeless problem of the self can be
studied from different angles (What makes me a Jew? Why am I a
traitor? Whose son am I?). But there is much more to his retrospection than this. It can also be seen that he looks back to the *années
noires* out of personal necessity, for his writing manifests eloquent
signs of a desperate, compulsive exorcism. Nowhere is this better
illustrated than in *La Place de l'Etoile*, which allows him on the one
hand to exteriorise the nightmare of the Holocaust and on the other
to take a measure of revenge on the oppressors of his race (Raphaël
kills Gérard le Gestapiste and then proceeds to put the best-known
collaborators and Nazis on show in Port Said). Yet *La Place de
l'Etoile* is hardly exceptional in this respect; a similar analysis can be
made of *La Ronde de nuit*, because here, too, the author is visibly
trying to lay one of his ghosts to rest:

> Parfois la nuit . . . je me pose cette terrible question . . . si j'avais vécu en
> quarante . . . moi Modiano? . . . Qu'est-ce que j'aurais fait? . . . Je crois
> bien . . . franchement . . . que j'aurais été un salaud . . . Enfin, j'aurais
> d'abord été un salaud . . . et puis j'aurais changé . . . après . . . comme les
> autres . . . j'aurais fini . . . non pas en héros . . . mais en martyr . . .
> Franchement, je le crois! Ça m'obsède . . .[10]

In the light of this 'Ça m'obsède', it comes as no surprise to discover
that *Les Boulevards de ceinture* is another act of self-purging. But now it
is perhaps not the Occupation itself that the novelist needs to put
firmly behind him but his own *infatuation* with the period, for he
confides (through his narrator) that this book will be 'le dernier
concernant [son] autre vie' (p. 162). And in his next novel, *Villa
Triste* (1975), he is perceptibly true to his word.

Unlike the three works which predate it, *Villa Triste* centres
mainly on the 1960s, so it is quite apparent that the author has
indeed abandoned the other life he 'lived' during the *années noires*.
But this is not to say that there has been a radical change of
direction in his fiction. On the contrary. Notwithstanding a more
linear, less circular narrative, the continuity of the preceding texts is
maintained, for there is 'un climat trouble qui rappelle l'Occupation

9. Victor Malka, 'Patrick Modiano: un homme sur du sable mouvant', p. 2.
10. Bernard Pivot, 'Demi-juif Patrick Modiano affirme: "Céline était un véritable
    écrivain juif" ', p. 16.

par sa teinte crépusculaire',[11] and, moreover, all the familiar themes recur. The (anti-)hero – Victor Chmara – is again a fearful, rootless individual in search of family ties; a number of father figures – Pulli, Yvonne's uncle – can once more be identified; and the basic subject matter of the novel remains unaltered: 'C'est la nostalgie de quelqu'un qui se fabrique des souvenirs imaginaires, parce qu'il en a le temps', the novelist himself affirms, 'c'est la nostalgie de quelqu'un qui puise dans cette vie rêvée les ressources qui manquent à la sienne. [. . .] J'essaie simplement de montrer comment le temps passe et recouvre tout, choses et gens.'[12] Thus, when all is said and done, Modiano's approach has deviated little from the pattern established earlier. He can still confess: 'C'est moi, mais à travers une autobiographie complètement rêvée.'[13]

One specific example will help to illustrate the dearth of thematic innovation in *Villa Triste* – the use of a neutral country to symbolise an unattainable state of emotional tranquillity. Switzerland is the country involved and Chmara is, predictably, the character enticed by the mirage-like comfort it represents:

> Moi, j'avais peur, encore plus qu'aujourd'hui et j'avais choisi ce lieu de refuge parce qu'il était situé à cinq kilomètres de la Suisse. Il suffisait de traverser le lac, à la moindre alerte. Dans ma naïveté, je croyais que plus on se rapproche de la Suisse, plus on a de chance de s'en sortir. Je ne savais pas encore que la Suisse n'existe pas. (pp. 14–15)

This concept of a refuge that cannot be reached harks back distinctly to Modiano's previous work, and in particular to *La Ronde de nuit*, for Swing Troubadour/Lamballe initially thinks that he can dispel his anguish by running away to Lausanne, but then eventually comes to concede: 'Lausanne ne me suffirait pas' (p. 174). Similarly, in *Lacombe Lucien*, Horn makes costly arrangements to flee to the safety of Spain, only to admit in the end: 'L'Espagne, l'Espagne! Ça n'existe pas l'Espagne . . .' (p. 114). In fact, so persistent is this leitmotif that the same procedure re-emerges in the text that follows *Villa Triste*, *Livret de famille* (1977).

Livret de famille is a seemingly disjointed but subtly unified collection of *récits*, in one of which the narrator actually manages to enter Switzerland and announce 'J'avais atteint cet état que j'appelais: "la Suisse du cœur"' (p. 98). However, his peace is soon troubled by D., 'le personnage le plus hideux du Paris de l'Occupation' (p. 105), and so disillusionment inevitably sets in: 'Il n'y avait plus qu'à se

---

11. J.J., 'Patrick Modiano à la question', p. 14.
12. Jean-Louis Ezine, 'Sur la sellette: Patrick Modiano ou le passé antérieur', p. 5.
13. Dominique Jamet, 'Patrick Modiano s'explique', p. 27.

laisser submerger par cette léthargie que je m'obstinais à appeler: la Suisse du cœur' (p. 120). Once again, then, the so-called haven does not offer the relief it seemed to promise.

But this is not the only manner in which *Livret de famille* builds on what has gone before; Modiano also returns to the obsession with paternal surrogates. The registry office man is seen to have 'un regard très doux, presque paternel' (p. 20); Le Gros openly declares 'J'ai envie de vous adopter' (p. 125); of Marignan it is noted: 'Parfois il me semble même qu'il fut l'une des multiples incarnations de mon père' (p. 23); and the list goes on, not least because innumerable contacts in the film world have to be included, as Georges Rollner indicates:

> 'Vous êtes parent avec Stocklin?'
> 'Je . . . je ne crois pas', lui dis-je.
> Il me souriait et me tapotait le crâne, d'une main paternelle.
> 'De toute façon . . . Nous sommes tous parents entre nous . . . Le cinéma est une grande famille . . .' (pp. 89–90).

What all this signifies in more general terms, of course, is that, as is now usual, an identity is being sought through the creation of family ties.

In spite of these echoes of previous texts, *Livret de famille* is anything but a simple rehash of old material, for it contains clear evidence of an authorial state of mind that is in many ways new. For the first time in his work Modiano makes lengthy, explicit reference to his own real-life situation. Pages are devoted to his grandmother, his mother, his wife and his daughter, and there is mention, too, of his father, his grandfather and his brother Rudy. Furthermore, the narrator is even called Patrick or Modiano on occasion. Why should this be? There are, it would appear, two perfectly good explanations. First, as irrefutable facts, the intimate personal details help to confer a psychological *vraisemblance* on the book as a whole and hence make it, as its title suggests, an appealing substitute for the full *livret de famille* after which the author hankers. Second, it could well be that marriage has transformed Modiano's outlook, and that he has become more confident, and hence more forthcoming, about the strength of his *état civil*. Certainly, his comments on his engagement tend to imply that he has found the roots he longs for:

> On entendait le ressac de cette mer et le vent m'apportait les derniers échos d'Alexandrie et de plus loin encore, ceux de Salonique et de bien d'autres villes avant qu'elles n'aient été incendiées. J'allais me marier avec la femme que j'aimais et j'étais enfin de retour dans cet Orient que nous n'aurions jamais dû quitter. (p. 162)

This impression of stability and contentment further emerges from his portrayal of his daughter Zénaïde, whose birth is presented as a vital turning point: 'En somme, nous venions de participer au début de quelque chose. Cette petite fille serait un peu notre déléguée dans l'avenir. Et elle avait obtenu du premier coup le bien mystérieux qui s'était toujours dérobé devant nous: un état civil' (p. 22). Consequently, the family heritage is secure for the future, no matter how fragile it may have been in the past.

Another benefit of the confessional nature of *Livret de famille* is that Modiano provides many useful insights into his literary obsessions. For instance, repeating remarks he has made in interviews, he reveals exactly why, in essence, he is so absorbed with the Occupation – the period is, he states, 'ce terreau d'où je suis issu' (p. 169), because 'sans cette époque, sans les rencontres hasardeuses et contradictoires qu'elle provoquait, je ne serais jamais né' (p. 173). When he evokes the *années noires* in his work therefore, associating them, as has been seen, with anguish and a need for exorcism, what he is really doing is conveying the uncertain, distressing nature of his origins.

But Modiano is also doing something more besides, as has likewise been seen – he is reliving a past which is not his. The question accordingly arises as to how he manages to do this, and here once more *Livret de famille* contains some illuminating information: 'ma mémoire précédait ma naissance. J'étais sûr, par exemple, d'avoir vécu dans le Paris de l'Occupation puisque je me souvenais de certains personnages de cette époque et de détails infimes et troublants, de ceux qu'aucun livre d'histoire ne mentionne' (p. 96). Such a disclosure can hardly be acknowledged as credible, but this does not mean that it is totally lacking in significance. If one accepts – and there is no reason not to – that Modiano has put his own thoughts into the mouth of his narrator, then he has undoubtedly come a long way since he admitted in 1968:

> Il y a longtemps que je baignais dans cette atmosphère, elle a fini par s'intégrer à moi [. . .]. Ce n'est qu'*a posteriori*, en réfléchissant à cette époque, que j'ai vécu de manière hallucinatoire la période 35–45. J'en ai fait mon paysage naturel que j'ai nourri de lectures appropriées: Mémoires, pamphlets, romans, études historiques.[14]

Obviously, the fruits of this early research have been mixed with family anecdotes, augmented by his imagination and then forged into the prenatal remembrance to which he now lays claim. His

14. Jean Montalbetti, 'La haine des professeurs: Instantané Patrick Modiano', p. 2.

avowed goal has thus been successfully achieved – he has indeed made a new memory for himself out of the memories of his elders.

Modiano gains no comfort, however, from this bizarre ability to remember things he has not experienced. As *Livret de famille* again demonstrates, the power of recollection (like the Occupation to which it is linked) is synonymous with torment in his eyes, and he would gladly be rid of such a burden: 'j'essayais de lutter contre la pesanteur qui me tirait en arrière, et rêvais de me délivrer d'une mémoire empoisonnée. J'aurais donné tout au monde pour devenir amnésique' (p. 96). After such a heartfelt cry, it is surely no coincidence that Modiano's next novel, *Rue des Boutiques Obscures* (1978), is narrated by a man who has in effect lost his memory.

The amnesiac in question is Guy Roland, or rather that is the name he has adopted; he has positively no idea at all who he is. Nevertheless, being a private detective, he is accustomed to unearthing missing persons, so he duly applies his skills to his own intriguing case. And as the mystery slowly unravels (with the linearity befitting a *roman policier*), Modiano's major preoccupations resurface. The search for an identity through the re-creation of the past, the uncertainty and menace represented by the *années noires*, the impossibility of ever fleeing to Switzerland, the tendency of time to leave nothing in its wake – these are just some of the perennial themes that are conspicuously reiterated. Against this background of thematic cohesion, the judges of the Prix Goncourt appear to have got things absolutely right. When they awarded their 1978 prize to Modiano, it was not for *Rue des Boutiques Obscures*, they announced, but for his fictional work as a whole.

In addition to the leitmotifs listed above, there is another factor which makes *Rue des Boutiques Obscures* so resonant, a factor which it will be useful to reflect on at this juncture: the presence of Denise Coudreuse. Plainly and simply, Denise gives rise to an impression of *déjà vu* because she is a model, for as such she fits neatly into the long line of mannequins and starlets who punctuate Modiano's *œuvre*. From the anonymous film star who is sent the 'Courrier du cœur'/ 'Lettre d'amour' to Yvonne Jacquet in *Villa Triste*, and on through Arlette d'Alwyn in 'Johnny' and '1, rue Lord-Byron' to, say, Maddy Contour in *Memory Lane*, the cast list is undeniably numerous. Reading between the lines of *Livret de famille*, such emphasis on the world of high fashion and the cinema is not hard to elucidate: Modiano's mother was an actress and a model, so he is clearly basing these characters on her.[15]

15. This is not the case for Annie Murraille (*Les Boulevards de ceinture*) or Betty

The reason for Modiano's wanting or needing to depict his mother like this could doubtless be related to her frequent absences while he was growing up (she regularly went off on tour with her fellow actors), but to see him employing the starlet/mannequin figure as a compensatory maternal presence, in much the same way that he uses paternal surrogates to replace the father who abandoned him, is not entirely satisfactory.

In the context of this cult of parental substitutes, *Rue des Boutiques Obscures* proves to be a high point in Modiano's career. Being the only one of his texts to contain the dedication 'Pour mon père', it can be interpreted as his final attempt to investigate his origins, all the more so in that shortly after its publication he proclaimed: 'A 33 ans je ne peux pas rechercher toute ma vie l'image de mon père. Quand on a des enfants, on est père à son tour, et l'on peut oublier un peu le passé. [. . .] je ne crois pas que je vais parler tout le temps de la guerre.'[16] Sure enough, his next novel, *Une jeunesse* (1981), translates these words into action. Out goes the once ubiquitous narrator figure, ever lonely and isolated, and in come Louis and Odile, a happily married couple with two children. Furthermore, although the major themes of time, memory and the past remain, the basic temporal setting is now one which is unambiguously up-to-date.

The same conscious effort to break new ground can also be discerned in Modiano's subsequent work. *De si braves garçons* (1982) revolves around two different narrators, both of whom look back over the last twenty years of their lives, recalling their schooldays together in the 1960s and recounting what has since become of their former classmates and teachers. Encapsulating a largely negative vision of parenthood in general, and motherhood in particular, this collection of doom-filled *récits* finds the author at his most melancholy. *Quartier perdu* (1984) and *Dimanches d'août* (1986) similarly give notice that some sort of corner has been turned, for like their predecessor, they have a time-scale that is securely anchored in the 1980s.' And that is not all. The central character in the first of these novels, Ambrose Guise, is a contented husband and a doting father (notwithstanding the troubled 'vie antérieure' (p. 13) he led until 1965), while his counterpart in the second, Jean, is refused police aid when his girlfriend goes missing, because, as is stated quite explicitly,

---

Beaulieu (*Lacombe Lucien*), however. These two actresses are modelled on Corinne Luchaire. For details of other historical figures evoked in Modiano's early work, see Patrick Modiano, 'Un roman sur Paris en été . . .,' p. 5, and Françoise Jaudel, 'Quête d'identité,' p. 61.

16. Patrick Modiano, 'Patrick Modiano', p. 79. This statement may have been prompted in part by the recent death of his father.

the person he is searching for is not a member of his family. In this latter instance especially, the contrast with the earlier works could not be more pronounced.

This is not to say, though, that previous practice has been totally ignored, for the texts Modiano has published since 1978 bear strong resemblances to those that came before them. The intricate overlapping of characters and décors persists (the Collège de Valvert in *De si braves garçons* was introduced in *Rue des Boutiques Obscures*, albeit under the name of Collège de Luiza et d'Albany); the authorial presence shows no sign of diminishing; the role of retrospection is as marked as ever – and this is to emphasise only the major constants.

Taken together, then, *Une jeunesse*, *De si braves garçons*, *Quartier perdu* and *Dimanches d'août* form a vital part of Modiano's universe; their compatibility has been rigorously ensured, and their integration skilfully crafted. But for all their numerous interlocking features, one telltale characteristic makes them stand out: the move away from the Occupation. This development represents a distinct, if limited, change of tack, and nowhere is the cause of such a transition better seen than in a comment made by Modiano himself. 'Il vient un moment', he confides, 'où on peut parler de soi-même, où l'on commence à posséder un passé à soi et où l'on n'a plus besoin de celui des autres.'[17] Most palpably, then, his original project has been abandoned, and understandably. Marriage and fatherhood have had their effect. He no longer needs to lay down roots through his fiction.

It is not only because his *œuvre* is so acutely personal, however, that Modiano distinguishes himself as a novelist. He also catches the eye on account of his technical mastery. The sense of precocious genius which emanates from his very first novel is truly overwhelming. Take for example his pastiche of Céline:

> . . . Schlemilovitch? . . . Ah! la moisissure de ghettos terriblement puante! . . . pâmoison chiotte! . . . Foutriquet prépuce! . . . arsouille libano-ganaque! . . . rantanplan . . . Vlan! . . . Comtemplez donc ce gigolo yiddish . . . cet effréné empaffeur de petites Aryennes! . . . avorton infiniment négroïde! . . . cet Abyssin frénétique jeune nabab! . . . A l'aide! . . . Montjoie-Saint-Denis! . . . Tralalilonaire! . . . qu'on l'étripe . . . le châtre! . . . Délivrez le docteur d'un pareil spectacle . . . qu'on le crucifie, nom de Dieu! . . . Rastaquouère des cocktails infames . . . youtre des

17. Gilles Pudlowski, 'Modiano le magnifique', p. 28.

palaces internationaux!... des partouzes *made in Haifa*!... Cannes!...
Davos!... Capri et *tutti quanti*!... grands bordels extrêmement
hébraïques!... Délivrez-nous de ce circoncis muscadin!... (pp.
9–10)

It could almost have been Céline himself who composed this extract.
The foreign language borrowings, the use of slang and onomatopoeia,
the *points de suspension*, the neologisms, the exclamations – Modiano
has captured nearly every aspect of his predecessor's technique. And
his parody of Proust (among others) is no less impressive.

It is neither by accident, nor entirely through youthful bravura,
that Modiano engages in such mimicry. He holds the authors of
Voyage au bout de la nuit and *A la recherche du temps perdu* in high esteem,
and from the very first he has sought to emulate their emphatic
achievements, most notably by developing a 'style émotionnel' as
personal as theirs.[18] The extent of his success here can best be
judged by a perusal of the French press, for there is hardly a
reviewer who does not acknowledge, and acclaim, 'l'atmosphère
Modiano'.

This journalistic consensus is well justified. All Modiano's works
have their own unrivalled atmosphere, as the following passage from
Les Boulevards de ceinture illustrates:

L'ombre des cornes dessine au plafond un entrelacs gigantesque. La
lumière s'affaiblit. Baisse de courant? Ils demeurent prostrés et silencieux
dans la pénombre qui les ronge. De nouveau cette impression de regarder
une vieille photographie, jusqu'au moment où Marcheret se lève, mais de
façon si brutale qu'il bute parfois contre la table. Alors, tout recommence.
Le lustre et les appliques retrouvent leur éclat. Plus une ombre. Plus de
flou. Le moindre objet se découpe avec une précision presque insouten-
able. Les gestes qui s'alanguissaient deviennent secs et impérieux. (pp.
17–18)

Note how the variations in sentence length establish a distinctive
rhythm, a rhythm which conjures up the scene described, unsure of
itself at first, but then finding both momentum and direction. Note
too how there is a poetic blending of long and short, soft and harsh
sounds, from the evocatively sibilant *silencieux* to the savagely abrupt
brutale qu'il bute. And above all note how a sense of dreamlike ebb
and flow emerges from the interaction of these two techniques. It is
this diaphanous haze which is Modiano's trademark.

Such haziness could never have been created without a specific
type of formal approach, as Modiano himself reveals:

18. See Jean Montalbetti, 'La haine des professeurs: Instantané Patrick Modiano', p.
2, and Josane Duranteau, 'L'obsession de l'anti-héros', p. 13.

j'écris dans la langue française la plus classique, non par une insolence droitière, non plus par un goût des effets surannés, mais parce que cette forme est nécessaire à mes romans: pour traduire l'atmosphère trouble, flottante, étrange que je voulais leur donner, il me fallait bien la discipliner dans la langue la plus claire, la plus traditionnelle possible. Sinon, tout se serait éparpillé dans une bouillie confuse.[19]

It is therefore pointless to look for linguistic experiment in Modiano's fiction, but this does not mean that modernism has been rejected out of hand. Quite the opposite. As may be apparent by this stage, *La Place de l'Etoile, La Ronde de nuit* and *Les Boulevards de ceinture* collectively have much in common with the novels of the *nouveaux romanciers* – the use of a circular structure and the abandonment of conventional chronology, for instance, not to mention the splintering of the narrative viewpoint or 'un double mouvement de création et de gommage'.[20]

This comparison must not be pushed too far, however. Ever since he shot to fame in 1968, Modiano has carefully distanced himself from Robbe-Grillet and his colleagues, primarily on artistic grounds: 'Je ne m'intéresse à aucune école expérimentale et je reproche notamment au Nouveau Roman de n'avoir ni ton ni vie. Je suis étranger à la littérature désincarnée. Car [. . .] je suis hanté par le souci du ton et du style.'[21] Furthermore, he has often suggested that the New Novelists regard writing as a dispassionate, intellectual exercise and not as an emotional necessity, whereas for him, as has been seen, the converse is true: 'la littérature pour la littérature, les recherches sur l'écriture, tout ce byzantinisme pour chaires et colloques, ça ne m'intéresse pas: j'écris pour savoir qui je suis, pour me trouver une identité.'[22] So there is nothing theoretical about the stance Modiano adopts. His formal modernism derives not from a wish to extend the boundaries of literature, but rather from an identity crisis which can only be expressed through confusion and uncertainty. The ultimate demonstration of this, of course, is the fact that his work has become less circular and less convoluted as his *état civil* has strengthened. Indeed, so linear and uncomplicated have his recent novels become – and so conscientiously correct has his use of French remained – that a new epithet is now regularly bestowed upon him: novelist in the classical tradition.

19. Jean-Louis Ezine, 'Sur la sellette: Patrick Modiano ou le passé antérieur', p. 5.
20. Alain Robbe-Grillet, *Pour un nouveau roman*, (Editions de Minuit, 1963), p. 127.
21. Jean Montalbetti, 'La haine des professeurs: Instantané Patrick Modiano', p. 2.
22. Jean-Louis Ezine, 'Sur la sellette: Patrick Modiano ou le passé antérieur', p. 5.

Patrick Modiano is an author who has slowly worked himself through a state of crisis, without once ceasing to exploit the same rich literary vein. At the start of his career, he uses his fiction as an instrument of self-discovery, a means of seeking out the roots he lacks but so desires. It is certainly not for nothing that, during this early period, his texts are suffused with parental substitutes, nor is it a coincidence that he tends to home in on the *années noires* – being the time when his mother and father met, the Occupation holds the key to his exotic origins. But this harnessing of literature to therapeutic ends proves, understandably, to be less than permanent. As he finds stability in marriage and parenthood, his initial anguish subsides, and he comes to abandon his painful, emotional soul-searching. This improved mental outlook diffuses into his later novels quite noticeably – in the shape of increased linearity and the adoption of more-modern settings – yet despite this, there is no radical change of direction in his work. The thematic focus on time, memory and the past is retained, and, moreover, his unique atmosphere continues to be very much in evidence. If one thing above all others brings a sense of cohesion to his *œuvre*, though, it is the unflaggingly high level of his stylistic craftsmanship. In fact, such consistency has he shown in his mastery of his medium that one critic has not hesitated to opine: 'Modiano s'affirme comme "le" grand jeune auteur, comme le plus brillant de sa génération et peut-être aussi de celles des autres.'[23] This assessment may be too exclusive and too hyperbolic to meet with everyone's approval, but its basic sentiment can hardly be faulted.

Bibliography

Novels by Patrick Modiano (all works published by Gallimard)

La Place de l'Etoile (1968)
La Ronde de nuit (1969)
Les Boulevards de ceinture (1972)
Villa Triste (1975)
Livret de famille (1977)

23. Jacques-Pierre Amette, 'La Piscine', p. 105.

Rue des Boutiques Obscures (1978)
Une jeunesse (1981)
De si braves garçons (1982)
Quartier perdu (1984)
Dimanches d'août (1986)

Other Works

'Courrier du cœur', *Les Cahiers du chemin*, 20 (15 Jan. 1974), 35–40

Lacombe Lucien (filmscript) [with Louis Malle] (Gallimard, 1974)

Emmanuel Berl, *'Interrogatoire par Patrick Modiano' suivi de 'Il fait beau, allons au cimetière'* (Gallimard, 1976)

'Johnny', *La Nouvelle Revue Française*, 307 (1 Aug. 1978), 1–5 [cf. *De si braves garçons*, 125–9]

'Lettre d'amour', *Paris-Match*, 1 Dec. 1978, 80–1 [cf. 'Courrier du cœur']

'1, rue Lord-Byron,' *Le Nouvel Observateur*, 23 Dec. 1978, 56–7

'Docteur Weiszt', *Le Monde du dimanche*, 16 Sept. 1979, p. XX [cf. *De si braves garçons*, 93–101]

'Memory Lane', *La Nouvelle Revue Française*, 334 (1 Nov. 1980), 1–30

Memory Lane, with drawings by Pierre Le-Tan (P.O.L./Hachette, 1981)

'La Seine', *La Nouvelle Revue Française*, 341 (1 June 1981), 1–17 [cf. *De si braves garçons*, 58–77]

Poupée blonde [with Pierre Le-Tan] (P.O.L./Hachette, 1983)

'Mes vingt ans', *Vogue* (Paris), 642 (Dec. 1983), 188–93

Une Aventure de Choura, with illustrations by Dominique Zehrfuss (Gallimard, 1986)

Interviews and Articles by Modiano

Cau, Jean, 'Patrick Modiano marié, un enfant et un livret de famille de 180 pages', *Paris-Match*, 12 Aug. 1977, p. 13

Chalon, Jean, 'Patrick Modiano: le dernier promeneur solitaire', in *La Ronde de nuit* (Cercle du nouveau livre, 1970), *postface*, 6–23

Duranteau, Josane, 'L'obsession de l'anti-héros', *Le Monde*, 11 Nov. 1972, p. 13

Ezine, Jean-Louis, 'Sur la sellette: Patrick Modiano ou le passé antérieur', *Les Nouvelles Littéraires*, 6–12 Oct. 1975, p. 5

Geille, Annick, 'Patrick Modiano m'intimide!', *Playboy* (Paris), 9, no. 5 (May 1981), 65–6, 127–8, 130

J., J., 'Patrick Modiano à la question', *Le Figaro (Littéraire)*, 20 Sept. 1975, I–II/13–14

Jamet, Dominique, 'Patrick Modiano s'explique', *Lire*, 1 (Oct. 1975), 23–5, 27, 29, 31–2, 35–6

Jaudel, Françoise, 'Quête d'identité', *L'Arche*, Oct.–Nov. 1972, p. 61

Malka, Victor, 'Patrick Modiano: un homme sur du sable mouvant', *Les*

Nouvelles Littéraires, 30 Oct.–5 Nov. 1972, p. 2

Modiano, Patrick, 'Patrick Modiano', *Paris-Match*, 1 Dec. 1978, p. 79

——, 'Un roman sur Paris en été . . .', in *La Ronde de nuit* (Cercle du nouveau livre, 1970), *postface*, 3–5

Montalbetti, Jean, 'La haine des professeurs: Instantané Patrick Modiano', *Les Nouvelles Littéraires*, 13 June 1968, p. 2

——, 'Patrick Modiano ou l'esprit de fuite', *Magazine Littéraire*, 34 (Nov. 1969), 42–3

Pivot, Bernard, 'Demi-juif Patrick Modiano affirme: "Céline était un véritable écrivain juif"', *Le Figaro Littéraire*, 29 Apr. 1968, p. 16

Pudlowski, Gilles, 'Modiano le magnifique', *Les Nouvelles Littéraires*, 12–19 Feb. 1981, p. 28

Rambures, Jean-Louis de, 'Comment travaillent les écrivains: Patrick Modiano: "apprendre à mentir"', *Le Monde*, 24 May 1973, p. 24

Selected Critical Studies

Amette, Jacques-Pierre, 'La Piscine', *La Nouvelle Revue Française*, 240 (Dec. 1972), 104–6

Bersani, Jacques, 'Patrick Modiano, agent double', *La Nouvelle Revue Française*, 298 (1 Nov. 1977), 78–84

Chasseguet-Smirgel, Janine, *Pour une psychanalyse de l'art et de la créativité* (Payot, 1971), 217–55

Dormann, Geneviève, 'Modiano apprivoisé', *Le Point*, 16 Oct. 1972, p. 100

Duhamel, Betty, '*Les Boulevards de ceinture* par Patrick Modiano', *Magazine Littéraire*, 72 (Jan. 1973), 36–7

Duranteau, Josane, 'Un début exceptionnel: *La Place de l'Etoile*, de Patrick Modiano', *Le Monde*, 11 May 1968, p. II

Galey, Matthieu, 'A la recherche du temps rêvé', *L'Express*, 8 Oct. 1982, p. 26

——, 'Roman: Modiano, l'Hoffmann des villes', *L'Express*, 7 Feb. 1981, 30–1

Gaudemar, Antoine de, 'Une inépuisable nostalgie: Patrick Modiano: *De si braves garçons*', *Magazine Littéraire*, 192 (Feb. 1983), p. 65

Labre, Chantal, '*Livret de famille* par Patrick Modiano', *Esprit*, 7–8 (July–Aug. 1977), 115–17

Montalbetti, Jean, 'Patrick Modiano: *Rue des Boutiques Obscures*', *Magazine Littéraire*, 141 (Oct. 1978), p. 47

Morris, Alan, 'Attacks on the Gaullist "Myth" in French Literature since 1969', *Forum for Modern Language Studies*, 21, no. 1 (Jan. 1985), 71–83

Nettelbeck, Colin, 'Getting the story right: narratives of World War II in post-1968 France', *Journal of European Studies*, 15 (1985), 77–116

——, and P. Hueston, *Patrick Modiano: pièces d'identité: écrire l'entretemps*, Archives des lettres modernes (Minard, 1986)

Ory, Pascal, 'Comme de l'an quarante. Dix années de "rétro satanas"', *Le*

Débat, 16 (Nov. 1981), 109–17

Poirot-Delpech, Bertrand, '*Livret de famille*, de Patrick Modiano; *Le Sommeil agité*, de J.-M. Roberts', *Le Monde*, 29 Apr. 1977, 17, 20

——, 'Un nouvel *Etranger*: *Villa Triste*, de Patrick Modiano', *Le Monde*, 5 Sept. 1975, p. 11

Steegmuller, Francis, 'Occupational therapy', *Times Literary Supplement*, 15 July 1977, p. 872

–8–

Monique Wittig

JEAN H. DUFFY

The close association between Monique Wittig's literary career and the Editions de Minuit is in no way fortuitous, Jérôme Lindon's progressive publishing house having provided an outlet for some of the most radical and experimental fiction published since the 1950s, including the work of the *nouveau roman*, the *nouveau nouveau roman* and ultimately unclassifiable authors such as Beckett and Jean-Philippe Toussaint. The appearance of Wittig's first novel *L'Opoponax* (1964) at a time when the importance and durability of the much-maligned *nouveau roman* were beginning to be recognised, the warm approval it prompted from Claude Simon[1] and, above all, its ingenious use of narrative point of view and total disregard for conventionally recognisable characters and plot might well have suggested that Wittig was a late-comer to the camp of Robbe-Grillet, Butor and Simon. The publication of her subsequent work, however, left no doubts about the limitations of such a comparison. For although undoubtedly indebted to and influenced by the formal experimentation of these writers, Wittig distinguishes herself clearly from the *nouveau roman* on one fundamental issue – the question of commitment. Wittig shares none of the *nouveaux romanciers'* reluctance to align themselves with a particular political, philosophical or social standpoint; nor does she share their distaste for the committed novel which harnesses its art to a contemporary cause. Wittig has no scruples about axe-grinding or about using the novel as a platform for polemical provocation. The staunchly feminist fiction which followed her deceptively innocent first novel was to exploit the lessons in formal versatility offered by the contemporary novel, not to produce self-conscious reflections upon form itself, but to produce a discourse which exposes and subverts the sexist and heterosexual assumptions underlying the prevalent discourse.

The radical and uncompromising nature of Wittig's feminism has

---

1. 'Pour Monique Wittig', *L'Express*, 30 Nov.–6 Dec. 1964, pp. 69–71.

precluded a wide general readership or critical vulgarisation, while the dearth of biographical detail, so characteristic of recent generations of French novelists, has discouraged spurious speculation about the psyche behind such apparently outlandish literary products. The relative prominence achieved with the publication of *L'Opoponax* and the award of the Prix Médicis was fairly short-lived, though her later writing – both literary and polemical – has made a qualified impact among feminist and post-modernist scholars in France, Britain and the United States. The few serious and sympathetic articles which have been generated by Wittig's fiction have tended to focus on individual works, at the expense of a sustained analysis of thematic constants. The aim of this essay is to redress that balance and to show something of the coherence and evolution which underpin an *œuvre* which may sometimes seem erratic and rebarbatively experimental.

Like all feminist writers, Wittig is preoccupied with the concept of sexual difference. In her explicit statements on the issue in 'On ne naît pas femme',[2] Wittig clearly aligns herself with the school of thought which sees difference as being a cultural construct to be abolished as opposed to a natural state to be tolerated. In 'La pensée straight',[3] she takes to task the high priests of contemporary anthropology and psychoanalysis – Lévi-Strauss and Lacan – arguing that, despite the sophistication of their analyses of cultural and symbolic codes, these luminaries have simply reinforced traditional sexual codes based on heterosexual assumptions:

> Et bien qu'on ait admis ces dernières années qu'il n'y a pas de nature, que tout est culture, il reste au sein de cette culture un noyau de nature qui résiste à l'examen, une relation qui revêt un caractère d'inéluctabilité dans la culture comme dans la nature. C'est la relation hétérosexuelle ou relation obligatoire entre 'l'homme' et 'la femme'. Ayant posé comme un principe évident, comme une donnée antérieure à toute science l'inéluctabilité de cette relation, la pensée straight se livre à une interprétation totalisante à la fois de l'histoire, de la réalité sociale, de la culture et des sociétés, du langage et de tous les phénomènes subjectifs. (p. 49)

For Wittig, as for Simone de Beauvoir, a person is not born a woman but becomes one through a process of heterosexual socialisation and ideological indoctrination. Quoting the now famous passage from *Le*

2. *Questions féministes*, no. 8 (May 1980), pp. 75–84.
3. *Questions féministes*, no. 7 (Feb. 1980), 45–53.

Deuxième Sexe, 'Aucun destin biologique, psychique, économique ne définit la femelle humaine; c'est l'ensemble de la civilisation qui élabore ce produit intermédiaire entre le mâle et le castrat qu'on qualifie de féminin', Wittig argues in 'On ne naît pas femme' that the polarising division of humanity into two least common denominators known as 'l'homme' and 'la femme' is but a product of heterosexual mythology.

Wittig's first novel shows an early, if undeveloped, interest in the question of sexual difference. *L'Opoponax* offers what she sees to be the child's-eye view of the world and charts the development of a little girl and her peers from the first day at school to early adolescence. Significantly, the development of heterosexual attraction is totally absent, the novel concluding with the blossoming of an adolescent crush for a member of the same sex. Heterosexuality not only does not figure as the norm, it is, in fact, ignored.

Wittig's child *is* aware and curious about sexual discrepancies. However, she perceives them as relative, as opposed to essential, differences which will be eliminated rather than reinforced in time. The possession or lack of a penis is conceived as being a question of age, and Catherine Legrand does not doubt that she too will grow an equally interesting anatomical feature. 'Le petit garçon qui s'appelle Robert Payen dit, regarde ma quéquette. Pourquoi tu as ça toi? Parce que je suis grand. Moi, j'en aurai aussi? Oui quand tu seras comme moi. Mais quand? Je te dis quand tu seras comme moi' (p. 19).

The empirical experience of physical difference does not produce in Wittig's little girl the sense of lack and traumatic reassessment provoked in the Freudian or Lacanian child by similar experiences. It is just one detail in the very rich fabric of the child's life; it is certainly not something to be dwelt upon and is almost immediately displaced by other demands upon the child's attention (p. 15).

That sexual difference is, according to Wittig, a social and cultural invention is suggested early in the novel by Catherine Legrand's discomfort and discomfiture when she is made to wear a pair of trousers. Difference for her until this point has consisted not in the recognition of a biological discrepancy but in the acceptance of a binary vestimentary code. Her definitions of 'boy' and 'girl' have clearly been based on conventions of dress, and the transgression of that arbitrary social code causes her anxiety about sexual identity that the sight of Robert Payen's penis does not: 'On ne met pas de pantalon quand on est une petite fille . . . Peut-être que Catherine Legrand est la seule petite fille à porter un pantalon et à n'être pas exactement une petite fille' (pp. 18–19).

But perhaps the clearest indication of Wittig's impatience with heterosexual assumptions is the fact that after these opening pages which establish her own premises, she ignores the subject totally for the rest of the novel, devoting her attention to the group dynamics of the childish micro-society. Sexual attraction, when it does manifest itself, is seen as part of a complex pattern of individuation, rather than a polarisation of the group into two distinct classes. The evolution of the adolescent crush coincides with the dawning awareness of the *multiple* differences between the self and the Other and the development of a sense of discrimination. This process involves a much greater attention to the characterising details of the Other's physique. The peer becomes an object of appreciation rather than simply a numerary playmate: 'On voit que les cheveux qui tiennent bien à la tête ont des lueurs d'acier dans leur blond' (p. 213); 'Catherine Legrand regarde Valerie Borge tirer sur son pull-over à travers lequel les seins sont vus' (p. 257).

The acknowledgement of individual preference is accompanied by a significant increase in introspection and the development of an aesthetic sensibility. It is a typical parting shot from Wittig (and one which anticipates her later work) that the novel closes with the appropriation of a line from Scève expressing heterosexual love by Catherine Legrand in the expression of her love for Valerie Borge: 'On dit, tant je l'aimais qu'en elle encore je vis' (p. 281). The school curriculum may promote heterosexual assumptions and censor, by omission, the expression of homosexual culture, but it cannot confine interpretation within the limits of its own divisive frame of reference.

Wittig continues her onslaught on the concept of natural difference in *Les Guérillères* (1969), *Le Corps lesbien* (1973) and *Virgile, non* (1985). A true feminist materialist analysis demonstrates, according to Wittig, that, as with racial differences, we have confused the material manifestations of oppression with its cause, that we have taken the contingent for the essential:

> Aujourd'hui . . . race et sexe sont appréhendés comme une donnée immédiate, une donnée sensible, un ensemble de 'traits physiques'. Ils nous apparaissent tout constitués comme s'ils existaient avant tout raisonnement, appartenant à un ordre naturel. Mais ce que nous croyons être une perception directe et physique n'est qu'une construction mythique et sophistiquée, une 'formation imaginaire' qui réinterprète des traits physiques . . . à travers le réseau de relations dans lequel ils sont perçus. ('On ne naît pas femme,' p. 77)

An indispensable stage in any destabilisation of heterosexual oppression involves the transformation of the way in which these 'traits physiques' are viewed. Wittig tries to effect this perceptual transformation through the promotion of parts of the female body normally eclipsed in the prevailing discourse and a demotion of those features previously seen as being inalienably and distinctively feminine. The discussion of the female genitalia in fiction has in general been restricted to the marginal and male-dominated domain of pornography. In Wittig's fiction, however, it occupies a high profile position. In *Les Guérillères*, the importance of body-awareness is signalled again and again through extended descriptions of body-functions and female sexual organs. The fascination which basic bodily functions held for the culturally uninitiated and uninhibited children of *L'Opoponax* is shared by the lesbians of *Les Guérillères* and recorded in a startlingly direct opening paragraph: 'A la longue quelqu'une dit que c'est comme un bruit de miction, qu'elle ne peut pas y tenir, en se mettant accroupie. Certaines alors font cercle autour d'elle pour regarder les nymphes chasser l'urine' (p. 9). It is the clitoris and vulva, however, which dominate the first half of the novel. Traditionally, woman has been defined in terms of a lack, in particular a lack of a penis, and the concept of penis-envy gave Freudian and Lacanian psychoanalysis considerable mileage. Wittig's women experience no such covetousness or sense of incompleteness; on the contrary, they see it as an important part of their task to undermine phallocentricity and the longstanding equation of women with absence: 'Elles disent, tu ne seras jamais trop nombreuse pour cracher sur le phallus . . . Elles disent . . . je refuse de marmotter après eux les mots de manque de pénis' (p. 153). For them, the vulva is not only an admirable physical phenomenon worthy of meticulous and loving description (pp. 41–2), but also the centre-pin of the whole symbolic code. The female genitalia are the primary tenor in a complex network of analogies encompassing the most diverse aspects of nature:

> Elles disent que les poils du pubis sont comme une toile d'araignée qui capture les rayons. (p. 24)
> Elles disent que le clitoris a été comparé à un noyau de cerise, à un bourgeon, à une jeune pousse, à un sésame décortiqué, à une amande, à une baie de myrte, à un dard, au canon d'une serrure. (p. 42)

The importance of body-awareness and of the frank acknowledgement of parts of the anatomy normally hidden from view and shunned by respectable discourse also figures prominently in *Virgile, non*, a parody of Dante's *Divine Comedy* which catalogues mercilessly the sins committed against women by men and by themselves. Here Wittig's didacticism is no less serious than in *Les Guérillères* but the earnestness of conviction is alleviated by a humour and irony which deflate as they attack and by Wittig's playful fusion of Dantean allusion and modern Americana.

The full weight of prejudice against the female body is exposed in the exaggerated outrage and violence of the women when Wittig, the protagonist, naïvely tries to give them a lesson in body-awareness by stripping in the middle of a launderette: 'Une d'elles rugit en pointant le milieu de mon corps: (Regardez, il est long comme un long doigt. Coupez-le, coupez le)' (p. 18). The logical conclusion of a rationale which ignores the reality of the female body and turns it into an object of shame is, according to the radical feminist, clitoridectomy. Clitoridectomy – generally carried out by midwives – is an important motif in *Virgile, non* and illustrates the way in which female sexuality and satisfaction have been denied by both men and women. The notion of carnal sin has been radically reworked in Wittig's version of the *Divine Comedy* to denote not excessive passion but rather pleasureless and mechanical sex which subordinates women to men and thereby reinforces the 'difference' between them. Wittig's description of the mutilating act on pp. 95–6 spares the squeamish no detail and belies the whimsicality of the incongruous scene in the launderette.

The open verbalisation of female sexuality is, however, but a stage in the raising of consciousness. The women of *Les Guérillères* have to recognise the danger of falling into the same trap as men. Vulvacentricity is as divisive and restrictive an ideology as phallocentricity. Wittig is keen to pre-empt any accusation that her Utopia is based on the same principles of subordination and division that she sees in reality. Self-contemplation and self-congratulation are a step in the right direction, not a destination, and her constant revision and reassessment are a crucial part of development. Hence, the women systematically subvert the metaphors and similes by which they had inserted female sexuality into discourse: 'Elles disent qu'elles ne privilégient pas telle [partie du corps] sous prétexte qu'elle a été jadis l'objet d'un interdit . . . Par exemple, elles ne comparent pas les vulves au soleil à la lune aux étoiles. Elles ne disent pas que les vulves sont comme les soleils noirs dans la nuit éclatante' (pp. 80–1). The promotion of sexual difference, whether to the advantage of the male or of the female, is the source of the problem. Wittig's aim is, on the contrary, to demote it. It is, therefore, not surprising that even in the first part of *Les Guérillères* the clitoris is described in terms normally reserved for the penis: 'Elles disent que dans le féminaire le gland du clitoris et le corps du clitoris sont décrits comme encapuchonnés. Il est écrit que le prépuce à la base du gland peut se mouvoir le long de l'organe en provoquant une vive sensation de plaisir. Elles disent que le clitoris est un organe érectile' (p. 29). Ultimately, it would seem, the fuss about genital difference has been for nothing.

Le Corps lesbien makes this point even more forcefully in the evocation of the relationship between the narrator and her female lover. Here, sexual intercourse involves loving, penetrating and fusing with every organ of the partner's body, not just those which have been culturally designated as erogenous. The point Wittig seems to be making is that the partner is first and foremost a human being, not a man or a woman. The repetitive, over-lengthy and often rather gruesome lists of the essential organs involved drive home relentlessly the point that the human body, whether it is male or female, is composed for the best part in the same way and that genital and reproductive differences are irrelevant in the act of love.

Physical issues are, however, not the only ones at stake, though the denial of physical difference is a prerequisite for the elimination of social and cultural difference. The next target in Wittig's programme is the male monopoly of power and the control over women's lives that it permits. Wittig takes to task the idea of ontological difference, arguing that it is simply a convenient disguise and spurious justification for an historical, and therefore contingent, situation based on self-interest and the greed for power: 'La différence n'a rien d'ontologique, elle n'est que l'interprétation que les maîtres font d'une situation historique de domination. La différence a pour fonction de masquer les conflits d'intérêt à tous les niveaux idéologiquement compris' ('La pensée straight', p. 50). Difference is another word for slavery, a premise which calls for a redefinition of the war between the sexes as a class-struggle. Women themselves are guilty in so far as they have been party to the naturalisation of the institutions which bespeak their oppression. In particular Wittig attacks the social conditioning which persuades the female of her procreative role. She makes a clear distinction between the concept of 'la femme', the mythical creature manufactured by heterosexual culture, and 'les femmes', the class within which women must struggle: '"La femme" n'est pas chacune de nous mais une construction politique et idéologique qui nie "les femmes" (le produit d'une relation d'exploitation). "La femme" n'est là que pour rendre les choses confuses et dissimuler la réalité "femmes"' ('On ne naît pas femme', p. 80). Although the ultimate aim is to abolish both the myth and the class, the development of a class awareness is in the teleological perspective of feminist materialism a necessary stage in the destruction of that class.

It is precisely this lack of awareness which characterises the damned souls of *Virgile, non*. Wittig's voyage of discovery exposes a hellish world in which men dominate and brutalise women and women passively acquiesce. Although a far cry from Dante's *Divine Comedy*, *Virgile, non* is a highly moral book. The theme of responsibility is central to every episode. In the great balance-sheet of mortal sins, the entries are fairly evenly distributed. The Utopian dimension of Wittig's earlier fiction resulted in a neglect of concrete grievances – a fact which may explain her sado-masochistic exposure of her fictional alter ego to an apprenticeship in despair. Here she is more than ready to point a finger. Men, it would seem, are characterised by violence, greed and deception. The camouflage of social institutions has been removed to reveal the slave-market that is the reality; the relationship between men and women is seen in classical Marxist terms as that between master and slave and is paralleled by the subordination of other ethnic groups by the white man. The war between the sexes is literally a war but one where the odds are scandalously weighted against women. Wittig's parade of the injuries inflicted on women – a black parody of the beauty contest – testifies to the many ingenious and perverse ways in which women of all cultures have been mutilated and disfigured to satisfy whimsical male 'norms'. The catalogue of female sins is even more specific, though the source of them all would seem to be a reluctance to take responsibility for their own fates. Like the inveterate sinners in Dante's Inferno, many hurtle on towards their damnation and are ready to assault anyone who attempts to dissuade them. Those who seem to be succeeding in the male-dominated world of technology are simply being assuaged by baubles, by cast-off, outdated science and equipment, and fail to recognise that trying to be a man is to miss the basic point.[4]

The damned souls of *Virgile, non* stick together, but theirs is a flimsy solidarity based on fear, herd instinct and a common aimlessness. In contrast, the 'amantes' of *Les Guérillères* channel their energies into a corporate struggle against the oppressor. *Les Guérillères*, with its island community of female warriors modelled on the mythical societies of the Lemnians and Amazons, is clearly an attempt to create a feminist epic, an epic whose outcome is radically different from those of classical epics where, as Mandy Merck has pointed out, the Amazons are not seen as an autonomous corps 'but as the vanquished opponents of heroes credited with the establishment and

4. Compare 'On ne naît pas femme', p. 78.

protection of the Athenian State'.[5] The divisive, patriotic dimension of the traditional epic has no place here, and the catalogues of national heroes, a standard set-piece in the epic, have given way to lists of female names drawn from a wide range of cultural sources and juxtaposing the recognisable and the obscure, the mythological and the historical, the ancient and the modern. Furthermore, the wars waged in the second half of the novel refute categorically the premise whereby the phallus is equated with power, ferocity and strength, while the myth of 'la femme' is contradicted by the aggressiveness and energy of these warriors. This aggressiveness has none of the aimlessness which characterises that of the damned souls in *Virgile, non*; its targets are the social institutions and structures on which patriarchy has been based. In razing the 'tall buildings' (clearly an attack on architectural phallic symbolism) and houses, they are attacking the principle of possession, at once an index and a source of difference between men and women. The huge circle which, like the lists of female names, punctuates the text, is no longer the insignia of vulvacentricity as it was in the first part of the text: it has come to represent the zero point of departure. The war has made a clean sweep, and the women, at the end of the novel, are offering men a second chance, an opportunity to participate in the inception of a new society in which difference and its inevitable side-effect – warfare – will be eliminated. Conquest here does not consist in the obliteration of the opponent, nor does it result in his subordination. Conversion is the key word – the 'amantes' are victorious only when they have transformed the way in which men view the world. The co-operative renaming of the elements of this pristine world signals that that is being achieved.

The admission of male converts to what has been a lesbian community clearly refutes any hypothesis that in Wittig lesbianism is isolationist. The Utopian lesbian communities of *Les Guérillères, Le Corps lesbien* and *Virgile, non* are to be clearly distinguished from the gay subculture as it exists and has existed on the edge of the heterosexual culture throughout the centuries. As her polemical articles make clear, the gay subculture, in so far as it has always threatened and denied the validity of heterosexual institutions, is the locus in which the fight against difference can take place; it is 'la seule forme sociale dans laquelle nous puissions vivre libres' ('On ne naît pas femme', p. 83). Her position is not a self-congratulatory one, however, and in *Virgile, non*, she takes to task in humorous but

---

5. Mandy Merck, 'The city's achievements' in *Tearing the Veil*, ed. Susan Lipschitz (London, Routledge and Kegan Paul, 1978), p. 96.

clear-sighted terms the staticism of the gay subculture. Wittig's Limbo is inhabited by an ineffectual lesbian coterie, whose attacks on heterosexual culture are uncoordinated sallies into male territory and who counter arbitrary and gratuitous violence with the same. They are 'enfants terribles' rather than Amazonian warriors, and their self-indulgence and narcissism are only pointed up by the plight of the damned souls. Unlike the warriors of *Les Guérillères*, they fail to see the perils of self-admiration and the sterility of vindictive attacks upon individual men, when the real enemy is difference. If lesbianism is to be constructive, it must transcend issues of sexual preference and factionalism. Wittig's definition operates a semantic shift in which the question of sexual preference is largely eclipsed by the political attitude it implies – one which quite simply rejects the interest- and ideology-laden division of people into 'men' and 'women':

> 'Lesbienne' est le seul concept que je connaisse qui soit au-delà des catégories de sexe (femme et homme) parce que le sujet désigné (lesbienne) *n'est pas* une femme, ni économiquement, ni politiquement, ni idéologiquement. Car en effet ce qui fait une femme c'est une relation sociale particulièrement à un homme, relation que nous avons autrefois appelée de servage, relation qui implique des obligations personnelles et physiques aussi bien que des obligations économiques. ('On ne naît pas femme', p. 83)

> Qu'est-ce que la femme? Branle-bas général de la défense active. Franchement, c'est un problème que les lesbiennes n'ont pas, simplement changement de perspective, et il serait impropre de dire que les lesbiennes vivent, s'associent, font l'amour avec des femmes car 'femme' n'a de sens que dans les systèmes de pensée et les systèmes économiques hétérosexuels. Les lesbiennes ne sont pas des femmes. ('La pensée straight', p. 53)

The importance that Wittig attaches to solidarity and class awareness is illustrated by the fact that her novels focus upon group dynamics and the role of the individual within a large community. The die-hard themes of much traditional fiction – the development of a clearly characterised protagonist or the relationships within the nuclear family – are absent. Thus, although *L'Opoponax* adopts as its main point of reference the child Catherine Legrand, it can in no sense be considered her story. Catherine Legrand is simply a point of access to the world of childhood. Her experience is representative, not specific. In Wittig's later work the narrative formula of 'one woman's fight against oppression' preferred by Anglo-American feminism holds no interest for her. These are symbolic, cerebral and

highly stylised works which deal in ideas and ideals rather than in
the nuances of everyday living.

L'Opoponax – on the surface a benign illustration of a familiar
literary theme – anticipates Wittig's subsequent radical approach
to her subjects. Childhood in *L'Opoponax* is seen not as a phase in the
continuum of life but as a world in itself, in which adult emotions,
interests and priorities are irrelevant. Throughout the book parents
occupy a purely marginal position, virtually disappearing altogether
when the children start boarding. Even on her first day at school,
frequently seen in traditional fiction as a traumatic break in the
nucleus of the family, Catherine Legrand regards her mother as
being an intruder: 'Il y a beaucoup d'enfants qui jouent dans la cour
de l'école mais pas du tout de grandes personnes seulement la mère
de Catherine Legrand et il vaudrait mieux qu'elle ne rentre pas dans
l'école c'est seulement les enfants' (pp. 7–8). Parents can be called
upon in extreme emergency, as on pp. 32–3 where Denise Joubert is
in danger of drowning, or they may intervene in childish affairs, as
on p. 131 where they appear briefly to reprimand the children who
have been throwing purée at one another. Even here, however, the
very fact that they are sitting at a different table only highlights the
boundary between the two worlds. If, as occasionally happens, a
child's parent momentarily invades the school territory, this is
perceived as a disruptive event inspiring curiosity on the part of the
children and a strong territorial instinct in the teacher, who invariably keeps the parent at the door of the classroom. Very occasionally an adult will try to subvert the demarcation between the
two worlds and attempt to make the child a companion. Thus the
super-sweet Mme La Porte tries to ingratiate herself with the
children by simpering and grinning at them. Her efforts only accen-
tuate the gap, however; all they perceive is her excessive saliva (p.
75). A few have a very limited success, but they are lonely and a
little insane and have no function in the adult world (p. 28). The
parents do generate a certain amount of interest if the child dies, but
the experience of grief would seem to be alien to children, and their
ghoulish curiosity is perceived as an intrusion into the adult world,
as is made clear by Robert Payen's father when he slams down the
window on his childish spectators. When the children pay attention
to the encompassing adult world, its inhabitants and activities seem
unreal and one-dimensional. The people who live in the houses
opposite the school figure only as matchstick-people who stimulate
childish fantasy: 'Là habitent des hommes et des femmes tout petits
dont on ne voit pas la figure parce qu'elle est couverte de sang [. . .]
Ils sont dans les maisons qui ressemblent à des châteaux de cartes.

On les voit aussi grouiller entre les maisons, c'est quand ils rentrent ou sortent de chez eux' (p. 49).

Within the childish world it is the centripetal forces of peer pressure and gregarious instinct that interest Wittig. In contrast to the traditional novel, characters are not seen in the round with distinctive attributes or failings. The first-name familiarity characteristic of the traditional author and his child protagonist is replaced by a neutral identification by both Christian name and surname. Civil identity is preferred to paternalistic partiality. A child may achieve notability or notoriety after the death of a relative or some scandalous exploit, but that status is always temporary and contingent upon very specific circumstances; their short-lived prominence causes but a ripple in the otherwise smooth flow of their lives, and their reassimilation into the anonymity of the group is swift.

The absence of a strongly delineated central character does not, however, preclude an interest in the process of individuation. Ostracism within the peer group acts as an index of the fact that one is trapped within oneself and of the emergence of more 'adult' feelings such as shame and embarrassment which isolate: 'C'est tout lourd au-dedans d'elle, c'est immobile à la hauteur des yeux, ça regarde dehors, à travers les orbites, c'est pris, ça ne pourra jamais être autre chose que Catherine Legrand' (p. 95). With the onset of adolescence begins a more radical process of differentiation. Significantly, the emergence of a sense of individuality comes not from within but from interaction with the Other. The relative prominence given to Valerie Borge in the concluding chapters of the novel charts the development of a discriminating capacity. Psychologically the character of Valerie Borge is not studied in any depth. She is essentially a catalyst who stimulates in Catherine Legrand feelings and emotions specific to herself and distinct from group response. The evolution of preferences intimates the transition from childish general interest to adolescent individualism, a transition which is also registered in the displacement of the anonymous narrative voice 'on' by the 'je' of the final sentence.

This process of individuation is paralleled by a dissolution of the barriers which divided the world of the child from that of the adult and the gradual elevation of barriers within the group. The world of the child is surrounded by barriers imposed by adults – concrete physical barriers limiting freedom of movement (pp. 8, 15, 38) and abstract moral ones taking the form of explicit interdictions (pp. 8, 9, 15). As these external barriers disappear, new ones appear demarcating personal territory. Thus the religious retreat on pp. 177–81 puts the emphasis on privacy and personal meditation as opposed to communal physical activity, while the establishment of preference is accompanied by the desire to create special secrets and exclusive relationships, barriers which cut across the barriers imposed from the outside by the teachers: 'les correspondances particulières sont des motifs de renvoi' (p. 232).

The barrier is also an important, if implicit, motif in Wittig's feminist work. The sexual barrier which divides men and women in the real world is replaced by symbolic ones which separate the ideal Utopian community from that real world. The *amantes* of *Les Guérillères* inhabit an island in which are concentrated the richest elements of the natural world and none of the evils of the man-made social world. In *Virgile, non* Dante's linear three-part progress through the distinctly demarcated strata of his metaphysical universe has been replaced by a much more erratic structure in which Wittig is unceremoniously projected back and forth among Hell, Limbo and Paradise. The barriers in *Virgile, non* are no less real for being invisible and unpredictable than those in the *Divine Comedy*, but it is a crucial part of Wittig's education that she learn to recognise with precision and nuance the differences among the various strata and the types of behaviour and degrees of understanding that determine condemnation or access to them. The more fitful structure of *Virgile, non* highlights the difficulty of such an undertaking, where every two steps forward are matched by one step backward. Ultimately these barriers are self-imposed – the acceptance of subordination by the damned souls which produces an uncoordinated, quarrelsome herd, the self-indulgent individualism which characterises the Limbo-stranded gay subculture. It is significant that when Wittig finally gains access to Paradise, it does not, as she anticipated, take the form of a reunion in an exclusive relationship with her beloved but a welcome into a Utopian community in which that relationship has its place but does not eclipse other bonds. The speaker of *Le Corps lesbien* has to undergo a similar arduous apprenticeship, whereby from an initial position of isolation and unrequited love she is gradually integrated into the society of 'amantes' to which her beloved belongs and which was originally perceived as an obstacle to the fulfilment of her love and a source of rivalry. At the close of *Le Corps lesbien* the exclusive proprietorial instinct of the jealous speaker has given way to an expansive capacity to share the self and the partner with the community. Commitment to solidarity must be the foundation of the ideal society, and the monogamous lesbian relationship is shown to be as potentially divisive as its heterosexual equivalent. Fulfilment can be achieved only through the collectivity, not through competition with it: 'j/e te cherche m/a rayonnante à travers l'assemblée' (p. 188).

Despite the priority Wittig gives to solidarity and the absence of conventional personalised characterisation, she does not overlook the demands of the individual:

> Se constituer en classe ne veut pas dire que nous devions nous supprimer en tant qu'individus. Et comme 'il n'y a pas d'individu qui puisse se réduire à son oppression' nous sommes aussi confrontées avec la nécessité historique de nous constituer en tant que sujets individuels de notre histoire. ('On ne naît pas femme', p. 81)

It is this concern for a relative balance which determines to some extent the inclusion in *Les Guérillères* of the lists of female proper names in a narrative otherwise dominated by the anonymous pronoun 'elles'. It also explains the curious sacred machine for recording divergencies described on pp. 32–3 and the idea of unity in diversity running through many of the short texts.

In *Le Corps lesbien* and *Virgile, non*, the individual subject is even more in evidence, the first an often moving record of the frustration and distress accompanying a relationship, the second a personal apprenticeship and test of belief for the protagonist Wittig, this 'lesbienne de papier' (p. 33) who, it seems to be suggested, has lived in the two-dimensional world of Utopian writing and must now address herself to some of the concrete realities of woman's situation. Like the *Divine Comedy*, *Virgile, non* can be interpreted as a drama of the mind where the poet scrutinises his/her assumptions and failings and the *décalage* between reality and his/her ideals. The brackets which enclose the dialogue between Wittig and the other characters make it plain that this is an internal debate in which Wittig revises her own arguments and anticipates counter-arguments.

The theme of apprenticeship – whether physical, ideological, practical or moral – is the linch-pin of Wittig's *œuvre*. In both *L'Opoponax* and her subsequent feminist work she is focusing on sections of society – children and women – who have been regarded as incompetent and marginal to serious adult male activities but where the potential for development is at a maximum.

The superficial amorphousness of *L'Opoponax* conceals a tight thematic structure in which the childish acquisition of skills is rigorously charted. In the first half of the novel the emphasis is on incompetence, and the child is constantly and mercilessly made aware of the ground to be covered. The gap between intentions and physical competence and coordination is nowhere more apparent than in the arduous process of learning to write. The letters exceed the lines above and below and run into one another in spite of the writer's attempt to control them (p. 27); if the pencil is too sharp, it makes holes in the paper; if the point is too blunt, it results in thick unseemly letters (p. 29). Even once the basic skills are acquired, aesthetic considerations leave a feeling of dissatisfaction: 'Catherine Legrand trouve que ça fait bien sauf qu'elle n'a pas une belle écriture et qu'elle ne sait pas mettre les mots en ligne droite' (p. 196). Tying one's shoe-laces (p. 45) or picking garden peas without squashing the pods (p. 27) presents apparently insurmountable problems. Adults manage to impinge upon the child's perception because they possess enviable and inaccessible skills: 'Ma sœur épluche les oranges. Avec son couteau, elle découpe la pelure concentriquement et ça se détache du fruit en ronds. Quand elle a fini elle accroche à la porte les plus grands ronds, les pelures qu'elle a réussi à garder entières sans les casser' (p. 9). Tree-climbing is a qualified success, if one does not fall into nettle-beds (p. 82). A new role or responsibility invariably exposes new areas of incompetence, as when Marie-José Broux is asked to ring the school-bell in the absence of the usual monitor (p. 244). Some children, such as the accident-prone Nicole Marre, never quite get to grips with the world around them and remain clumsy to the end of the novel (pp. 243, 262, 270). The examples are trivial and predictable, but they do show an appreciation of the physical hurdle-course of growing up and an attempt to reproduce the conditions and details of childish perception that is surprisingly rare in novels on childhood. Wittig's novel can be described as a phenomenological work in so far as it suspends adult assumptions and knowledge about the world and tries to re-create something of the surprise and difficulty of the unfamiliar. Repeatedly in *L'Opoponax* the child is caught in mid-gesture as he or she grapples with new dimensions of his *Lebenswelt*.

Gradually, of course, the child's control and understanding of his environment increase and are refined, and Wittig meticulously records the progress made. At an early stage the children's keenness to adapt and exploit the material available and turn it into new useful objects is seen in their manufacture of home-made walking-sticks:

> Des bouts de bois on en trouve de part et d'autre dans le sous-bois ou même au milieu du chemin [. . .] Quelques-uns sont assez grands pour faire des bâtons. On s'appuie dessus de toutes ses forces pour en éprouver la solidité. Il y en a qui se cassent. [. . .] C'est le bois pourri. On se met à en fabriquer en coupant avec des canifs des branches de noisetier. [. . .] On les prend le plus longs possible. On les dépouille de l'écorce. On les prend flexibles. (pp. 68–9)

The role of adults remains minimal, and the children's own experiments with the natural world and self-instructional activities predominate. They learn a great deal from each other and through group activity. Catherine Legrand learns the skills involved in tickling trout from Vincent Parme (p. 108), while the construction of a shelter in the woods is a successful combination of practical shrewdness and coordinated action (p. 149). Not all of their enterprises meet with such success. Their attempts to pan for gold in the river and to make a mud kiln are doomed to failure because of the inadequacy of their tools and materials, but both show an enterprising readiness to exploit and experiment with the substances and elements of their environment in a creative and constructive way. This creative instinct is nurtured in a more structured way during the retreat at school where the children are encouraged to pursue personal projects which interest them, such as book-binding and the construction of a herbarium, for which they are provided with suitable materials. The children reach a peak in physical competence at the end of the novel, where they not only are able to swing athletically from tree to tree but have attained a mastery of gesture and movement which permits them in their school drama productions to conjure up with great precision a whole imaginary world:

> Véronique Legrand se déplace sur la scène suivant des directions données qu'on ne connaît pas, elle va, elle vient d'avant en arrière, elle est en train de parcourir une oblique qui devient la tangente d'une courbe ou d'un cercle [. . .] il semble que les mouvements des filles qui l'entourent soient déterminés par les siens, et qu'ils lui servent de décor, on voit comme des remous autour d'elle, qu'elle arrête d'un geste de la main [. . .] On ne voit pas un sourire sur sa figure. (p. 210)

The transition from a purely functional to a symbolic use of their bodies testifies to a grasp of highly complex gestural codes and patterns.

Of Wittig's feminist work, it is *Les Guérillères* which devotes most space to the development of practical and physical skills. Here the acquisition of new areas of competence previously denied to women is accompanied by a process of unlearning and the rejection of domestic crafts and the subservient instrumental roles which have been traditionally delegated to women. The ritual burning of tools and materials conventionally associated with women's work (pp. 102–3) is a prerequisite for their further development which will culminate with the capture and control of the entire industrial world:

Elles sont dans les aérodromes dans les maisons de la radio. Elles contrôlent les communications. Elles ont mis la main sur les usines d'aéronautique d'électronique de balistique d'informatique. Elles sont dans les fourneaux les chantiers navals les arsenaux les raffineries les distilleries. Elles se sont emparé des pompes des presses des leviers des laminoirs des treuils des poulies des grives des turbines des marteaux-piqueurs des arcs des chalumeaux. (p. 137)

The domestication of women has eclipsed innate survival skills which now must be relearned: 'il y a eu un temps où tu n'as pas été esclave, souviens-toi [. . .] Tu cours pour attraper les jeunes lièvres que tu écorches aux pierres des rochers pour les dépecer et les manger tout chauds et sanglants. Tu sais comment ne pas rencontrer un ours sur les pistes' (pp. 126–7). Thus in the first part of the novel we find the women engaged in a wide range of activities, some – such as hunting, farming, engineering – to ensure their survival and others, which involve the fabrication of strange substances and objects, to improve the quality of life (pp. 36–7, 49–50). Women are no longer seen as instruments. The invention of silk is attributed to a woman (pp. 115–16), while the *amantes* of this Utopian community produce strange and wonderful objects which are both useful and aesthetically pleasing, such as a multi-coloured weather vane which catches and retains the light of the sun.

In the second part of the novel the women's inventiveness and practical inspiration turn to the manufacture of more lethal objects. The account of their struggle against the enemy testifies to a progressive sophistication in the production of weapons. From the outset they are seen wielding with consummate skill an infinite variety of both modern and traditional instruments of warfare: rifles, machine-guns, rocket-launchers, man-traps, lances, halberds, double-edged swords and sabres. By the climax of their war, however, they are confronting the enemy with strange new, highly effective weapons with remarkable and highly effective capabilities. The ospah (pp. 149–50) combines the features of the cowboy's bolas, the invisible weapon of myth and fable, the stink bomb and the laser gun, while the apparently innocuous sphere which they carry with them would seem to belong to the world of selective nuclear weaponry (pp. 154–5).

The learning process in *Les Guérillères* is, however, not restricted to the invasion of male strongholds. As in *L'Opoponax*, an appreciation and knowledge of the natural environment is given considerable weight. From the beginning of the novel the richness and complexity of the natural world is stressed. In the long list of aromatic substances on p. 10, exotic and strange figures alongside the familiar draw attention to the existence of natural phenomena of which most people are at best only marginally aware. A similar point is made on p. 10 in the description of the visit to the market, where the women are presented with a dazzling display of both banal and unusual fruit. The enumeration of the names of a whole range of different types of palm-trees on p. 69 highlights the variety within a single species and makes the average reader aware of his or her ignorance. Realism never being at a premium for Wittig, she brings together in one Utopian landscape sub-species native to several different countries. Her taste for the outlandish is not gratuitous ostentation – the reader's own recourse to the encyclopedia makes him or her aware of the gaps in the range and specificity of his or her general knowledge.

The theme which ultimately dominates Wittig's work is that of the relationship between language and perception. Its exploration informs both her fictional work and the feminist dictionary, *Brouillon pour un dictionnaire des amantes* (1976), written in conjunction with Sande Zeig.

L'Opoponax opens at the point when Catherine Legrand has reached an adequate level of communicative and comprehension skills to participate in the micro-society of school and closes at the point when she and her peers have a mastery of language which permits them to challenge authority and confidently plagiarise from the classics in the expression of personal feelings. The acquisition of linguistic skills is the most reliable indicator of the passing of time in the novel, the various exercises in literacy providing a kind of temporal punctuation in a novel where time is experienced in a highly elastic and impressionistic way.

The acquisition and extension of vocabulary are meticulously charted. The prominence of concrete vocabulary and active verbs in the early stages of the novel reflects the children's active exploration and identification of the elements of their environment. Vocabulary relating to nature is prominent throughout the book, but there is a discernible progress in differentiation and the assimilation of labels and categories, which is promoted by their various nature trips (pp. 68, 70, 80). Each new 'leçon de choses' opens up new lexical areas and allows them to break mystifying areas of adult activity into comprehensible units: 'il y a des scies à bois, des scies à métaux, des scies circulaires, il y a des égoïnes de taille différente, des limes à bois, à métaux, un compas d'épaisseur, il y a une chignole, il y a des poinçons de toutes les tailles et de toutes les sortes' (p. 78). The geology lesson (pp. 169–70) introduces them to unfamiliar terminology referring to phenomena which are not immediately verifiable but which they have to accept as real (p. 170). The manipulation of abstract vocabulary is seen as a late development, and the *décalage* between the child and the adult in this respect is highlighted by the difficulties which the children have in distinguishing between the concepts of animate and inanimate (pp. 20, 46, 51, 59). The study of mathematics is a landmark in so far as it both offers them a whole new language for the analysis and description of their world (pp. 208–10) and takes them beyond the level of concrete, verifiable reality to an abstract plane and challenges the assumed identification between sign and referent.

Interest in the vocabulary relating to the emotions and psychological phenomena is also introduced relatively late in the novel, the study of the introspective poetry of Charles d'Orléans (pp.175–6) and the emotionally charged tragedy of the seventeenth century (p. 222) providing a literary cue. Here Wittig's view is borne out by Piaget's analysis of the relatively late development of introspective thought processes: 'One feature of adolescent thought is the capacity to think about thinking, to introspect . . . The adolescent becomes secretive about his thoughts. He recognises that his thought is private'.[6] Thus Catherine Legrand's personal interest in Charles d'Orléans coincides with the retreat in which the children are encouraged to devote their attention to private reflection and to give some thought to difficult and sophisticated concepts such as the Pascalian argument about the 'disproportion de l'homme' (p. 178). Similarly, the discussion of seventeenth-century views on passion coincides with Catherine Legrand's own awakening to the power of love in her attraction for Valerie Borge. At this point, too, the children are exposed to a new dimension of language: the contrast between the specificity of the concrete vocabulary they have learned elsewhere and the multivalence of the abstract word. The abstract vocabulary may be less varied, but the connotations of a single abstract are shown heavily to outweigh its denotative value.

The appreciation of polyvalence and the acknowledgement of the absence of a one-to-one relationship between word and referent are the culmination of a long initiation into the complexity of definition. Definition causes the children considerable difficulty in the early sections of *L'Opoponax*. From her first day at school Catherine Legrand has to contend with the discrepancies between connotation and denotation. On p. 8 she finds that the associations and expecta-

---

6. D. Elkind, *Children and Adolescents: Interpretive Essays on Jean Piaget*, 3rd edn (London, Oxford University Press, 1981), p. 102.

tions which she has attached to the word 'école' are not borne out by experience. The radical opposition she has set up in her mind between 'school' and 'home' is much too crude and cannot cope with the nuances of reality nor of linguistic differentiation. Her inability to make the distinction between common nouns and proper names manifests itself in a circular definition on p. 10 which tries to establish a one-to-one correlation between a word which has no universal referential meaning and a word which *is* descriptive and does have a generalised definition: 'La grosse petite fille qui s'appelle Brigitte parce qu'elle est grosse'. The same tendency to associate words with one another in apparently absolute relationships is seen on p. 20 in an equation of 'mort' and 'trou' which confuses cause and effect, contingency and necessity. An inability to ideate and a susceptibility to the simplicity of binary oppositions produce ingenious but uninformative glosses which disintegrate into confusion when a third term is introduced: 'Qu'est-ce que c'est un pays, c'est où on est, et où on n'est pas c'est pas un pays' (p. 15); 'Alors il n'y a pas de totems où on n'est pas si c'est pas un pays dis, je ne sais pas, alors où on est c'est un pays et il y a des totems' (p. 15).

The discrepancy between the children's impressionistic and experiential definition of apparently innocuous words such as 'fleuve', 'rivière' and 'torrent' and the teacher's precise, differential definition of these words in relation to each other constitutes another semantic eye-opener for them and demonstrates the differential foundation of the linguistic system. Gradually, as the relative nature of signification dawns on them, the children become aware not only of the restrictions of language but also of the room for play within the system. This awareness crystallises in Catherine Legrand's deformation of and investment of personal significance in the word 'opoponax'. She has identified a little used and therefore vulnerable element in the system and conferred upon it a private but potent significance, using it to denote all that is incomprehensible to her, all that is not covered by familiar taxonomical vocabulary.

The formulation of areas of experience uncharted by existing discourse is central to Wittig's feminist novels. The subordination of women and the imprisonment of their thought and expression within man-made language are seen as being inextricably associated. The derogatory epithets which have been applied to woman, as to blacks, testify to the white male's cultural domination (*Les Guérillères*, p. 146).

The docile servitude of woman is to be attributed largely to a male linguistic conspiracy which has refused to record or has destroyed evidence that she might have enjoyed an alternative status: 'il y a eu un temps où tu n'as pas été esclave . . . Tu dis qu'il n'y a pas de mots pour décrire ce temps, tu dis qu'il n'existe pas' (ibid., pp. 126–7). The prevailing man-made linguistic code precludes the recognition of dimensions and possibilities not articulated by that code. Wittig challenges the ostensibly natural but in fact arbitrary relationship between the existing linguistic system and reality, claiming that reality contains things which have not been formulated and which have been conveniently consigned to oblivion: 'Ce sur quoi ils n'ont pas mis la main, ce sur quoi ils n'ont pas fondu comme des rapaces aux yeux multiples, cela n'apparaît pas dans le langage que tu parles' (ibid., pp. 162–4). The act of renaming at the end of *Les Guérillères* is the Utopian goal which gives direction to Wittig's exposure of the patriarchal assumptions enshrined in language and her plea for a discourse in which women's experience can be accommodated. The zero which punctuates the text so conspicuously is a polyvalent symbol – at once a graphic cipher for the female genitalia, the number nought signalling a new beginning *and* a reference to the holes, absences and lacunae in the male discourses. The recurrent O points to the gaps in which a female discourse may take root.

Brouillon pour un dictionnaire des amantes is a blueprint for such a Utopian discourse and belongs to a now well-established genre – the feminist dictionary or lexicon, founded on the assumption that the entries in existing dictionaries are at once aimed at and determined by men. The entry under the word 'mot' offers a crucial key to the selection criteria underpinning the dictionary. Wittig and her collaborator, Sande Zeig, aim to establish a lexical least common denominator, retaining, inventing and redefining words which are seen to be indispensable.

Words such as 'énergie', 'antenne' and 'circulation' have been redefined to denote specifically lesbian faculties not covered by received definitions. The superficial facetiousness of such definitions is highly disingenuous. The attribution to lesbians of special powers unknown to men opens up a whole can of linguistic and ideological worms. The female-specific faculty or power has traditionally been denied, ignored and misrepresented or has incurred severe persecution. The word 'sorcière' provides a measure of the gap between feminist and non-feminist definition. Wittig and Zeig provide a definition which discards the traditional image of the malign old hag to replace it with that of a healthy nature-loving athlete.

Typically, the *Brouillon* concludes with an entry which points forward to an ideal future salvaged from the debris of the past. 'Voyelle' is used as a convenient peg on to which Wittig and Zeig hang their implausibly ambitious conception of a hypothetical language composed of elemental and freshly combined sounds. Far-fetched and impractical their conception may seem; however, it is firmly founded in post-Saussurian linguistic theory. If one accepts that language in general is a system where meaning is produced and perceived through differentiation between related phonemes, then one also has to accept that any new language will be founded on the same principle. Wittig and Zeig's project may seem outlandishly idealistic, but their grasp of linguistic principles has allowed them to expose the purely conventional nature of the relationship between word and established meaning and the deterministic role of ideology in that tenuous and shifting relationship.

Furthermore, Wittig's ambitious injunctions are accompanied by a modest and self-critical scrutiny of her own position. *Virgile, non* is an exercise in self-exposure in which Wittig, the protagonist, is made to confront her own ignorance. Language is given thematic prominence at the outset of the novel in Wittig's fight with the robotic eagle (a modern parodic equivalent of Dante's eagle of justice) which plummets to the ground vomiting clichés. Victory for Wittig rarely comes easily, and it is not long before we realise that the cliché is an Aunt Sally and that little glory is to be derived from knocking it down. The articulation of male offences is equally straightforward, given their obviousness. The naming of the hitherto unnamed is another problem altogether. Words such as 'compassion' and 'beauty' are found wanting in Wittig's attempts to formulate her fellow-feeling for the damned or the overwhelming gorgeousness of paradise. Words simply elude her on her entry to Paradise, and their conspicuous absence forms a concrete barrier between her and her beloved. Readily available words are to be regarded with suspicion: they are treacherous allies and seduction by them is likely to precipitate Wittig into Hell at any moment. Access to Paradise presupposes the expunction of the trite, careless and facile. Language is full of unforeseen dangers, and Wittig's oversights and loose usage stand as a warning to the linguistically naïve reader. Wittig gives vent to her own frustration in an emphatically placed central passage, where she laments the gulf between her verbal facility in the enumeration of Hell's atrocities and her inarticulacy in the face of Paradise. Destructive critique comes easily; the construction of a Woman's Language is beset by monumental difficulties.

Once again, however, the final note is a positive one. As in the *Brouillon*, Wittig is prepared to sift and salvage. The literal and the concrete survive where the abstract and metaphorical failed, as the final section with its enumeration of utensils, weapons and natural species demonstrates. These, we must assume, are the essentials for a state of well-being. The inessential, the distortive and the conno-tatively suspect are, as in the *Brouillon*, expunged. Wittig's perverse variation on the passage in the last canto of Dante's *Divine Comedy*, where all the leaves of wisdom and knowledge are united in a single volume, is instructive. In the Paradise of *Virgile, non* language disintegrates and is scattered like the leaves of the sibyl in Virgil's *Aeneid*. Ultimately, Wittig retains but a single abstract – 'passion' – which eclipses the wan 'compassion' and 'beauty' which were pre-viously found so unsatisfactory. 'Passion' is at the centre of Wittig's Utopian language and of her work as a whole. It alone can en-compass the intensity, urgency and harmony that constitute the core of her feminist philosophy.

Wittig's salvaging and re-invention campaign also extends beyond language to encompass the fairy-tales, myths, literary classics and historical accounts which, as prominent elements of our cultural code, condition our perception of the world and reinforce certain ideological assumptions. An early instance of Wittig's sceptical and critical approach to the received version is to be found in the historical lesson on Charlemagne in *L'Opoponax* (p. 104), where the discrepancy between the children's observant 'Il n'y a pas de petites filles sur l'image' and the teacher's platitudinous interpretation of the history-book illustration in terms of benevolent paternalism highlights the way in which the female sex has been erased from history.

In *Brouillon pour un dictionnaire des amantes* Wittig and Zeig use the bibliography and illustrative quotations to rewrite the history of literature and at the same time attack the monopoly that male writers have on illustrative quotations. The relative unfamiliarity of the bibliographical references reinforce, rather than invalidate, the fiercely defended view that women have been eclipsed from histori-cal consciousness. The poetry of Virgil and Baudelaire has been reduced to a few fragments salvaged from the debris of androcentric culture which do not weigh very heavily against the host of women writers, the citation of whom widens the authorship beyond the named signatories and turns the work into a collective enterprise.

The world of folklore and fable is subject to even more radical 'correction'. In *Les Guérillères* the tale of Sleeping Beauty is given a surprising and risqué twist – Sleeping Beauty is the passive, un-conscious woman whom Wittig so abhors, while the spindle on which she pricks her finger symbolises the clitoris, her spellbound sleep being a fit punishment for her lack of body awareness. The story of Drapaudi with her five subservient husbands is a malicious reworking of part of the Hindu epic *Mahabharata*, where a character named Drapaudi was won by one man and shared with four others.

The appropriation of names and stories from a wide range of cultures and the inclusion in *Les Guérillères* and the *Brouillon* of references to cross-cultural mythological figures show Wittig's debt to contemporary structuralist anthropology and at the same time strengthen her and Zeig's argument that there was once a single harmonious culture which disintegrated in the face of territorial acquisitiveness. Thus in the *Brouillon* Wittig and Zeig have rewritten biblical and factual history to explain the disappearance of Amazonian culture and language. The wanderings of Noah's people recounted in the eleventh book of Genesis and the standard school-book history of the great tribal migrations are the pre-texts for Wittig's evocation of the idyllic period when Amazons roamed the earth freely. The building of Babel and the tribal settlement signal the start of a process of confining domestication and the rise of anti-social, acquisitive territorial instincts. The universal tongue which prevailed in the early books of Genesis and in the mythical Amazonian society disintegrated when Noah's descendants and the *mères* betrayed the principle of freedom and openness for security and exclusive possession. The civilisation which has produced society as we know it has been a divisive process to which can be attributed physical conflict and linguistic difference. From being a transparent vehicle, language became a source of ambiguity and distrust, requiring constant interpretation. 'Big' historical events do not in themselves interest Wittig and Zeig; like their structuralist contemporaries, they are looking for general principles, trends and structures, for only the recognition of the essential underlying the contingent can pave the way for a different sort of history.

The search for trend and pattern leads Wittig and Zeig back to fundamental texts – to Daniel and Ovid's *Metamorphoses*, which inspire their recasting of history in terms of a decline from the age of gold, through silver, brass and iron, to the age of clay. Once again, however, the inclination to carp is not allowed to prevail at the expense of the positive, constructive perspective. The rise of lesbian feminism is seen as a signal of the Second Coming and the eclipse of the past by an age of glory.

The subversion of date- and event-centred historiography and the irreverent reworking of the Bible constitute a blatant refusal of the 'facts' and an unashamed appropriation of one of western man's most powerful and time-honoured ideological weapons. Wittig's rewriting of the Song of Songs in *Le Corps lesbien* provides an even clearer example of an apparently boundless irreverence, backed by a firm grasp of contemporary reinterpretative strategies. In recent studies of the Song of Songs, literary analysis has tended to displace finicky and ingenious exegesis.[7] In such analyses the Song of Songs is no longer seen as an obscure allegory on the relationship between man and the church, but as a candid affirmation of human love and sexuality in which the female speaker is quite capable of taking sexual initiative. Wittig's variation on the sacred poem flouts the church's taboos on homosexuality, but it shows a grasp of the source's structure and spirit. On the level of superficial detail the two works present no similarities whatsoever, but the emotional phases – the unquenchable fire of passion and the sickening weariness following consummation – and the obstacles encountered by both speakers in their quest for union – separation, the unaccountable disappearance of the beloved, the obstructive enmity of the city-dwellers – are remarkably similar. Even the startling fragmentation of the body in long physiological catalogues in *Le Corps lesbien* has an equivalent in the *wasfs* of the Song of Songs. The *wasf* (signifying 'description' in Arabic) has been appropriated by criticism on the Song of Songs to refer to the set pieces within it describing parts of female and male bodies, which are distinguished from the rest of the poem both by the nature of their content and by their absence of grammatical structure. Similarly, for Wittig the enumerative lists which punctuate the text, but are not syntactically integrated into the text, highlight the sensual and physical dimension of love. The emphasis given to the body by the accentuation of the formal distinction between narrative and description and her elimination of the metaphorical formulation of the Song of Songs show a desire to nail her own interpretative colours to the mast rather than to achieve a radical transformation of her source. In neither work is a traditional plot- or character-based interpretation fruitful or apt. The reader who tries to establish a single, logical, syntagmatic sequence will be eternally frustrated. In both the Song of Songs and *Le Corps lesbien* the narrative springs from a single seminal paradigm and its variations. The trials and tribulations of a single, identifiable couple hold no interest either for Wittig or the writer of the Song of Songs. The lovers in both are representative figures who are constantly adopting, dropping and qualifying the multiple poses and personae of love; their story is not a smooth chronological progression but a gamut of discrete, contrapuntal scenes and situations in which passion is considered from multiple

7. See, for example, Francis Landy, *Paradoxes of Paradise* (Sheffield, Almond, 1983).

angles and explored exhaustively through a wide variety of combinations.

Of Wittig's variations on spiritual and literary milestones, *Virgile, non* is undoubtedly the most humorously playful. The world of *Virgile, non*, like that of the *Divine Comedy*, is a microcosm bringing together the real and the fantastic, the ancient and the contemporary, the finite and the infinite. Modern San Francisco has replaced Dante's sinful city of Dis, and Wittig leads us through a universe where classical allusion and twentieth-century kitsch and Americana rank equally as coordinates. The Acheron, the Lethe, the Phlegethon and Orpheus coexist alongside launderettes, gay bars, cheer-leaders, joggers and the subway. Biblical episodes are given modern technological twists or are updated in line with contemporary fashion. Thus the 'flaming sword' of Genesis is replaced by a laser beam, while Wittig has to face a final test of faith which is reminiscent of Jacob's struggle with the angel, the tactics of which show the influence of the modern western craze for Oriental martial arts. The angels in Wittig's Paradise are a gang of biker lesbians who, nevertheless, bear names taken from the Old Testament and the Book of Enoch. Wittig's fusion of the sacred, classical and ancient with the profane, kitschy and new-fangled is not simply the gratuitous whim of an outrageous iconoclast. The location of her *Divine Comedy* in an America full of excess and bad-taste is determined by the fact that women and America share a common feature – a longing for a cultural history which would put them on an equal footing with the rest of the world. In her synthesis of the Old and New Worlds, Wittig is robbing the rich to give the poor a few cultural points of reference.

This essay has attempted to give a perspective on the work of a writer who has made few, if any, concessions on the level of either content or form. As a self-appointed consciousness-raiser, Wittig has refused to pander either to moderate ideological reformists or to the aesthetic and narrative tastes of the reader-consumer. The stridency of her arguments and the formal difficulty of her work will, however, figure as no more than an occasional irritation to the reader who is willing to acknowledge the sophisticated wit, remarkable erudition and technical courage which, in different measures, characterise all her novels. The pragmatic feminist who can see no further than equal opportunities and a discursive space within a social structure that has been engendered by men will find little or no constructive guidance in Wittig. The reader – male or female – who accepts the broader lessons offered by contemporary feminist linguistic and anthropological theory on the matrices underlying apparently discrete sexual, social and discursive phenomena will appreciate the sophistication of Wittig's polemics. Wittig does not aim to satisfy a pre-existing audience; a true innovator and radical modern moralist, Wittig can only hope to create her own readership.

Bibliography

Works by Monique Wittig

Books

L'Opoponax (Editions de Minuit, 1964)
Les Guérillères (Editions de Minuit, 1969)
Le Corps lesbien (Editions de Minuit, 1973)
Brouillon pour un dictionnaire des amantes, written in collaboration with Sande Zeig (Grasset, 1976)
Virgile, non (Editions de Minuit, 1985)
Le Voyage sans fin (Blasta, 1985)

Short Stories

'Banlieues', *Le Nouveau Commerce*, 5 (1965), 113–17
'Yallankoro', *La Nouvelle Revue Française*, 177 (1 Sept. 1967), 559–63
'Un jour', *Questions féministes*, 2 (1970), 31–9
'Une partie de campagne', *Nouveau Commerce*, 26 (1973), 13–31
'Les Tchiches et les Tchouches', *Le Genre humain*, 6 (1983), 136–46
'Paris – La – Politique', *Vlasta*, no. 4 (1985), 36–41

Radio Plays

'Le Grand – Cric – Jules', 'Récréation', 'Dialogue pour les deux frères et la sœur', short plays written for Radio Stuttgart

Essays, Articles

'Lacunary films', *New Statesman*, 15 July 1966, 102
'Bouvard et Pécuchet', *Les Cahiers Madeleine Renaud – Barrault* (1976)
'Paradigm', in *Homosexualities and French Literature*, G. Stambolian and E.

Marks, ed. (Ithaca, Cornell University Press, 1979), 114–21
'La pensée straight', *Questions Féministes*, 7 (1980), 45–53
'On ne naît pas femme', *Questions Féministes*, 8 (May 1980), 75–84
'The Category of Sex', *Feminist Issues* (1982)
'Universal or particular? The point of view', *Feminist Issues* (1983)
'Le lieu de l'action', *Digraphe* (1984)
'The Trojan Horse', *Feminist Issues* (1984)
'The place of the action', in *Three Decades of the French New Novel*, Lois Oppenheim, ed. (Chicago, University of Illinois Press, 1968), pp. 132–40

Selected Critical Studies

Bazon, L., 'Le faussaire: *L'Opoponax*', *Etudes*, (Feb. 1965), 232–7
Crowder, D. G., 'Amazons and mothers? Monique Wittig, Hélène Cixous and theories of women's writing', *Contemporary Literature* (Summer 1983), 117–44
Duffy, J. H., 'Language and childhood: *L'Opoponax* by Monique Wittig', *Forum for Modern Language Studies*, XIX (1983), 289–300
——, 'Women and language in *Les Guérillères* by Monique Wittig', *Stanford French Review* (Winter 1983), 399–412
Durand, L. G., 'Heroic feminism as art', *Novel*, VIII (1974), 71–78
Duras, M., 'Une œuvre éclatante', *France Observateur*, 5 Nov. 1964, 18–19
Gotham Davis, R., 'Invaded selves', *Hudson Review*, XIX (1966–7), 659–68
Higgins, L., 'Nouvelle, nouvelle autobiographie: Monique Wittig's *Le Corps lesbien*', *Sub-stance*, 14 (1976), 160–6
McCarthy, M., 'Everybody's childhood', *New Statesman*, 15 July 1966, 90, 92–4
——, *The Writing on the Wall and Other Literary Essays* (London: Weidenfeld and Nicolson, 1970), pp. 102–112
Marks, E. and I. de Courtivron, *New French Feminisms: An Anthology* (Amherst, University of Massachusetts Press, 1980)
O'Flaherty, K., *The Novel in France: 1945–65* (Cork, Cork University Press, 1973)
Ostrovsky, E., 'A cosmogony of O: Wittig's *Les Guérillères*', in *Twentieth Century Fiction*, G. Stambolian, ed. (New Brunswick, Rutgers University Press, 1975), pp. 241–51
Simon, C., 'Pour Monique Wittig', *L'Express*, 30 Nov.–6 Dec. 1964, 69–71
Spraggins, M.P., 'Myth and Ms. Encroachment and liberation in Monique Wittig's *Les Guérillères*', *International Fiction Review*, 3 (1976), 47–51
Vlasta, no. 4, 1985
Wenzel, H. V., 'The text as body/politics: an appreciation of Monique Wittig's writings in context', *Feminist Studies*, 7 (Summer 1981), 264–87

Patrick Grainville

DAVID GASCOIGNE

'Nos rapports avec le pays natal sont toujours chargés d'ambiguïté. Une tendresse puissante qu'avive une imperceptible agressivité. Une relation amoureuse en somme' (*Au long des haies de Normandie*, p. 1).[1] Patrick Grainville was born in 1947 in the Calvados area of Normandy. The stretch of coastline around Honfleur and Deauville is very much his home country, and his writing, however widely it may range, seems impelled to return periodically to the evocation of its landscapes and seascapes, as though to reassure itself of its origins. He went from the lycée at Deauville to the lycée Henri IV in Paris, participating in the 1968 'events' but, he says, 'nullement engagé'. He obtained his *agrégation* at the Sorbonne and became a teacher.

He chose as a thesis topic 'Le donjuanisme chez Montherlant'. Montherlant was scarcely a fashionable writer to choose to study in the 1970s, and this is already evidence of Grainville's resistance to conventional canons of judgement and cultural fashion. He has no patience with 'cette emprise de la tradition romanesque française, celle du roman court, précis, sentimental, psychologique'. He particularly abhors the 'nouveau roman': 'des textes disloqués, incompréhensibles, absolument refermés sur eux-mêmes'.[2] The writers he loves include Céline, Proust and Saint-John Perse, for their refusal to remain within prudent, economical limits: all writers who are, in different senses, 'baroque'. 'Baroque' is, with 'epic', a term of high praise in Grainville's vocabulary: 'Je crois qu'il y a un courant baroque et qu'il est libérateur.'[3]

---

1. References in the text are to the editions listed in the Bibliography, with the following exceptions: *Les Flamboyants* (Livre de poche, 1978); *La Diane rousse* (Livre de poche, 1980); *Le Dernier Viking* (Editions du Seuil, *Points*, 1982); *Les Forteresses noires* (Editions du Seuil, *Points*, 1983); *La Caverne céleste* (Editions du Seuil, *Points*, 1986).
2. Interview with Jérôme Le Thor appended to the Cercle du Nouveau Livre edition of *Les Flamboyants* (Tallandier, 1977), pp. 7, 8.
3. Interview, *Nouvelles littéraires*, 2558 (10 Nov. 1976), p. 5.

Grainville sent a copy of his first novel, *La Toison* (1972), to Montherlant who read it shortly before his death. The novel can be seen as a fictional extension of Grainville's research and reflection on 'le donjuanisme'. The unnamed narrator is a student living in a residence at the Cité Universitaire, between visits to his home territory in Normandy or to the Vosges. The Parisian setting is presented in a frequently surrealistic light. Something akin to the events of May 1968 takes place, but in midwinter; the city is invaded by deer, the population lives on nutritional pills, and the Eiffel tower keels over. These dream-like elements are in keeping with a narrative which is centrally an exploration of the narrator's desire for women. Everywhere he conjures up his fantasy-spectacle of women undressing, spontaneously offering him an erotic exhibition. His desire flits between three groups of women students – Swedes, Africans, Japanese – and more specifically between three other, particular women: Lise, Jana and Laura.

Lise, an ample, pale-complexioned girl from his home province, sometimes accompanies him on his long game-shooting expeditions across the marshland. The theme of hunting is firmly established in the opening chapter where he pursues and kills a hare, and it is closely associated with his endless Don Juan 'chasse aux femmes'. The 'toison' which fascinates him is a feature of both types of prey. For him, hunting is erotic and sex is predatory. The second girl, Jana, presents a contrast: she is dark-haired and inhabits a dusty flat in Paris. She is less responsive to his advances, remaining irritatingly elusive. She evokes even more insistently the furry coat of the animals he hunts with such determination. The third and youngest girl, Laura, is still at convent school, and with her he enjoys an idyllic 'honeymoon' at her home in Lorraine while her parents are away.

Each of these young women, with a certain physique, a certain sexuality and placed in a particular characteristic setting, constitutes a potentially self-contained fantasy for the promiscuous male. As the narrative progresses, however, the links between the women, the overlapping of features, complicate and blur the picture. Lise develops her own fantasy life, asserts her independence and leaves him with mocking words, and Jana refuses to soothe his wounded ego. The fantasy project of male desire is thus frustrated, and it suffers another setback at the moment of what ironically should have been a long-desired victory. As the deer invade the city, Jana takes the initiative and comes finally to his room. His desire for her has been infused by a fetishistic vision of fur ('un pelage t'irait bien . . . un petit peu bestiale Jana' – p. 150), but when he finds this all too abundantly realised in the luxuriant growth on Jana's body, his desire vanishes, overwhelmed: 'J'avais voulu rôder aux marges de la féminité et je devais tout bonnement faire face à un règne différent' (p. 229). The relationship collapses after this débâcle, and while the narrator's spirits rise again with a card from Laura announcing her imminent arrival, the mention of her growing maturity and independence leaves the reader with the possibility of another eventual failure. *La Toison* starts as a confident celebration of male sexual fantasy, but it ends by sowing the seeds of a critique of 'donjuanisme' and its conventions.

La Toison is typical of many first novels in that it is autobiographical in temper, if not in actual substance: it presents the emotional life of a young man of the same age and status as the author. In *La Lisière* (1973), Grainville visibly set himself a greater challenge, that of widening his exploration of this rich texture of emotion and fantasy to include both earlier and later points in the cycle of life. Whereas *La Toison* reflects fundamentally one character's point of view, there are in *La Lisière* two characters whose visions of the world dominate the narrative: Gildas, a boy of thirteen on the verge of puberty, and Paulin, a writer on the verge of middle-age.

The novel is set in Nancy and in the surrounding countryside of Lorraine. Paulin is staying with his wife Claire at a hotel overlooking the Place Stanislas. Nearby is the museum housing sequences of engravings by the seventeenth-century Lorraine artist, Jacques Callot, on whom Paulin plans to write an essay. The relationship between husband and wife is strained. Claire describes Paulin to a fellow-guest as manic-depressive, and much of the narrative conveys Paulin's unstable, fantasy-ridden temperament. His reactions to Callot's powerful engravings, in the course of several visits to the museum, are carefully traced. At first these are negative:

> Paulin n'aime guère les gravures des sièges. Il en réprouve le mélange d'extrême précision et de désordre. Minutie des combattants [. . .] mais confusion du terrain déchiré de mer [. . .] Seule, la répartition des armées, cavalerie, marine, arquebusiers, archers, impose à l'amalgame de terre et de mer un quadrillage, des différences, une géographie d'emplacements. (p. 132)

This reaction reveals a need for order, system, geometry and a fear of chaos, of a mingling of elements: 'la lisière', the frontier, the borderline is precisely the point of peril. Claire comments on his 'manie de découper le monde en tranches et en contrastes'(p. 127), and he himself indulges his hypersensitive reactions to the city streets: 'Jusqu'à l'angoisse il remplit son regard d'horreur: coulées aveugles, envahissantes d'hommes, d'autos [. . .] quand le paroxysme est atteint et qu'il éprouve le vertige, il s'arrache à sa contemplation pour regagner rapidement le décor intemporel de la Place . . .' (p. 92). The structured architecture of the Place Stanislas is reassuring, but that reassurance seems threatened by the contorted faces of the carved caryatids or the stone monster in the fountain. The order he perceives brings with it stress and suffering, as in the zoo where the animals seem repressed, their very bestiality an inappropriate encumbrance. What he sees in the city around him is akin to what he discerns in Callot's drawings of massacre and nightmare: an extreme tension between the ordered precision of the form and the violent forces of pain and emotion which it seeks to contain. As he rereads the notes he has made on Callot's work, he finds that the images he has retained often bear little resemblance to what is actually in the engravings: the original drawings have become a 'pretext' to the free play of his own imagination: 'des négatifs incolores, des empreintes sèches, que son délire irrigue et travestit . . .' (p. 136).

Paulin's capacity for fantasy is further stimulated by newspaper and radio reports of the mysterious disappearance of a passenger liner, which gives rise to feverish media speculation. The narrative is periodically punctuated by spectacular evocations of shipwreck and disaster, an inner cinema of sensual surrender to death and disorder.

The temptations of disorder begin to impinge on his everyday life. He steals a statuette of Venus from the museum and starts looking for sexual adventures. He is particularly attracted to Servane, a café waitress, and his pursuit of her causes a serious rift with Claire, who has an affair of her own in revenge. Servane comes from Champenoux, in the heart of the forest. The forest, too, has an aura of fear and violence, with its buried debris from the battles of the Great War and its disquieting population of snakes and gypsies. Grainville sets up a consistent analogy between the expanses of forest and sea, so that the lure of Servane is echoed by the seductive dream of shipwreck, a traditional metaphor of erotic surrender. These progressive disorders of the imagination presage nothing good for Paulin. When Servane vanishes back into her home in the forest, Paulin cannot get past the redoubtable man and his three (Cerberus-like) dogs who guard the stream he must cross to reach her. He is cast in the role of an Orpheus who lacks the power to retrieve his Eurydice, the image of a failed writer who lacks the discipline to control and shape his dreams. When, in the closing pages, drainpipes burst beneath the Place Stanislas and that cherished symbol of order is flooded with mud and water, Paulin experiences a sense of personal devastation. Paulin's career, like that of Aschenbach in Thomas Mann's *Death in Venice*, testifies to the subversive power of Dionysus, a threat which the writer, as a creature of fantasy, must always confront.

While Paulin's evolution and the issues it raises form the most complex element in the novel, it is not the whole story. The book begins and ends not with Paulin but with the young Gildas, whose equally intense emotional adventures are narrated in parallel to those of Paulin. Gildas is on holiday in the countryside just outside Nancy with Vivie, a girl of the same age. He excitedly explores the forests, farms, fruit-trees and trout pools and impatiently anticipates the onset of sexual potency. Analogies are suggested between the experience of these two male characters, the middle-aged intellectual and the adolescent. While Paulin reflects on Callot's massacres, Gildas and Vivie observe the deaths, deliberately or accidentally caused, of worms, frogs and grasshoppers. Gildas, like Paulin, hears the news of the missing liner and dreams of it as an adolescent erotic paradise. He, too, seeks to be 'unfaithful' to Vivie when he is violently attracted to Laura, a young woman on whom he spies as she sunbathes in her garden with her lover Felix. This leads only to humiliation when Laura rejects his clumsy proposition out of hand: she is as inaccessible to him as Servane finally is to Paulin. The outcome of Gildas's story is, however, in sharp contrast to that of Paulin's, and the two strands are held in subtle balance. Each has confronted a difficult transition, but while Paulin seems to have been laid waste, Gildas emerges into sexual maturity with increased confidence and self-awareness. As he and Vivie set up their den on the edge of a graveyard, it is clear that the powers of love and death, Eros and Thanatos, hold for the moment no terrors for them.

Grainville describes his first three novels as a loosely structured 'autobiographie mythique', of which *L'Abîme* (1974) is the third self-contained section. It constitutes a satisfying structural close to the trilogy, completing the study of what one might call the four Ages of Man: the passage from childhood to adolescence (Gildas), the prime of youth and sexual power (*La Toison*), the uncertainties of middle age (Paulin) and, here, the crisis of old age. Grégoire, in his early seventies, is a respected resident in an old people's home in Normandy, close to the salt marshes of the estuary. In the shadow of death he pursues two distinct love affairs. He feels particularly close to Geneviève, a frail elderly woman with whom he plays draughts and discusses the relative merits of the poetry of René Char and Saint-John Perse. More critically, his sense of vitality is sustained by a final, passionately physical love affair with a young student, Laura. The Laura of *L'Abîme* echoes aspects of the role of Lise in *La*

Toison: for instance, she accompanies her partner as helpmate on his water-fowl hunts, and they make love in their hide in the marshes. Laura is 'issue de la mer' (p. 86): their first sexual encounter is initiated by her inviting him to bathe in the sea with her, and she is insistently associated with water. The 'abîme de mer' (p. 342) is here again an erotic abyss. To snatch love from the element of death – that, for Grégoire, is the wager, and as in *La Lisière* it takes on an Orphic dimension as he and Laura cross the motorway – 'un méandre noir et douteux entre la vie et la mer' (p. 356) – and pick their way across rickety bridges over the black water of the canals towards the refuge of the hide.

Grégoire struggles to maintain a positive perspective on death, to see it as a stimulus to a final burst of vitality, as a life-enhancing, not a life-denying, conclusion. This is the mission he undertakes also in his pastoral role towards the other inmates of the residence. He introduces himself in the opening pages as 'le pâtre des vieillards' (p. 16); to the others he is 'notre bon Mage' (p. 266). Legendary episodes of his life have added to his shamanistic or heroic status: we are told of his war-wound, and of the subsequent act of self-mutilation which led to the loss of his leg, and of how he put thieves to flight by brandishing his artificial limb. Shaman-like, he spends a night stretched out on the grave of his fellow-inmate Marguerite, newly dead. There he perceives the harmonious presence of nature and conjures up a vision of the layers of dead of different ages stirring beneath him: the conjunction of life and death. This experience of 'voyance', another journey in imagination into the 'abîme' of death, confers on him, however momentarily, a decisive sense of metaphysical knowledge: 'L'aube me surprit. J'avais fait le tour complet du temps. J'avais tout compris' (p. 170). It is this exorcism of the power of death which he seeks to communicate to his fellows: 'On est tous magiques les vieillards. On a à remplir notre fonction de pure magie, de grands, d'authentiques éveilleurs de l'essentielle méditation . . . On doit être les vrais, les chauds, les amicaux, les profonds désenchanteurs . . .' (p. 234). The 'désenchanteur' seeks to undo the baleful spell of death itself. Grégoire's method is to tell each 'patient' a story or weave a web of words that will console them and outweigh their fears. He peers into the anus of each: it is, he says, a window to the body as the eye is to the soul.

But as his own powers wane and his own death approaches, his doubts about the rightness and efficacy of his mission grow. He comes into conflict with other 'prophets' who pronounce their own, more doom-laden truths. The man known as 'Le Comte' is from the start his most respected rival. Le Comte's diatribes against facile humanism carry echoes of Céline, Beckett, even Nietzsche. His suicide is a turning-point, after which the Mage progressively loses his authority and lapses into irresponsibility. A nocturnal expedition he leads to massacre a flock of sheep is, as Tournier might have put it, an 'inversion maligne' of his vocation as 'pâtre', and he sabotages his therapy by suggesting nonsensical remedies to his remaining clientele. In the last few pages he takes his farewell of Laura, feeling by now distanced, detached from her, and as he lies alone in the hide for the last time, her image dissolves in his mind: 'Laura fuit, se mue en images factices que mon cerveau fabrique et la douleur lancine, le manque . . .' (p. 356). He arrives back at the residence to find that Geneviève, too, has died; he cannot discover any human significance in the expression on her dead face. The language of the final two pages dissolves into a formless monologue, a shifting play of rhetorical leavetaking, irony, physical detail, grandiose metaphor, fragments of memory. The last word(s) '. . . Laura-ruban . . .' (p. 360), which conclude the trilogy of novels, may remind us that the name Laura is the only one to occur in all three, and that this recurrent positive image of a lively, sexually attractive young woman is, as it were, a ribbon which binds the three parts of the 'mythic autobiography' together. 'Ribbon' may also suggest the highly coloured, continuous fabric of language which is all that remains at the end and whose production has been associated throughout with the erotic. The thread of narrative snaps once Grégoire's love-affairs with the old Geneviève and the young Laura end and as their images dissolve. Just as the Mage strove to exorcise death with the only real power he has, the murmur of words to his anxious flock, so Grainville, it is clear, is seeking to subdue the power of death in advance with the fire-power of poetry. It is the vocation of Orpheus.

Grainville is not a writer who modestly conceals himself behind his text. Near the beginning he refers jokily, through the voice of Grégoire, to the genesis of the novel in adolescent scribblings, and later to the interruptions and discouragements which beset the author. The text thus contains an awareness of the process of its own creation, the feverish joys and exasperations of the writer himself. Some will find this self-indulgent, others may accept it as part of the particular fabric of Grainville's writing and a legitimate extension of emphasising the theme of language.

Grainville's next novel, *Les Flamboyants*, brought him literary fame, winning the Prix Goncourt in 1976. The trilogy of novels which preceded it can be seen as an apprenticeship, developing the writer's ability to convey the experience of characters progressively distanced in age and situation from his own, to explore the relationship between landscape and fantasy and to experiment with the resources of language and narrative. This learning of a craft and forging of a style now bear full fruit in a novel which carries an unmistakable sense of assurance. Grainville wanted to write an adventure story, to renew a vigorous and popular tradition of story-telling, and he found in Africa a setting and a subject that offered an even richer stimulus to his imagination than Lorraine, Paris or Normandy. 'J'ai trouvé là le terrain propre à mon baroque. [. . .] Avec l'Afrique j'ai pu me permettre des libertés jusqu'alors inédites.'[4] The epic breadth which he wanted to confer on the novel generated a manuscript of 800 pages which Gallimard refused, and they maintained their refusal even when he had re-edited it to more manageable proportions by eliminating an extended study of the copper mines, cotton plantations, multinationals and the European population. In the final form of the text (where no sense of pruning is likely to be apparent to the reader!) the concentration is on black Africa, and in particular on the central portrait of mad King Tokor.

The personality of Tokor is a focal centre of energy in the novel. He is impressive in physical stature and deploys a charismatic power over those around him and over his people, who are in superstitious awe of him. His nature is childlike, or childish: a capacity for naïve delight and emotional generosity has as its counterpart a fundamental irresponsibility and a horrifying capacity for casual violence and mayhem. Tokor is viewed for the most part through the eyes of a young and very white European visitor, William Irrigal, and the way Tokor is presented seems designed to evoke the same paradoxical reactions of fascination and repulsion in the European reader as in William himself. This may reflect the sense in which the novel is less a documentary study of an archetypal independent black African state than an expression of the European myth of Africa, which has always seemed both threatening in its aspects of brutality, superstition and raw physical energy, and attractive in its promise of release from European neurosis, introspection and puritanism. The novel's power lies, in part, in its incarnation of the Rimbaudian dream of a *terra incognita* of the imagination.

Tokor represents a total rejection of European intellectuality and moralism ('vos éducations judéo-chrétiennes vous ont crétinisés, rationalisés' – p. 231). He seeks to abolish intellectual detachment altogether and to commit himself totally and perilously to absolute physical contact with the raw elements that compose his environ-

4. Ibid.

ment. He plunges into the slums of Mourmako to take what Baudelaire called a 'bain de multitude', unprotected except by his own awesome prestige: 'Je voudrais les étreindre et fouiller la splendeur de ce viscère lugubre et massif! . . .' (p. 98). In episodes which combine grotesquery and a kind of heroic folly, he wallows with a herd of animals in the suffocating, fecal mud of the Maloumbé River; he kills and slits open an impala, whose bloody corpse he then drapes round himself like a cloak; he is finally scorched almost to death by a volcanic eruption which he witnesses from a suicidally close position. When it is not near suicidal, this immediate contact is often murderous. His visit to Mourmako culminates in his strangling of the soothsayer Molimbo: 'Il voulait faire jaillir de ce réceptacle charnel la vérité tellurique, une révélation à la fois mystique et matérielle, celle qu'il s'était acharné à poursuivre tout le long de son règne' (p. 109). He persuades himself that the remote and elusive tribe of the Diorles are the holders of this mysterious knowledge, but any contact he has with them degenerates almost at once into frenzied slaughter. The text seems to be making a moral point here. Tokor may be, as Grainville has described him, 'une force de la nature', but we are reminded that such forces are blindly, violently self-seeking.

Tokor thus rejects psychology, reflection, analysis in favour of spontaneity and physical engagement, and Grainville has sought to create a narrative which reflects this *parti pris*: 'J'ai essayé de faire coller une écriture tropicale avec ce pays et, comme je n'aime pas la psychologie, j'ai préféré faire une espèce de bande dessinée, d'épopée, de chanson de geste, où les personnages sont dans l'espace, n'existent que par ce qu'ils manifestent dans l'action.'[5] As these references to epic, chanson de geste and strip-cartoon suggest, Grainville is quite consciously concerned with modes of narrative, ancient and modern, on which he draws both seriously and ironically. A number of conventional narrative patterns are used to underpin the novel's construction. There is the mode of tragedy, the downfall of the larger-than-life hero through hubris or *démesure*. There is the political drama, the weaving and bringing to fruition of a conspiracy to overthrow the tyranny of an absolute monarch (both these elements might recall, for instance, *Macbeth*). There is the 'roman d'éducation' of William, the novel of a young man's initiation into an intense and life-enhancing relationship with Tokor and the ethos of Africa. Not least, *Les Flamboyants* is a quest narrative. Tokor's obsession with the Diorles, his conviction that they

5. Ibid.

possess the 'révélation à la fois mystique et matérielle' which he has always longed for, leads him to launch a huge military expedition into their territory. There is a clear contradiction between the quest, which is private and metaphysical, and the arsenal of destruction he uses to pursue it. Like Lancelot in the Grail legend, he will never achieve the quest himself: the vision of the mysterious sacred creatures, the Ludies, will be vouchsafed only to his protégé William, who has progressively distanced himself from Tokor's manic and murderous progress.

Certain of Tokor's specific traits reflect, on the level of the plot, characteristics of Grainville's narrative voice. They share, for instance, a taste for the spectacular. Tokor instigates lavish displays of wealth and power – fireworks, receptions, military displays, bombardments – both out of a naïve pleasure in the grandiose and colourful and as a glorification of his personal régime. These events in turn give Grainville the writer a pretext for sumptuous set-piece descriptions to add to those of the palace, the capital city and the natural spectacle of tropical rain-forest, its flora and fauna. Tokor's philosophy of life parallels Grainville's philosophy of language: it should be above all sensual rather than rational, mythopoeic rather than analytic, a pursuit of poetic vision, not sober assessment. It must be extravagant, risky, excessive. To find one's style as a writer, Grainville once commented, one must take Cocteau's advice to 'cultiver ses défauts'. Tokor, in his life, takes the same advice. He cultivates his prestige, for instance, by spectacularly outraging the conventions of European hierarchy and decorum: he leads a gang of slum children on an invasion of the exclusive country club, Bel Azur, and greets a newly appointed consul with a preposterous display of his ability to swallow live humming birds. Tokor revels in and seeks out the clash of opposites, the drama of sharp contrast. He delights in bringing the world of vermin-ridden slum children and that of pampered European bathing beauties into collision and falls into a state of erotic frenzy at the idea of his sinuous mistress, Hélène, kissing La Méza, the fat procuress of Mourmako. Likewise, Grainville's narrative is vitalised by his delight in bold contrasts, especially between characters. Tokor himself is thrown into relief by a series of contrasts, with the pale northerner William, with the socialist reformer Lalaka, with his anxious, diplomatic foreign minister Tiélibili. Grainville displays a Hugolian verve in the oppositions of wealth and squalor, high technology and primitive nature.

The contrasts are achieved and heightened by a simplification of the elements opposed. Tokor generates a whole series of epithets to refer to the people he loves or respects – William Néant Blanc, Hélène la Malachite, Lalaka le Taï-Ping, Moanda le Serpentaire, among others – which suggest that they are epic incarnations of a principle, part of an equation which he himself constructs. He thereby confers a poetic significance on them of his own choosing, often of an arcane or allusive kind. This process is suggestive of a fetishistic or talismanic use of language of which Grainville was evidently much aware: 'Les Africains ont été très sensibles à mon emploi d'un vocabulaire coloré, ouvert. Pour eux le mot a une valeur propre, presque magique. Prononcer un mot, c'est déjà posséder la chose qu'il désigne.'[6] Tokor's titles are thus an act of possession, and the multiplicity of epithets which he applies to himself and which accumulate during the novel into a celebratory catalogue of titles – 'le Babouin Léopard / le gros Bitis / le Pansexuel / ou l'Egout / et le Souimanga Malachite / le Seigneur Tellurique . . .' (p. 232) – constitute a systematic effort to transform his life, moment by moment, into poetry and the substance of epic myth. He is writing the script for posterity.

One of Tokor's titles for himself is 'le grand Analogique'. His taste for analogy leads him to infer unpredictable links particularly between human beings and the natural world of mineral elements (Hélène Malachite) or of living species (Méza Cantharide, Moanda Serpentaire). This power of analogy is fundamental to Grainville's poetic imagination and serves constantly to shift the attention away from the immediate and documentary and towards the metaphorical and symbolic.

La Diane rousse (1978) is a home-coming for Grainville: the setting is once more the Seine estuary and its environs. The scale of the book, compared to that of its predecessor, is modest and its structure more controlled. The (unnamed) voice of the first-person narrative is that of another would-be 'mage', a man blinded in a hunting skirmish and who now feels that this mutilation has, by compensation, endowed him with a brilliant inner vision. The patterns he perceives in his life centre on his awe-struck adoration of Hélianthe, an independent, sensual, red-haired young woman who disappeared mysteriously while bathing in the sea. She is the presiding goddess of his life and his text. He hymns her beauty, transmutes into private legend her provocative behaviour and outrageous caprices and recounts his systematic idolisation of her memory. He cherishes relics of her and builds her a shrine, with her mink as its centrepiece. He recruits two rebellious teenagers, Judith and Christophe, who for

6. Interview with Le Thor, p. 17.

a while partly fill the gap Hélianthe has left in his life and act as acolytes in the mystic–erotic rituals he ordains. Hélianthe becomes for him a supernatural principle, an incitement to increasing exaltation and a divinity who will brook no rival in his allegiance.

The title *La Diane rousse* and the name Hélianthe (the botanical name for the sunflower) suggest the interlocking networks of associations Grainville plays on here: that of hunting, of which Diana–Artemis is the goddess, untamed, haughty and vengeful on occasion; and that of the redness of the sun, scorching at midday and flame-coloured at sunset. Hélianthe, as befits the huntress, had a dog, a red setter called Diane, who remains in the narrator's loving care. The title thus applies even more directly to the setter bitch than to her mistress, and this ambivalence is part of an extended equivocation whereby dog and woman – both flame-haired, physical, impulsively instinctual – tend to form a common focus for the narrator's adulation and erotic attraction: 'Je m'allongeais dans les fougères serrant dans mes bras nus le grand corps malhabile et jubilant de Diane rousse, d'Hélianthe . . . Chienne ou Femme je ne savais plus. Sa langue s'abattait sur ma joue, sur ma bouche, sur ma langue avec une fébrilité joyeuse' (p. 32). The loving enumeration of the features of Hélianthe's body (pp. 17–18) is matched by a similar eulogy of the setter (pp. 64–6). Just as Hélianthe escapes from his presence to bestow her favours on a farmer, a fisherman or a bank clerk, so too Diane leaves him fretting with jealousy when she runs off for several days to mate with 'un chien marginal, un chien bohème, un peu hippie' (p. 148). The bitch is in the image of her mistress, loving yet beyond restriction, beautiful and a little wild.

The story takes its starting point from the disappearance of Hélianthe and ends with the shooting of Diane by a posse of outraged neighbours and the blinding of the narrator as one of their bullets grazes his eyes. The narrative covers, therefore, the period when Hélianthe's brilliant presence has been withdrawn yet in a sense continues to be with him in the form of Diane. It is as though he sees her in Diane, so that, when Diane is no more, logic demands that sight itself be withheld. 'Hélianthe, c'était le regard' (p. 143). 'Je mesure à quel point Hélianthe, Diane et moi nous formions un bloc divin. Trois dans nos étreintes. Toisons, cheveux. Peau nue, fourrure. Rires, abois . . . Triple regard vivant' (p. 189).

Hélianthe's sun may have set, but for the narrator portents abound which betoken the continuing power of her presence, writ large on the scenes and events around him. They start with the plague of ladybirds which comes in from the sea at the moment of her eclipse. She becomes a focus for local legend and superstition and is linked to a series of spectacular incidents of arson for which a tall, red-haired girl is arrested. Her spirit is said to survive in the forest, from which errant schoolchildren return wide-eyed and corrupted. Her signs are those of the cataclysmic power of nature, of fire let loose and of the capacity of the young for exemplary, anarchistic disruption of the society ordered by their elders. May 1968 turned into a religion . . .

If a single name is to be given to this religion, then Grainville provides it in an epigraph from Artaud:

> Le vieux totémisme des bêtes, des pierres, des objets chargés de foudre, des costumes bestialement imprégnés, tout ce qui sert en un mot à capter, à diriger et à dériver des forces, est pour nous une chose morte . . . Or toute vraie culture s'appuie sur les moyens barbares et primitifs du totémisme dont je veux adorer la vie sauvage, c'est-à-dire entièrement spontanée . . . (p. 5)

The text enacts this adoration. In Hélianthe, whose face has 'une laideur racée de totem' (p. 18), this 'vieux totémisme des bêtes' takes the form of a special affinity with animals appropriate to a hunting goddess, and the narrator's cult reflects this. Her shrine is peopled with carvings of totemic beasts, and in the final grand ritual of the 'bal masqué' to which Judith and Christophe invite a tribe of their friends, the masks are animal ones, imposing their own symbolic gestures and actions on the wearers. Two of the most important totem creatures are the hare and the trout, which have a special childhood significance for the narrator, and these in turn signify earth and water, of which the estuary is the conjunction. Hélianthe, too, is perceived as both marine and terrestrial, and from the earth beneath her shrine rises a salt-water spring.

Hélianthe is seen, then, as a bewilderingly multiform natural deity – of sun, sea, earth, forest. This polyvalence is reflected in the disordered references to numerous ancient mythologies: 'notre Anubis, notre Sphinx, la Madone, la Braconne, notre Artémis de vie et de mort' (p. 172). Like Tokor's in *Les Flamboyants*, Hélianthe's attributes and titles are inexhaustible because she represents a primal force which can take on infinite manifestations.

What follows her presence can only be a poor reflection of it. The very names of Judith and Christophe suggest a Judeo-Christian posterity which proved inadequate and unsatisfying compared to the totemic religion it replaced. The narrator's blindness can be seen in this light as the textual equivalent of the loss of the power to perceive the 'vieux totémisme' which, Artaud says, is now 'chose morte' for us. The only compensation is to re-create this perception in our imagination, in dreams, ultimately in language, in order to restore a sense of immediacy, of wonder at the divinity of the natural which contemporary culture is deemed to have suppressed.

The estuary which featured in *La Diane rousse* is even more powerfully present in Grainville's next novel, *Le Dernier Viking* (1980). The strong Viking associations of this part of Normandy are alluded to in passing in some earlier novels, with the Viking ship or 'drakkar' emerging already as one of Grainville's recurrent images. It is obvious that he found this a rich vein of history and legend waiting to be worked.

What might have been attempted was an epic narrative retelling of the Viking raids up the Seine, and indeed elements of this historical saga are embedded in the present text. Grainville, however, opted for something more ambitious: a novel which confronted anachronism and used it as a generating principle. The narrative begins in the mode of the magical and supernatural, in mock-heroic tone and, like *La Diane rousse*, centres on the powerful imaginary world of one man. Martel is obsessed with the Viking past. He is irresistibly attracted to the ethos of the Vikings as he perceives it, a spirit of quest and adventure, of violence without guilt, of heroic energy and of oneness with the forces of nature.

As in *L'Abîme* and *La Diane rousse*, Grainville places his main character at the centre of a small colony of people on the margin of modern civilisation. But like Grégoire, Martel becomes increasingly estranged from those around him as he enters further and further into the spirit of his implausible project to re-create Viking values. Besides his family, three further characters are caught up in Martel's personal saga: Odile, a local doctor, Gabriel, the idiot bee-keeper, and above all Lucas, a perverse and clever young scholar who will play Mephistopheles to Martel's Faust. From this duo of opposites Grainville draws a play of contrasts and dialectic as rich in its way as that between Tokor and William in *Les Flamboyants*.

Martel shares Tokor's appetite for contact with nature. He is a Panic being, reminiscent in many respects of characters in Giono's early fiction. He surrounds himself with living creatures with whom he has a passionate and sensual relationship: his horse Asa, his snake Cléopâtre, his dogs Fenhir and Fafnir, his goshawk Harald. (The use of totemic creatures as attributes of the hero is character-istic of Grainville, from Tokor's leopard and baboon, to the nar-rator's trout and hare in *La Diane rousse*.) Martel establishes a network of magic sites, points of reference in a personal symbolic geography. There are nine such sites altogether: the church, the river, a tree, a pool, an island, a wall, a dangerous bend, a fortress and the estuary itself. Within this private fiefdom the sceptre he holds takes the form of a hammer, a mark at once of brute force, of phallic power and of the gift of craftsmanship. The hammer is present in his name, Martel, which was also that of a Frankish king, Charles Martel. Clearly the hammer evokes also the Norse god Thor, whose attribute it was. Martel's hammer, like Thor's, returns magically to the hand of its owner when he hurls it aloft.

Beside Martel, and against him, is set Lucas, the Loki to Martel's Thor. Loki was another Norse god, but legend portrays him as seductive, eloquent, wilful, perverse, selfish and even satanic, always prepared to betray his friends or stir up mischief. This persona gives Grainville the basis for his character. Like Loki, Lucas demonstrates a 'méchanceté supérieure et magnifique' (p. 21); his urge is always to replace order by disorder, harmony by dissonance. He makes a Faustian pact with Martel, offering him the means to discover a hidden treasure of Viking gold in exchange for access to Martel's strength, and to his daughter-in-law Alice. Lucas has Loki's Don Juan attractiveness to women and seduces Alice without delay (though not before she has scored some points off him). She experiences her intensely erotic relationship with him as a kind of devil-worship.

There is another aspect to Lucas, with an implied echo not in Norse mythology but in Greek legend. Lynceus was renowned as the sharpest-eyed of the Argonauts: in Goethe's *Faust* he keeps watch from a tower. Lucas, too, gazes at the stars, from a turret in the manor house, and his apparent power of prophesy derives from the way he can discern danger or catastrophe approaching from afar. The constant references to the constellations and to supposed runic inscriptions reinforce Lucas's function as a reader of signs, a decoder of the world, a character who stands at an ironic and critical distance from life and its progress. Lucas is anti-life: he revels in pollution, decomposition, all the portents of ecological disaster.

Martel's unprincipled greed, his Viking hunger for treasure, gives rise to two episodes which loosely recall Norse legend. Martel has cheated and intimidated the mason who restored his manor house, just as Odin and the gods sought to wriggle out of the contract they had made with the giants who built Asgard. Later Martel fakes the theft of the family's horde of gold and precious objects and conceals them for himself in the trunk of his great ash tree. (Both motifs, breach of contract and theft of gold, feature strongly in Wagner's opera *Das Rheingold*.)

The nearer the story approaches to its end, the closer the characters are tied in to the Nordic legend of 'the twilight of the gods'. There it is the death of Baldr, engineered by Loki, which heralds the fall of the gods: in this novel it is the murder of the innocent Gabriel. After a swarm of wasps hurtles in from the sea like latter-day Viking predators and destroys all but one of Gabriel's hives, Lucas with calculated malice uses a drug to enrage the remaining bees. Gabriel is stung to death by the very creatures he has loved and trusted all his life. When Lucas boasts of this crime to Martel, the final cataclysm is unleashed. Thunderbolts, the manifestations of Thor's rage, strike the tree, and Lucas is killed. The tree splits open, showering Lucas's body with the hidden, illicit gold, thus making explicit its causative, corrupting power. The great ash-tree, like the World Ash-tree (Yggdrasil) of Norse myth, is riven asunder, and its fall is accompanied by earthquake and civil riot. According to legend, Thor met his end in this chaos, in a final battle with the serpent of Midgard. Martel, in a final dream-like episode, descends into an underground cavern and finds, as Lucas had promised, a Viking treasure-ship. His snake Cléopâtre seems to swell to fill the space as the text ends:

> Le Serpent s'élargit. La caverne n'est plus qu'un foisonnement d'anneaux géants.
> Maintenant l'océan s'ouvre, bleu, immobile. Les grands navires et les rois vont accueillir Martel. (p. 252)

Martel, seen for all his faults as the embodiment of vitality and life, seems to be promised his Valhalla, and as in Wagner's *Götterdämmerung* the cataclysmic downfall of the prevailing order yields finally to a sense of expansive serenity.

The achievement of *Le Dernier Viking* lies fundamentally in the ambivalence which flows from its central idea of anachronism. It plays with the notion of a continuity of values and patterns between the ninth century (or the myths of that age) and our own day, and in doing so, it succeeds in placing the values it explores firmly outside the Judeo-Christian framework. This exploration of a possible return to an earlier moral order based on archetypal patterns linked firmly to the natural world is a constantly developing theme in Grainville. The ambivalence is expressed in the text, too, in the balanced binary opposition of Martel and Lucas. If Martel is the 'last Viking', then Lucas is in a sense the spirit of modernism. Versed in the perverse logic of Sade and eighteenth-century materialism, he opposes Martel's passion and elemental vigour with his intellect and irony, with his play of language and decoding of signs. He is the principle of abstraction and fancy which needs the raw material of natural energy to work on, just as Martel needs Lucas's imagination and insight to tell him the Viking stories and nourish his dreams. Faithful to this balance, Grainville has produced a very modern narrative, heavy in primal symbolism, yet light in its play of rhetoric. It is at once serious and preposterous. However eccentric the subject may seem to start with, *Le Dernier Viking*, like the best of Grainville's writing elsewhere, has the capacity to surprise the reader with the richness of the resonances it sets up.

In *Les Forteresses noires* (1982) Grainville has moved away from the coastal setting of his previous two novels, this time to a firmly contemporary urban environment: La Défense, an area of sky-scraper office-blocks and apartments in Paris, which constitute the 'forteresses noires' of the title. It is a less frenzied, more genial novel than its predecessors. For one thing, it is less of a study in mono-mania: interest is diffused among a number of contrasting charac-ters. For another, the book plays down the poetry of cataclysm and disaster which was a dominant strand in the texture of Grainville's writing hitherto.

What remains unimpaired, however, is Grainville's taste for binary opposition as a motive force behind his narrative. At the top of one skyscraper, the 'tour de Mercure', is a control room where a bank of video screens offers all-round surveillance and a gleaming computer constantly monitors its circuits and systems. In the lowest basement of this same edifice there is preserved a fragment of rampart dating from six-thousand years ago, whose existence is known only to a few privileged individuals and specialists. This characteristically striking paradox suggests at once that, within the trappings of an ultra-modern décor and its futuristic technology, there remains, embedded in its depths, an ancient secret, a dimen-sion of primitive life, a sense of time past and passing that neces-sarily underpins the here and now.

The prestige of modernity that the 'tour de Mercure' represents is mirrored in different ways by two characters: the banker Raphaël and his daughter Elodie. Raphaël, an immensely successful financial speculator, has at the age of fifty reached a middle-age crisis. The symptoms of his unease are apparent to the professional eye of his wife Léone, a marriage guidance counsellor. His yearning for lost youth leads him into an affair with the fourteen-year-old daughter of the tower supervisor, and this relationship mirrors, in uncon-strained form, the sensual rapport he has with his own daughter. Raphaël is shown as grappling with the problems of age, death, the passing of time. While his day-to-day work concerns the fleeting currents of market forces, he is also a numismatist, hoarding (like the building itself) secret vestiges of the distant past: the coins that have turned from currency into talismans of history and myth.

Another symptom of his malaise takes the form of noises in his head, soft hallucinatory flute sounds that seem to intrude on his consciousness. That the music ('mélodie') is linked to the suppressed desire for his daughter Elodie would be clear even without the verbal clue. Raphaël admits himself fascinated by the ambiguous couple of father and daughter: 'Il y a du père dans la magie de la fille. Etrange miroir où le père se reconnaît rajeuni, féminisé, nocturne . . .' (p. 65).

Elodie's vocation as artist might seem a conventional contrast to her father's career as entrepreneurial capitalist. Yet strong similarities emerge. Elodie works in her vast studio on the elaboration of an immense mobile, a structure of indefinite proportions and meaning. Many different interpretations are offered, but Elodie is not content with any formulation: 'Le Mobile indiquait plutôt l'infinie cosmologie de ses états, la complexité inouïe de ses désirs et de ses peurs [. . .] tout ce flou gigantesque d'un moi ténébreux et solaire auquel nulle intelligence n'accéderait jamais' (pp. 40–1). The openness and abstraction of the structure she finds sometimes inspiring, sometimes derisory, but her attitude to it changes when she is visited by a handsome and precocious thirteen-year-old boy of Zairean extraction, Bidji. As he moves around within the vast hanging structure, he seems to confer life on it. She allows him to conceal a secret object (a rat's tooth) within it, in a spot unknown to her, and she becomes his lover for an afternoon.

Both father and daughter, then, are the creators of a vast and finely balanced system: she in art, and he in finance, about which he waxes eloquent. Neither, moreover, is content with success on a purely abstract level, and they both discover within themselves the secret desire for an adolescent lover, an element of erotic transgression.

This pattern of the disruption of intellectual equilibrium also emerges in the stories of two other characters. Léone, Raphaël's wife, is well known as a well-balanced and resilient woman, an acute observer and analyst of the behaviour of others. One day, however, she is the victim of a well-planned ambush in the metro in which her handbag is snatched by a juvenile gang headed by Bidji. This seemingly trivial incident reduces her to hysterical screams and sobs. The children discover with interest that the handbag contains a nude photo of Léone taken some years before (for what lover?). Once again it is the resurgence of the past and a buried erotic passion which is associated with the crisis, and it is the young who are the catalysts of self-awareness.

The remaining principal character is Chandor, a night doctor.

Like Léone he is expert at listening to the woes of others and making sense of them, and he seems infinitely self-possessed. He has an intense but hitherto chaste relationship with Elodie, fearing that to let Eros in would place at risk the finely balanced understanding they have. Risk, however, is not absent from another area of his life: on Sundays he slips away to a distant quarter of the city to bet on the races and to move in less respectable circles.

The final section of the novel, 'L'Ardeur', presents a combined dénouement of many tensions. Raphaël has discovered, via Bidji, that robbers are tunnelling towards the vaults of his bank in the basement of the tower-block. He decides recklessly to turn the alarm system off and to confront them himself as they break through. As he is waiting, he realises the significance of the flute sounds that have been haunting him. They are the music of Stravinsky's *Rite of Spring*, sounds associated with his daughter, with Panic desire and youth, with the 'impossible printemps de l'amour' (p. 274). As the vault walls give way it is Chandor who steps through. He is in league with the robbers, but what he has come to claim is not Raphaël's wealth but his daughter. The ordeal that faces Raphaël is that of surrendering any claim to Elodie and accepting that he has been displaced by a younger man. His desire to confront the robbers can be seen as a death-wish, to escape the issue of old age. The final section shows Chandor and Elodie joyously together, their relationship now carnal as well as intellectual, with the acceptance of life and death that that involves.

Again and again, on the level both of individual characters and of the community as a whole, this novel shows the precarious equilibrium of conscious structures that holds everyday life in place being disrupted and threatened by ancient, primitive, erotic forces which require to be expressed and accommodated. Elodie's Mobile can be seen as a central image of the novel. It is an abstraction that is given meaning by Bidji's rat's tooth and Elodie's clothes scattered within it, and by their afternoon of love: the carnal must be admitted into any system that claims to represent life. The fertilising relationship of Bidji and Elodie, the capitalist's daughter and the immigrants' child, can be seen as the creative point of contact between the sophistication of the First World and the raw energy of the Third. The Mobile is also a structure which is sensitive to the merest touch, the slightest vibration; it is 'à l'écoute'. It is an antenna tuned in to the world and its signals both overt and secret, and as such it is an admirable metaphor for the novel itself.

By this point in Grainville's output, it is possible to perceive that one of his recurrent character-types is that of a man past his prime, struggling against the weight of age and the past, enmeshed in his own fantasies and erotic appetites. Paulin in *La Lisière*, Grégoire in *L'Abîme* and Raphaël in *Les Forteresses noires* are variants on this type, and we meet another such at the centre of *La Caverne céleste* (1984). Simon, a journalist seeking to escape the guilt and pain of a past relationship, comes to Aguilar, a remote village in the Cathar country in the far south-west of France. The community there has its quota of scandal, past and present. One young woman, Iza, has been slightly mad ever since she was, seemingly, seduced by the curé and had a miscarriage in the forest. The local innkeeper, Alphonse, cycles off every afternoon for a rendezvous with his mistress, leaving his dying wife Paula upstairs in her room and Line the barmaid (and unmarried mother) in charge behind the bar. None of this, of course, escapes the chief collector of local gossip, the elderly spinster Agathe. Simon, however, has come to investigate not the village and its affairs but the excavations in the prehistoric cave not far away, where a skeleton half a million years old has been unearthed. After a brief flirtation with Line, Simon is drawn into a very physical affair with the striking black African, Myriam, who is attached to the archaeological team as an artist. Line reacts to her desertion by turning to a rather earnest, passive student, until she is literally swept off her feet and out of the village by Paloma, a red-headed member of a motor-bike gang, in a euphoric, whirlwind lesbian affair. Myriam the Black Venus and Paloma the flame-haired biker are incarnations of the Panic forces which surround the village and threaten to disrupt its routine order.

Much of the strength of Grainville's novel, as in earlier texts, derives from his sense of the tension between the distant past in its primitive otherness and the apparatus of modernity. This anachronism, the simultaneous presence of two eras, underlay *Le Dernier Viking* and accounted for the mention of the ancient rampart remains beneath the skyscraper in *Les Forteresses noires*. Through Simon, Grainville reveals a fascination with the paradoxes of archaeology: the remnants of a cannibalistic cave-man culture are picked over meticulously by peaceable young helpers and taken for analysis by the most advanced scientific techniques. Shiny chrome coaches bring tourists to view the ancient skull in the museum: it all represents, Grainville suggests, a new cult based on older relics than those of Christianity in the local church and inspiring greater reverence in the visitors of today. For Simon the cave is not just a prehistoric site of academic interest: it is a place of primal instincts, of hunting-lust and bloodshed, and self-evidently an erotic orifice, which finds its equivalents in Myriam's body.

Anachronism, then, is characteristically an aspect of the tension between the violence, chaos and vitality of the instinctual life and the rational moral order of civilisation. The narrative presents two other images of the forces of Panic subversion: a lynx, which has been released into the wild, and an escaped Basque terrorist. The police hunt for the terrorist merges with a fight against a bush fire. Grainville portrays the forces of violence, destruction and threatening sexuality which beset the village as a shifting conspiracy of disorder. Various links connect one element to another. Paloma's hair is red, like the fur of the lynx (reminiscent of Hélianthe and Diane). The lynx hunts down a hare and eats its brains, as the ancient cave-man devoured the brains of his fellow; the terrorist must hunt, too, seizing a lamb and tearing its raw flesh in his hunger. In Simon's mind, and in the ravings of the mad Iza, the cave-man has returned in the form of the terrorist. Myriam, who brings cave-men to life again in her drawings, also has a mysterious complicity with the terrorist. This nexus of forces of primitive power sows seeds of havoc in the village. The church is desecrated, and a statue of the Virgin beheaded: like the deranged, pious 'fille-mère' Iza, the Virgin too has 'lost her head'. Paula, Alphonse's dying wife, is roused to a final gesture of revolt and drugs herself sufficiently to walk miles to her death in the wilderness. Agathe, the gossipy spinster, climbs high towards the cave and, as one whose life has been devoted to curiosity, to storing facts and making patterns, is vouchsafed a supreme vision of the ordered interconnection of things. Death, frenzy, lusts and visions lure characters into the wild or strike unpredictably at the heart of order.

As the population watches and discusses the man-hunt for the terrorist, Grainville gives a sardonic commentary on the division in popular opinion between supporters of the police and those who, secretly, side with the outlaw: 'D'un côté, les partisans fervents de l'ordre, les férus de matraque policière; de l'autre, les individualistes romantiques, les jeunes gens oniriques, les Bovary impénitentes et les rêveurs violents' (p. 317). Grainville's sympathies, however ironically expressed, are not in doubt: he is a formidable poet of the forces of disorder.

> Heureux les obsédés car ils sont les seuls à posséder encore un Dieu. Les seuls qui s'agenouillent devant l'hostie d'un vice immense. Heureux les idolâtres car leur croyance a la beauté des divinités mythiques. [. . .] Heureux les fanatiques d'une foi unique, d'une faim sans limites [. . .]. Heureux les loups religieux . . . (p. 25)

This parody of the Beatitudes, placed early in *Le Paradis des orages*

(1986), suggests that the paradise of the novel's title is a rather particular one. This passage is just part of a stylised revelation of the nature of the obsession and the object of the worship: 'Je vous salue, ô fesses . . . Dolmens sur la mer. Sœurs immaculées. Joconde dédoublée au miroir de Vinci. Théâtre aux coulisses charnues. [. . .] Je te salue, ô cul, global et gémellaire' (p. 28). This sacrilegious abuse of the formulae of religious worship appropriately introduces a perversion which remains a source of scandal as the obverse of the normal: the ignoble, bestial and defecatory. The unnamed narrator of the text is a collector of bottoms. He imagines them when he has not yet seen them, and cherishes their memory or image once he has. His language in describing them is wholly unrestrained: it is by turns liturgical, scientific, mythic, racy, scatological. Such an obsession, in itself, might be seen as merely curious, comic or even tedious as the topic of a substantial novel, and certainly it does threaten sometimes to turn into a catalogue of erotic experiences and conquests. The narrator, though, insists that he is no mere Don Juan: you only possess what you understand, he argues, so that Don Juan, with his swift routine of seduction and abandonment, possesses nothing. 'Je ne prise que les longues aventures suivies. Celles qui viennent de loin, qui s'enracinent, qui vous possèdent et vous laissent des traces. Et vous ruinent tout en vous faisant naître' (p. 36). It is not mere self-indulgence he is concerned with, but this sense of suffering, self-discovery and love. 'Si le chemin du vice est long, plus périlleux, plus égoïste d'abord et morbide parfois, l'amour peut y gagner au bout. Emouvante victoire après un tel périple' (p. 28).

'Don Juan est un prurit. Je suis une belle et longue maladie' (p. 36). The 'belle et longue maladie' of love is most fully explored in his extended and increasingly anguished affair with Paule. She is a maths student, he a forty-year-old film critic, and the dominance of the older man suggests the complicity of a father-figure encouraging a daughter to act out the taboo desires of childhood and recalls Raphaël in *Les Forteresses noires*. Paule is vulnerable, caught between guilt and pleasure, submission and a will to independence, acceptance and resentment of the narrator's other partners. These inner tensions, and the man's aggravation of them, lead inexorably to dramatic scenes of rupture and recrimination. Paule's chief rival is Clo, who keeps a 'lingerie fine'. Clo is calmer, more self-possessed, yet that relationship too ends in pain and tears. The narrator seems determined to be marked by the wounds of Tristan, to bear the scars of love as though this were the necessary inscription of a higher knowledge. The third affair spoken of at the beginning of the novel has on the face of it an even more disastrous outcome: Mô is a psychologically disturbed girl abandoned by her mother in child-hood, and she moves from a phobia about pigeons to end in homicidal frenzy. Here again the narrator seems fascinated by the risk such a relationship represents, by the potentially irremediable consequences of any provocation.

A fourth exhibit in this Casanova's collection of partners is a double one, the twins Drusilla and Dorothée. They spring straight out of the world of the amoral thriller with its ingredients of sex, murder and drug-trafficking. They offer an insubstantial image of the narrator's Gidean desire to escape conventional moral categories and reassert an older freedom.

More importantly, the twins represent doubleness, 'gémellité'. 'Je te salue, ô cul, global et gémellaire.' The fascination with Dorothée and Drusilla stems from their incarnation of globality and twinship.

> Le monde lui-même possède deux hémisphères. Le Nord c'est Dorothée, le Sud c'est Drusilla. Sœurs et complémentaires elles sont à la mesure de la planète ronde. Deux filles, deux pôles. Un miroir coupe le cosmos où Dorothée reflète Drusilla et vice versa. Fesses de cristal branchées sur une unique fêlure noire. (p. 137)

This notion of doubleness is present throughout. The lover moves between Paule and Clo as between two complementary bodies: 'deux filles, deux pôles' (deux Paules?), and as he deliberately provokes Paule's jealous suspicions, he imagines the presence of the unseen rival as a stimulant for each lover. The actual presence of a third stimulates him too: he involves Paule's adolescent brother, Claude, and is later attracted to a mother and her daughter, Hélène and Lucy. Sister/brother and mother/daughter are variants on the central notion of twinship, of complementary mirror-images.

'Je vous salue, ô fesses [. . .] Théâtre aux coulisses charnues.' The erotic is in this text significantly theatrical. 'Je remonte lentement la robe le long des cuisses. Théâtre. L'événement pur est lever de rideau . . .' (p. 97). Paule likes improvising with him dialogues in mock Racinian or Claudelian language about, say, farting: 'Mes petits scénarios excitent toujours Paule' (p. 165). The rituals and props of striptease feature frequently, from Paule's 'robe d'amour' and suspenders to Clo's shopful of underwear, conventional and exotic. Later in the novel, visits to a friend's fashionable strip club lead to an argument about the aesthetics of stripping. The narrator argues that striptease should have its Playboy cellophane gloss removed: it should be basic, bestial, 'racaille et portuaire' (p. 331).

This return to the bestial, the shamelessly physical and anal beyond the coy fantasies which mask it, becomes a major theme in the book.

C'est parce qu'il chie que le derrière des madones et des reines intègre à sa sublimité une insolence, une impudeur, tant de sournoises implications, une souterraine anarchie indispensables à sa notion. Par cette étroite lucarne affleure l'énorme et magnifique machinerie du corps, son alchimie sainte et terrible. (pp. 264–5)

It is a 'caverne céleste', in fact, and we recall how Grégoire the Mage looked through this window into the bodies of his patients in *L'Abîme*. When the narrator swims across the polluted Seine from his house on one bank to Paule's on the other, or when he climbs down into a newly dug grave in the cemetery where his family lies buried, these are anal adventures, confrontations with the substance of corruption and death. This quest for primal truth culminates in a visit to Africa, a search for the Nuer tribespeople in the Sudan with a film-crew. What starts out as an idealistic quest for the spectacle of primitive mankind in all its beauty turns sour, as he finds that the Nuer have themselves been corrupted by the cheap detritus of modern industrial culture. Finally the film-crew is obliged to bribe them to take their clothes off and hunt elephant (an ironic strip-tease indeed). What should have been a vision of innocence becomes commercial theatre for the titillation of the armchair spectators of the west.

This final, African episode amplifies elements placed earlier in the book. The Nuer girls recall the black immigrant schoolgirl Léa in Paris, who is as happy as they are to pose for photographs. More significantly, the opening pages of the novel describe the narrator's collection of totems, mysterious carved or assembled figures, old and new, to whom he attributes supernatural influence. Seeming to preside over all these is the inexpressive Popol Vuh, a live, lizard-like creature he bought on the *quais*, imported from Guatemala or the Nile. It sits often on the encyclopaedic dictionary, and seems to symbolise for its owner a primordial life-force which precedes and founds language and knowledge. In the swamp at the very heart of the Sudanese marshes he encounters a larger version of Popol Vuh. He experiences a revelation, a moment of truth whose importance is underlined by the solemn rhetoric of the language used: 'Je sais que je suis parvenu au bout du voyage et qu'ici se reboucle l'estuaire de ma naissance et ma tombe natale. Je te salue vieux patriarche de ces eaux, joyau des commencements' (p. 413); 'Tu es le premier mot, tu es mon Nom. Je puis maintenant retourner vers l'estuaire, sans peur . . .' (p. 414). In a final dream he sees photographs, but not like the photographs of his collection: 'Ce ne sont plus fastes lombaires ni courbes gémellaires qui atteignent ce sommet de la brillance et de la beauté. Je reconnais de beaux visages de femmes' (p. 414). This suggests that he has transcended his obsession and has achieved the 'émouvante victoire' glimpsed at the end of the 'chemin du vice'.

Whether or not this affirmative ending carries the reader's conviction with it, it is of a piece with Grainville's ultimately optimistic stance as a writer. The quests he describes are life-affirming, given that one accepts that to affirm life is also to confront and absorb death, disaster, violence and pain. The quests culminate characteristically in moments of truth and insight for the searcher: the Mage in *L'Abîme* lying on Geneviève's tomb, William in *Les Flamboyants* granted the spectacle of the 'Ludies', Martel descending into the cavern of Viking treasure. Grainville asserts the power of a knowledge that must be struggled for. Wisdom lies in confrontation with the physical as well as the intellectual, with raw nature as well as abstractions, with corruption and death as well as life. It demands an imaginative awareness of the past and of what lies beyond the confines of European culture and Judeo-Christian morality.

Grainville's gift as a writer is above all vitality: his works celebrate the life of the senses and the inexhaustible richness of language. The baroque exuberance of his style may throw off ten or twenty words where another writer would have chosen one, but Grainville's clusters, cataracts of words, can, when cunningly assembled, generate a powerful collective energy, an open network of images which lives precisely because it defies precise definition. There is in Grainville no trace of fashionable despair over the possibilities of language or the function of narrative. His work represents a formidable, combative declaration of faith in the potential of the novel form:

> Le roman n'est ni une copie de la réalité, ni un exercice formel réservé aux initiés. C'est l'expression dynamique d'une imagination en travail. Le roman est une transformation subjective donc perverse de la réalité à laquelle on donne la couleur de nos désirs. C'est un abus de confiance. Un parti-pris éclatant. C'est l'histoire de l'enfant qui rêve et qui ment et ne trahit jamais si bien sa vérité que dans ses mensonges.[7]

---

7. Interview with Le Thor, p. 21.

Bibliography

Works by Patrick Grainville

Novels

La Toison (Gallimard, 1972)
La Lisière (Gallimard, 1973)
L'Abîme (Gallimard, 1974)
Les Flamboyants (Editions du Seuil, 1976)
La Diane rousse (Editions du Seuil, 1978)
Le Dernier Viking (Editions du Seuil, 1980)
Les Forteresses noires (Editions du Seuil, 1982)
La Caverne céleste (Editions du Seuil, 1984)
Le Paradis des orages (Editions du Seuil, 1986)
L'Atelier du peintre (Editions du Seuil, 1988)

Shorter fiction

Images du désir (Playboy/Filipacchi, 1978)
L'Ombre de la bête (Balland, 1981)

Other works

Au long des haies de Normandie (Editions du Chêne, 1980)
Bernard Louedin (Bibliothèque des Arts, 1980)

Reviews, articles on other writers

'Don Juan et le donjuanisme chez Montherlant', *La Nouvelle Revue française* 242 (Feb. 1973), 64–71
'Les tribulations d'un lecteur', *Les Nouvelles littéraires* 2622 (9 Feb. 1978), 15–16 (on Jules Verne)
'La révolution sidérale de Jean Cayrol', *Nouvelles littéraires* 2670 (18 Jan. 1979), 5
'Tournier au lycée', *Sud* (1980), 42–7 (special issue on Tournier)
'Ce qu'ils pensent de Flaubert (enquête)', *La Quinzaine littéraire* 324 (1 May 1980), 22

Interviews

'J'ai jonglé avec mes fantasmes et ceux de l'Afrique', *Les Nouvelles littéraires* 2558 (10 Nov. 1976), 5 (with Annie Daubenton)
'Patrick Grainville ou les mots en liberté', *Figaro* (16 Nov. 1976), 32 (with Gérard Guillot)

'C'est si indécent, le langage', *Le Nouvel Observateur* 628 (22 Nov. 1976), 78
(with Jean Freustié)
'Dossier' in *Les Flamboyants* (Tallandier, 1977) (with Jérôme Le Thor)

Criticism

Piatier, Jacqueline, 'Littérature de l'excès ou excès de littérature?', *Le Monde*
(11 Oct. 1974), 19, 21 (on *L'Abîme*)
Tournier, Michel, 'Pour saluer Grainville', *Le Figaro* (24 Nov. 1973), 14 (on
La Lisière)

List of Contributors

David Coward is Senior Lecturer in French at the University of Leeds.

Jean H. Duffy is Lecturer in French at the University of Sheffield.

Ann Duncan was until her death in 1989 a Fellow of Newnham College, Cambridge.

David Gascoigne is Lecturer in French at the University of St Andrews.

Leslie Hill is Lecturer in French at the University of Warwick.

Rosemary Lloyd is a Fellow of New Hall, Cambridge.

Alan Morris is Lecturer in French at the University of Strathclyde.

Michael Tilby is a Fellow of Selwyn College, Cambridge.

Index

Index

Gomez-Arcos, Agustin, 3, 4, **151–76**
Grainville, Patrick, 2, 5, **229–55**
Guyotat, Pierre, 104

Heath, Stephen, 116
Hemingway, Ernest, 41
Henric, Jacques, 104
Hitler, Adolf, 74
Hugo, Victor, 238
Huysmans, Joris-Karl, 137

Ionesco, Eugène, 50, 167

Jakobson, Roman, 117
Jaloux, Edmond, 8
Jarlot, Gérard, 54
Je suis partout, 179, 185
Jew Süss, The, 180
Joanovici, Joseph, 178
Joyce, James, 113, 116–17, 118, 119

Kafka, Franz, 41, 143, 178
Kristeva, Julia, 101, 103, 104, 105, 116, 118, 119

Lacan, Jacques, 44, 117, 202, 203, 205
Landru, Henri, 182
Laurent, Françoise, 129, 134, 138
Lautréamont, 104, 106, 115
Le Clézio, J.-M. G., 5
Le Pen, Jean-Marie, 157
Lévi-Strauss, Claude, 65, 117, 202
Lindon, Jérôme, 201
Lonsdale, Michael, 55
Lorca, Federico Garcia, 165n
Lucretius, 115

Mahabharata, 224
Mallarmé, Stéphane, 103, 104, 110, 111–12, 114
Malle, Louis, 182
Malraux, André, 5, 7, 65
Mann, Thomas, 17–18, 223
Mao Zedong, 104, 115, 116, 119
Margaret of Austria, 17
Marx, Karl (and 'Marxism'), 100–1, 103, 115, 208
Mauriac, François, 41, 180
Maurras, Charles, 179, 180
May '68, 8, 16, 50, 54, 113–14, 116, 157
Medici, Catherine of, 17
Merck, Mandy, 208–9
Michaux, Henri, 100

Mirandola, Pico della, 21
Modiano, Patrick, 2, 3, 5, **177–200**
Modigliani, Amedeo, 180
Montaigne, Michel de, 78
Monteverdi, Claudio, 113
Montherlant, Henry de, 5, 8, 229, 230
Moreau, Jeanne, 55
Munch, Edvard, 123, 142, 144

Nietzsche, Friedrich, 74, 116, 235

Orléans, Charles d', 219
Ovid, 224

Pascal, Blaise, 219
Perec, Georges, 5
Perse, Saint-John, 229, 233
Pétain, Philippe, 178, 182, 187
Petiot, Marcel, 182
Petronius, 20
Piaget, Jean, 219
Pindar, 7
Pinget, Robert, 175
Pleynet, Marcelin, 104
Ponge, Francis, 100, 105
Pound, Ezra, 116
Pourrat, Henri, 2
Proust, Marcel, 28, 34, 35, 95, 135, 137, 169, 180, 195, 229

Queneau, Raymond, 167, 175

Racine, Jean, 251
Rembrandt van Rijn, 184
Renard, Jules, 2
Renaud, Madeleine, 53
Resnais, Alain, 40, 54
Ricardou, Jean, 104, 105
Richardson, Tony, 54
Rimbaud, Arthur, 236
Robbe-Grillet, Alain, 1, 2, 3, 5, 49, 100, 105, 106, 107, 109, 159, 196, 201
Robespierre, Maximilien, 26, 30
Roche, Denis, 104
Roche, Maurice, 1, 104, **112–13**
Rousseau, Jean-Jacques, 41, 67
Rubens, Peter Paul, 26

Sachs, Maurice, 178
Sade, D.A.F. marquis de, 104, 244
Saint-Just, L.A.L., 26, 30
Sarraute, Nathalie, 1, 7
Sartre, Jean-Paul, 7, 41, 50, 65, 100,